THE SLAVE STATES

FREDERICK LAW OLMSTED

THE
SLAVE STATES

REVISED AND ENLARGED EDITION

—————

Edited, with an Introduction, by

HARVEY WISH

Professor of History,
Western Reserve University

CAPRICORN BOOKS

New York

THIRTEENTH IMPRESSION

Library of Congress Catalog
Card Number 59-9116

MANUFACTURED IN THE UNITED STATES OF AMERICA

CONTENTS

German Farms—A Free-Minded Butcher—Neu-Braunfels—An Evening Far From Texas—The San Antonio Road—San Antonio—The Missions—The Environs—The San Antonio Spring—Bathing—Town Life—The Mexicans in Texas—A Pause—A Norther —Neu-Braunfels—The Orphans—History of the German Settlements—Present Appearances

A Cotton Man—The Landscape-Rose Hedges—The Plantations—"Important to Business Men"—Hill-side Cotton Culture—Abandoned Plantations—A Mississippi Fast Man—Education—"Swell-Heads"—The Lower Law—Refusing a Noble Title—Where Are All the People?—Experience of a Foreign Tourist— Natchez—The Bluff—Labor and Wages–Town and Country—Food of the Slaves—An Overseer at Home —Review of a First-Rate Cotton Plantation—Deserters and Detectives—Driving—Days and Hours of Labor

Tennessee Copper Mining—A Smart Yankee—A Colonizationist—How They Talk

The Cotton Kingdom

Introductory—The Present Crisis

INTRODUCTION

FREDERICK LAW OLMSTED: HIS LIFE

As THE nation headed blindly toward civil war, the politicians were not alone in formulating compromises to bring North and South together. There were moderate journalists like Henry Raymond of the New York *Daily Times* who attempted to use their newspapers to eliminate slavery without war. Even ardent proslavery writers, like George Frederick Holmes and George Fitzhugh of Virginia, actually sought peace by suggesting that mass passions give way to a scientific temper. In fact, George Fitzhugh published *Sociology for the South* (1854), and the scholarly Holmes penned several articles on a science of society that would justify slavery in human nature and history. They proposed to the abolitionist Stephen Pearl Andrews of New York that they work together to solve the slavery controversy through a new social science. Not the least of those who tried to stave off the war by an appeal to reason was Frederick Law Olmsted, a journalist who was vigorously opposed to slavery, but who was at the same time hopeful that he could save the peace by proving to the slaveholders that slavery did not pay and that it corrupted Southern civilization.

Olmsted liked to speak of himself as an "unpractical man" of many unfinished careers, but he distinguished himself in at least two great fields—as an acute social critic of the Old South, and as the father of American landscape architecture. Historians who write of the antebellum years, even those who decry his bias against the South, lean heavily upon his detailed observations for their picture of the Cotton Kingdom. At the same time, a generation of artists ranging from Daniel H. Burnham and the Chicago School to other noted men, praised Olmsted as the imaginative designer of Jackson Park during the Columbian Exposition of 1893. The two fields were not really separated, for he describes many a Southern or English landscape in his travel books. Behind both careers

7

was a deep love of the out-of-doors and a desire to compensate for his physical frailties by undertaking strenuous activities, whether on foot, on horseback, or before the mast on a sailing vessel to China. So a connection existed between the author of *The Cotton Kingdom* (1861) and the great designer of New York's Central Park, who raised landscape gardening from its humbler beginnings to the architecture of landscape.

His life began on April 2, 1822 in Hartford, Connecticut in a New England family that traced its American pedigree to the very first settlers that came from England. One of the advantages of being the son of a well-to-do dry-goods merchant was that he had enough income to surmount many false starts and mistakes before discovering his true career. There were disadvantages also. While the elder Olmsted encouraged Frederick's love of the scenic, he showed an amazing ineptitude in educating his son, for he sent him to ministers who were sometimes so busy that they turned the boy over to others. Frederick managed to outgrow the cloying Calvinist orthodoxy of his environment picked up in these years, for he soon became an outspoken rationalist warring upon narrow sectarianism and church authority. These boyhood years with the miscellaneous tutors did give him many opportunities to know farm life and the country. Besides, he was able before his sixteenth year to make at least four trips by carriage, horseback, or canal, each of over a thousand miles in New York state, New England, and Canada.[1]

He had hoped to study at Yale, but an eye ailment prevented regular studies and led him to turn to private training in surveying and later a brief job as a dry-goods clerk in New York city—the latter his father's choice. For a time he attended lectures at Yale and then decided on an exciting adventure, a sailor's berth on a bark bound for Hongkong. But the experience was too strenuous and sometimes even downright unpleasant. Later, in writing *A Journey in the Back Country* (1860), he found space —however irrelevant for this book—to attack the myth of the jolly sailor. American seamen as a class, he asserted, "are more wretched, and are governed more by threats of force than any other civilized laborers of the world." He went so far as to claim that almost any sober sailor would say "that he habitually hates his ship, hates his officers, hates his messmates, and despises himself." [2]

When he returned, he attended Yale lectures in agricultural science and engineering, while his brother, John Hull Olmsted, to whom he was greatly attached, enrolled as a regular student. They became part of an unusually stimulating intellectual circle at New Haven which included Charles Loring Brace, destined to become a noted welfare worker and philanthropist. Meanwhile, Frederick tried to learn farming and with his father's aid, bought a 130-acre farm on Staten Island. There he gave particular attention to the cultivation of fruit trees, some of which he imported from France, became a scientific farmer, and published articles on rural subjects. A literary career greatly tempted him. As he became deeply absorbed in travels abroad and in the South, in journalism, and in publishing, he neglected the farm and was forced to sell it within a few years.

His first book, *Walks and Talks of an American Farmer in England* (1852), published by G. P. Putnam of New York, is significant not only for its intrinsic merit as a fascinating travel account but because it sheds light on the methods he used later in writing about the South. It was a thoughtful analysis of contemporary English life and grew out of the jaunt that he undertook with his ever-ailing brother, John, and Charles Brace. They had been encouraged to learn about European agriculture and landscape gardening by none other than Asa Gray, the distinguished Harvard botanist. John, who was to die within a few years of tuberculosis, suffered at the time from an eye ailment, but hoped to improve his health. Frederick's book proved that he had genuine literary ability, could construct revealing dialogue and authentic regional dialect, knew how to draw out information in interviews, and above all possessed a trained eye for social conditions as well as for the details of farming and landscape.

In a lengthy dialogue, he expressed his own rationalist beliefs and concluded: "True religion is not a machinery for fitting men with beliefs and morals . . . Let us remember too . . . that all churches and governments whose authority is not dependent on the untrammeled and honest judgment of free intelligent minds, are alike ungodly and degrading." [3] He favored the English cam-

paign for a national system of education free of church
influence and spoke caustically of the Conservatives who
fought it.

With his New England love of neat inns and efficient
service, he was quite taken with English towns and villages. These favorable comments contrasted greatly with
his later strictures against filthy Southern hotels and
cooking. Still he was shocked by Liverpool's slum, even
if the streets were cleaner than in New York. "You can
see nothing like such a dead mass of pure poverty in the
worst quarter of our worst city. In New York, such a street
would be ten times as filthy and stinking, and ten times as
lively . . ." He amplified this judgment: "There was
somewhat rarely an appearance of actual misery, but a
stupid, hopeless, state-prison-for-life sort of expression."
Prices were low, but so were living standards. "The labourers seem haggard and stupid, and all with whom I
have talked say a poor man can hardly live here." He dis-
agreed with those citizens who blamed low wages on the
Irish immigrants and upon free trade. His books on the
South would have been enriched greatly had he been able
to interview slaves as freely as he did the Liverpool workmen.

England's traditional rural life and poetic landscape
reminded him of home and charmed him in a way that
Dixie never did. "Land of our poets! Home of our fathers! Dear Old mother England!" he apostrophized. His
book gave the most favorable treatment to the farmers of
Southern England and parts of Ireland, but he character-
istically reported unfavorably upon the condition of farm
laborers.

Olmsted felt curious about English attitudes toward
America. Scarcely anyone in England expressed a hostile
recollection of the American Revolution, although he recalled that in his own youth anything British meant "the
enemy," especially to schoolboys, and that American national holidays dwelt almost exclusively on victories over
England. While lower-class Britons might know as little
about America as about Russia, the more intelligent of the
working class showed sincere admiration and friendship.
Currently, the active source of anti-Americanism came
from the slavery question which, he felt, was greatly mis-
understood due to abolitionist propaganda. Too many
Americans were thought of as wielders of bowie-knives

and devotees of the pistol. "I wish our Southern brethren would send a few lecturers on the subject to England," he wrote. "The abolitionists have it all their own way there now, and take advantage of it to give the ignorant people ideas about our country which it is very desirable should be contradicted." In keeping with the cordial tenor of his book, he concluded with an appeal for tighter ties between the two countries and asked everyone to go to work for Ocean Penny Postage—the then current cause of reforming internationalists.

The excellent reviews of *Walks and Talks of an American Farmer in England* fanned his desire for a literary career and helped to convince Henry J. Raymond, editor and co-founder of the New York *Daily Times,* that here was a highly perceptive reporter capable of handling so controversial an issue as slavery. The book had suggested an objective investigation of slavery, and Olmsted had argued in this vein with his abolitionist friend Brace, and even with Theodore Parker and William Lloyd Garrison, who represented the radical antislavery movement.

Henry Raymond had once thought of teaching in the South, but had turned to journalism as an associate of Horace Greeley on the weekly *New Yorker* and then on his New York *Tribune.* Greeley's radical social and economic ideas alienated him, along with many other moderate readers, and Raymond independently established a relatively non-partisan newspaper, the New York *Daily Times,* on September 18, 1851. Like Olmsted Raymond was an antislavery Whig who believed that the Free Soilers with their emphasis on restricting slavery in the territories should capture the party and save it from extinction.[4] Accordingly, while it was said that he did not ask Olmsted for his opinions on slavery, nor seek to commit him to his editorial policy, the close coincidence of viewpoints makes it clear that Raymond must have had a rather good idea in advance that he was dealing with a man with whom he could cooperate editorially—as he did.

Therefore on December 11, 1852, Olmsted took the train for Washington to begin a fourteen-month Southern tour that took him as far as Texas and across the Rio Grande, and which covered practically all of the southeastern states. He had agreed to report on "the influence of Slavery, as a mode of employing labor, on the devel-

opment of the general resources of the South." Within a
few months, starting with the *Times* issue of February 16,
1853, he was sending back lengthy letters on the South,
about fifty in all, under the name of "Yeoman." Raymond
displayed each one prominently in the very first columns
of the editorial page. Despite their length, the *Times*
promptly printed them with only brief intervals of three
to six days between them.

At the same time Raymond published long articles on
slavery by others, one of serial size and all reflecting a desire to end slavery in some gradualist way. Usually they
agreed with Olmsted's observations. One writer, for example, ("H.W.P."), corroborated these facts by comparing them with his own experiences during trips through
the South. He fully agreed that slave labor was more
costly than free labor because the slaves tended to lack
intelligence and motive.[5] "A Native Southerner," while
taking exception to a few comments, praised Olmsted's
candor and intelligence: "The general tone of his articles
is acceptable to unbiased Southerners, but nevertheless,
we can see very clearly that he is looking at things
through a pair of sharp Northern eyes." This Southerner
proposed a solution that would separate the races in "a
peaceable and profitable separation." [6] Others, such as a
visiting English scholar, suggested a version of the old
Whig idea of transferring and colonizing the freed slaves
in Africa.[7]

Southern newspapers tended to regard Olmsted as a
spy in their midst, although the critical New Orleans
Delta balanced its charge of prejudice by conceding that
the writer was "manly and honest." Actually, they had
little to complain about, for Olmsted in his articles leaned
far backward to avoid giving offense and to convert the
planters, even repeating dubious proslavery propaganda
at times. In fact abolitionist papers accused Raymond of
conducting a whitewash. Some of Olmsted's comments
which seemed to equate the evils of slavery to the exploitation of free labor in Ireland, England, and the North
were later toned down in his books.[8]

This investigation of the South which took fourteen
months was so enlightening to the North that it left a lasting record for historians as well as contemporaries, but it
was not wholly a unique enterprise. Horace Greeley had
sent many a reporter to spy out the land in Dixie. English,

continental, and Northern travelers, from Charles Dickens and Charles Mackay to Harriet Martineau and Fanny Kemble, the actress, were pouring forth books and articles on the South that were usually unfavorable to slavery. But too few—not even Dickens—displayed the accurate reportorial skill and background knowledge that the *Times* special correspondent possessed. Olmsted's comments on slavery took on added significance, as the pages of the *Times* reveal, because of the national controversy over Harriet Beecher Stowe's portrait of the land of slavery in *Uncle Tom's Cabin*, which had appeared in 1851-52. In fact, he discovered Southerners who were quite familiar and even in agreement with the forbidden book. He knew how to ask questions of the planters after winning their confidence, and he had read enough of Southern history for background to feel at home. To corroborate his statements, he often cited Southern newspapers and magazines at length.

His brother John, still in search of more robust health, accompanied him on the second stage of his journey, this time through western Louisiana and Texas. Later John was entrusted to write the second volume on the basis of Frederick's letters and journal. They returned partly on horseback from New Orleans through "the back country" of the Southern Appalachians to Richmond and finally New York. They were home by the summer of 1854. In these strenuous fourteen months, Frederick had traversed thousands of miles by train, then by stage, and finally on horseback. His health remained good despite his frequently expressed discomfort at untidy Southern inns, badly cooked meals, rural squalor, and inept slave service. He admitted that he was "a growler."

During 1854-56 (and even later), the years just preceding the appearance of *A Journey in the Seaboard Slave States,* an edited and expanded version of his earlier *Times* articles, he embarked upon a startling intrigue. His activities reveal quite another personality than the man of soft words and conciliatory temper that his readers knew. He had never concealed his Free Soil sympathies, his opposition to any expansion of slavery in the territories, but he went so far as to take serious risks to halt the advance of the slaveholder in Kansas and in Texas. The atmosphere was electric with tensions aggravated by the ill-conceived Kansas-Nebraska Act of 1854 which created "Bleeding

Kansas" by allowing the question of slavery or freedom to be settled by rival groups of settlers. When the militant New England Emigrant Aid Company tried to capture Kansas for freedom, they had the aid of Olmsted who busied himself in raising funds for heavy cannon.[9]

At the same time Olmsted tried to work together with the Company by attempting to unite the Kansas experiment in colonization with another one in western Texas. Usually the Company remained in the background while Olmsted took the initiative in promoting the antislavery colony without arousing the suspicions of proslavery forces as to the real intentions. The Texas experiment in building a free society grew out of Olmsted's contacts with the German cotton-raising farms around San Antonio, particularly in the model town of Neu-Braunfels, where he met some of the radical Forty Eighters who were foes of slavery. Not all of the Germans wished to become belligerents in the antislavery cause, and Olmsted tried to strengthen the Free Soil faction by collecting funds and newspaper subscriptions from Henry Ward Beecher and other antislavery friends on behalf of his harassed friend, Dr. Adolf Douai, editor of the San Antonio *Zeitung*. Together they hoped that a new state of West Texas would arise as a free state obstacle to slavery expansion.

While his articles on his Southern trip were still running in the *Times*, he either instigated or wrote anonymous articles on the West Texas project. Raymond and he both vainly urged the Texas Germans to back Dr. Douai and to colonize West Texas. In 1857, when his second book appeared as *A Journey Through Texas*, he built up propaganda for his project by distributing numerous free copies and specially bound pamphlets containing relevant portions of his book. His intense interest in the free colony experiments explains the unusual space and cordial tone devoted to the Texas Germans and the numerous clippings referring to the project that he included in his Appendix.

He turned to England for aid after personal consultation with the officers of the New England Emigrant Aid Company. In letters to the Cotton Supply Associations of Manchester and Liverpool, he asked their assistance in directing free laborers to Texas and other Southwest territories in order to increase cotton production in America. He even offered his personal services free if they would send an agent to investigate the project.[10] But the English were wary, for they realized the possibility of awakening Border Ruffianism on the turbulent Kansas model. Meanwhile the German Free Soil faction under Douai surrendered the fight amidst increasing resistance from conservatives, and even Olmsted's efforts to avoid publicity for himself and the Company did not avert open charges from Southerners that he was the head of an abolitionist plot.

When the colonization scheme collapsed and the Civil War began, Olmsted hurried through a condensation of his trilogy to be known as *The Cotton Kingdom* (1861). It was no longer addressed to the more tolerant slaveholders but to England, whose attitude toward the Union was a matter of life and death. Possibly because the propaganda value of his large section on the Texas Germans had ceased to exist, he and his editor, Daniel Goodloe, deleted most of it. So ended an episode in his life that revealed how thoroughly he was committed to the extermination of slavery even if it involved direct action and tortuous intrigue. It is true that he had followed the well-established Whig-Republican position, which had opposed federal interference with slavery in the South but also had emphatically opposed the introduction of slavery into the territories. Olmsted would advocate going somewhat further than this position by using the legal provision that permitted Texas to be divided into several states to stop the growth of slavery in the South. In this he had been in close touch and perhaps essential agreement with actual abolitionists as well as more moderate antislavery men, including John Greenleaf Whittier, Theodore Parker, and Dr. Samuel G. Howe.

In 1855, with the financial aid of his indulgent father, Frederick Olmsted became a partner of the publishers Dix and Edwards for whom he made a business trip to Europe for a year. Their shaky finances forced him to borrow money again from his father to pay the printer for publishing *A Journey in the Seaboard Slave States* (1856). At the same time he edited *Putnam's Magazine* which his firm had bought from George Palmer Putnam. Dix and Edwards also published Olmsted's second book on the South, *A Journey Through Texas* (1857), but the firm went bankrupt while the third volume, *A Journey in the Back Country*, was still in process, thus leaving the author to struggle with their debts. Fortunately, another American publisher, Mason Brothers of New York, issued the last volume, while a separate English edition appeared through Sampson Low, Son & Company of London.[11]

While the printings were usually small, the reception was gratifying and the reviews often enthusiastic. Even the abolitionists overlooked his concessions to proslavery arguments to praise his work. Whittier, William Lloyd Garrison, and Harriet Beecher Stowe thought highly of the books. Southern papers and magazines such as *De Bow's Review*, were correspondingly hostile. English reactions that had been so ardent over *Uncle Tom's Cabin* were also favorable to Olmsted's indictment of slavery. Charles Darwin added his warm endorsement. German demand for *A Journey Through Texas* resulted in at least three editions in that language. Over and over again reviewers paid homage to Olmsted's reportorial skill and his objectivity and sometimes contrasted these qualities with the violent tone of Hinton Rowan Helper's attack on the "slavocracy" in *The Impending Crisis* (1857).[12]

As the Civil War began, Sampson Low, Son & Company of London were encouraged by the English demand for *A Journey in the Back Country* to propose a condensation of the three volumes. Olmsted, eager to sway English opinion to the Union cause, gladly agreed. Aided by a special editor, Daniel R. Goodloe, the editor of the abolitionist *National Era*, Olmsted issued a special two-volume edition in 1861 which was entitled *The Cotton Kingdom* and published in this country by Mason Brothers simultaneously with the English edition. The London edition was warmly received and widely quoted by English statesmen and economists. It came at a time when the ministry seemed to favor the Confederacy and when the impression existed that the war had little to do with slavery, only with the subjugation of an area that wished independence. The American edition was undoubtedly handicapped by the bankruptcy of Mason Brothers in 1862, but the reviewers were generous. Charles Sumner called it "a positive contribution to civilization," and James Russell Lowell was not far behind in his appreciation; as a pioneer in the use of dialect in literature, Lowell recognized a fellow expert in the author.

For years, the praise continued. Charles Francis Adams Jr., investigating in 1862 the contraband slave problem around Beaufort, South Carolina, wrote home repeatedly of his indebtedness to Olmsted's books. He wrote in a letter to his brother, Henry Adams, "The contrabands were slaves yesterday and may be again tomorrow, and what slaves are any man may know without himself seeing, who will take the trouble to read Olmsted's Books." [13] Unfortunately, Olmsted himself discouraged suggestions for a later edition because the problems dealt with seemed to have been solved. In 1907, a second edition did appear, this time through G. P. Putnam's Sons. Thereafter it became a major source for historians dealing with the South.

Meanwhile, new changes came for Olmsted. His beloved brother, John, who had been his companion and publishing associate for so many years finally succumbed to the tubercular ailment. Frederick married his widow and turned to a new career as a landscape architect. In 1857, while he had still been engaged in publishing ventures, he had accepted a post as superintendent of the preparatory work on Central Park in New York and with an able partner, Calvert Vaux, won an important prize competition for a park design. Thus he became architect-in-chief of the project, but this career was interrupted by the Civil War in which his knowledge of the South made him invaluable to the Union cause. He took a leave of absence to go to Washington as Executive Secretary of the United States Sanitary Commission, visited armies in the field, and gathered information which enabled him to recommend remedial legislation regarding their condition. The Sanitary Commission was modelled after the British Sanitary Commission and the Crimean War experience of civilian agencies serving the soldiers. Olmsted sent out about five hundred agents to distribute food, clothing, and health pamphlets to the Union men, set up soldiers' homes, and performed various other personal services for them. It is easy to see why after the war he was encouraged to help organize and direct the Southern Famine Relief Commission. In recognition of such services Harvard awarded him an honorary degree.[14]

His interest in the Negro and the South continued throughout his life. When he assisted E. L. Godkin to establish *The Nation* in 1865, he had in mind a policy of sympathetic aid for the reconstruction of the South. During the war, he had given considerable attention to the federal plan for the freedmen along the lines eventually adopted by the Freedmen's Bureau, but he watched with mixed feelings while the Radical Republicans hastened to enfranchise the freedmen whom he regarded "as yet ludicrously unfit to be trusted with the ballot," though he saw little practical alternative to this. He saw the danger of a revival of the old sectional conflict and even reenslavement unless the vote was given to Negroes. Later, he explained his position more clearly:

> If I could have secured to the freedmen the full rights of intending citizens yet unnaturalized, I would have placed clearly before them, and at no indefinite or discouraging distance, perfect political equality with white citizens, but this upon conditions making such political equality a privilege to be earned.

He favored an effective literacy law on the Massachusetts model for the suffrage in the South and urged the use of machinery to make it apply equally to both races. Altogether, by 1889, when he reconsidered the postwar era, he felt that the Negroes were doing better than he had ever expected, and he hoped that the South would hasten to improve suffrage conditions.[15]

After the Civil War, he returned to his profession as a landscape architect, after struggling with ill-health and experimenting with various newspaper projects. The "unpractical man" embarked on vast landscape projects ranging from Yosemite Park to Boston's Back Bay. He pioneered in the creation of vast pleasure parks for the people on a regal scale at a time when most public parks were small unimaginative affairs. Disciples felt honored to be associated with him as he grew in fame. Andrew Carnegie and Leland Stanford were his clients. The federal government needed him to redesign the grounds for the nation's capitol. New York called him to complete Central Park, and to design Prospect Park, Morningside Park, and Riverside Park.

He travelled abroad to learn how to apply the aristocratic landscape arts to the needs of the common man's recreational needs. Perhaps the culminating point of his professional career—and it was more than just another professional assignment—was his majestic conception of the Columbian Exposition grounds in Chicago during 1893, when he introduced into Jackson Park a lasting and imaginative chain of lagoons, wooded islands, and cultivated shrubbery. That year an assemblage of artists gathered to honor Daniel Burnham, the organizer of the art work, and the men who contributed to the final result. Burnham reserved his highest praise for Olmsted: "Each of you knows the name and genius of him who stands first in the hearts and confidence of American artists, the creator of your own parks and many other city parks." There were still older men who remembered a former career, that of a great social observer of the South. But after a tragic mental breakdown in 1893, Olmsted disappeared from public notice until his funeral in 1903 when newspapers and magazines paid fresh homage to him.[16]

THE WRITINGS OF FREDERICK LAW OLMSTED

2

Olmsted's trilogy on the South and its condensation and revision in *The Cotton Kingdom* offered a notable record of travels that has been favorably compared with the penetrating classic account of the French peasantry by Arthur Young, *Travels in France* (1792). Although he was mainly concerned with the impact of slavery on Southern economic life, he was also greatly interested in discovering the effect that slaveholding had upon the white man, in fact upon every aspect of society in the Old South. He claimed that his books corrected many romantic ideas of the South and asserted that he had started out with a much more favorable picture than he was able to justify by the time he had returned home. His claim to objectivity for the reader rests upon internal evidence largely since it is now almost impossible to reconstruct the antebellum South of 1852-54 from purely objective historical sources.

He believed that everything he had seen indicated that slavery was wasteful and did not pay, that it injured the entire South by exhausting the soil and by driving away free labor and democratic institutions, that it held back many Southern communities to a primitive frontier level socially and culturally, and that it coarsened or brutalized the slaveowner's character. But he did not subscribe to the then popular abolitionist idea that the sectional conflict and the ensuing Civil War were part of a slaveholder's conspiracy. He criticized the responsibility of Southern leaders, but felt they had miscalculated their true interests. His picture of the Old South has dominated the writing of Southern history, even in the mid-Twentieth century.

Olmsted's influence may be compared with that of the noted Georgia-born historian, Ulrich B. Phillips, who went on to teach graduate students at the Universities of Wisconsin, Michigan, Tulane, and Yale. Although he criticized Olmsted as being prejudiced against the South, he could not avoid relying upon many of the facts and conclusions of *The Cotton Kingdom*. Both emphasized that slavery was inefficient and wasteful and that many Southerners would have liked to see emancipation but dreaded the prospect of racial conflict thereafter. They agreed in holding the abolitionists responsible for arousing tensions North and South, although Olmsted was an active Free-Soiler who raised funds for a howitzer intended for the Kansas Free State party and was ready to risk a second Bleeding Kansas in western Texas.

Phillips emphasized the economics of slavery no less expertly than Olmsted, but he apparently believed that in the final analysis, it was not the dollars and cents of slavery that mattered so much to the average Southerner as the fact that the institution preserved the security of the rigid biracial system that was otherwise difficult to justify. Olmsted was acquainted with this view, but believed until the very outbreak of war that if the planters could be shown how utterly wasteful slave labor was through such books as his that the institution would be on the way out. He was closer to modern science than the other in utterly rejecting the theory that climate and soil made slavery inevitable, and he was also more realistic because he did not confine his observations to the large plantations. Phillips was evidently influenced by the fact that the records of the large plantations were most accessible to historians; but Olmsted, a born reporter, deliberately chose "the back country" and the isolated highlands as well as the large plantations to study the small farms and the "poor whites" (which the other historians almost ignored) as well as the rich planters. Both agreed that the slaves were better off in bondage than in their native African home (neither knew much about West Africa, the source of slave exportation to America) and commented upon the backwardness of the Negro. However—and this is fundamental—Phillips thought that the Negro's savage traits were inborn and that little improvement could be expected; but Olmsted attributed such traits to the lack of incentive and opportunity under slavery and pointed out some gratifying exceptions to the low level of knowledge among the slaves. Together, despite these differences, the two did a great deal to create the modern historian's image of the Old South.[17]

A Journey in the Seaboard Slave States (1856) covered the first three months of his fourteen-month trip in 1853 starting from Washington, D. C. to Virginia, through the Carolinas, Georgia, Alabama, and Louisiana. Of 715 pages fully 288 were devoted to Virginia alone—not counting the section of the book treating his return to that state. The prefatory advertisement declared that the original Yeoman letters to the *Times* had been revised in the light of his later visits to the South and that much additional matter now appeared. A second preface apologized for his fault-finding but avowed his freedom from partisan bias. The revealing dedication from Alexander von Humboldt's *Cosmos* suggested how far Olmsted had gone since his *Times* articles, which were more deferential to slaveholders. Humboldt emphasized the idea of humanity in history, "the noble endeavor to throw down all barriers erected between men by prejudice and one-sided views, and by setting aside the distinctions of religion, country, and color, to treat the whole human race as one Brotherhood . . ."

As Olmsted looked out of a train window in Virginia, he was struck by the intimacy of the races. Negro women carried both black and white babies in their arms. "Black and white faces are constantly thrust together out of doors, to see the train go by," he noted. Children of both races could be seen at play. In the train itself, mistresses sat next to their slave girls and chatted freely with them, quite unlike the racial restraint practiced in the North. From all this, he shrewdly concluded, "When the negro is definitely a slave, it would seem that the alleged natural antipathy of the white race to associate with him is lost."

He regarded the Virginia field hands with distaste, finding them brute-like, dull, awkward, slow, and disgustingly dirty. Still, he saw nothing of the insolence that planters complained about. Wherever he could, he interviewed planters and people of other classes, but too seldom did he question the Negroes directly, for they were often evasive or too concerned with telling a white man what he wished to hear. Now and then in his travels a Negro dropped a revealing comment to him about brutal treatment.

Occasionally he met a planter harassed by the management of slaves and his large farm, frankly ready to admit that slaves were careless and wasteful and that free laborers if available might well be more profitable than bondsmen. One could trust the field hands only with the cruder and heavier tools. They did not work too hard and seemed well-fed, well-clad (if only in the white folks' cast-offs), and housed comfortably in good cabins. In fact, as he had first written unqualifiedly in the *Times*, they were better off than the starving Irish, the English poor who sold their children, or the struggling Northern workers. He now repeated the same idea, somewhat toned down, possibly borrowing the analogies from the proslavery writings of the extremist George Fitzhugh, who wrote editorials in the Richmond *Examiner* for certain national political campaigns, and who based his justification of slavery on the alleged historical fact that slavery, white or black, had always been right, normal, and necessary.[18]

In this and in later books Olmsted showed a keen awareness (as Phillips did to a lesser extent) of the possibilities of slave insurrections. If slaves rebelled, he observed, their rebellion was almost always betrayed by domestic servants. The discontented frequently ran away or disappeared into the swamps and raided the plantation storehouses. Those that worked required the most exasperatingly minute instructions, were unreliable, drank a good deal, and often went through the motions of labor without putting any real force behind this pantomime. At other places, he learned that slaves were disposed to sham illness or lameness and did as little as possible, for they lacked real incentives. Still, while preferring freedom, they were reluctant to make the change at once.

He was told again and again that the Negro was inherently improvident, but he refused to be convinced and argued that they were no more so than whites of the same cultural level. There was no question however that the system lacked incentives and that the slave usually withheld his full labor. After considering these factors and estimating the costs of real illness, disability, and runaways, he concluded that Virginia slaves did half as much work as free workers and that the system was uneconomic as well as inhumane.

While slavery did not enrich the planter, the system bore down heavily upon the poor whites, who were left out of the scheme of things. The stigma of "nigger work" prevented the development of these white workers. Falling back upon their limited economic and social resources, they corrupted the work habits of the Negroes also, thieved and drank heavily and were themselves more unreliable than the slaves. As one master observed in disparaging the poor white workers, "Slaves are the only reliable laborers—you could command them and make them do what was right." Here in Virginia and elsewhere, Olmsted reported that in certain types of employment masters preferred to use Irishmen rather than Negroes because the life of a slave was too valuable to expose to dangerous work such as draining flooded land. Free Negroes were not the best workers, however, because their work habits had been spoiled by the deliberate slow tempo of the nearby slaves.

He had an enlightening conversation with a Virginian planter who had freed his slaves on moral grounds and aided many of his former slaves to return to Africa and even kept in touch with them thereafter. Although he complained that the free Negroes were less efficient than they could have been due to contact with slaves, and he was turning to the introduction of Irish workmen, he was convinced that free labor was cheaper than slave. His dislike of slavery as an evil did not prevent him from condemning abolitionists as troublemakers, yet he condemned the return of runaway slaves and felt that *Uncle Tom's Cabin,* aside from some inaccuracies regarding Southern life, was truthful in its account of cruelty and suffering.

While Olmsted was primarily concerned with slavery and its social impact on society, he was too good a reporter to neglect other facets of Virginia life, but he tended to select drab situations and to assume that these grew out of slavery. Thus, in describing Richmond, then a town of 30,000, he sniffed at its unpaved though newly gaslit streets, its few sidewalks, and the cheap stucco imitation granite in Jefferson's State Capitol. He did not like the precious paintings of Washington either, dismiss-

ing the style as mere strut. At the same time, he seemed
unaware of such cultural landmarks as the *Southern Literary Messenger* building, where Edgar Allan Poe had so
recently held forth, the Virginia Mechanics Institute, the
University of Richmond, and the picturesque details that
had attracted visitors like Thackeray and Dickens.[19]

From Virginia he went on to North Carolina which
gave him an opportunity to observe the large turpentine
farms, the rosin works, and the piney-wood lands. He
seemed absorbed by the details of production even apart
from social implications. In describing the labor situation,
he contrasted the many intelligent, cheerful slaves with
the idle poverty-stricken poor whites living in the turpentine forest. Those employed were more inefficient and un-
manageable than the slaves. On the other hand, he found
that the slaves used in the glue-trade were so unreliable
that they were being replaced by Irishmen and Germans.

In South Carolina, Olmsted compared the labor costs of
a planter with his own in Staten Island where he used
Irishmen, and convinced the Southerner that slave labor
was far more expensive and that the low values of Southern lands reflected this situation. The slaves also had a
degrading effect on the planter's family, he noted, and
cited Southern newspapers on this score. He saw white
children listening to the obscene language of the slaves
and quoted Chancellor Harper of South Carolina who said
that in order to compensate for the degradation of slavery
it was necessary to show "a greater severity of decorum
than is required elsewhere." Olmsted's concern with conditions of the farms and plantations led him to cut his descriptions of Charleston and Savannah to a few para-
graphs, but he managed to single out the urban slums and
the prevailing quarrelsome spirit:

> I saw as much close packing, filth, and squalor, in cer-
> tain blocks inhabited by laboring whites, in Charleston, as
> I have witnessed in any Northern town of its size; and
> greater evidences of brutality and ruffianly character, than
> I have ever happened to see, among an equal population
> of this class before.

He went into the technical details of rice culture in the
Carolinas and Georgia. As in the tobacco and cotton
fields, he found innumerable instances of the wastefulness
and inefficiency of slave labor, and while he generalized

about the relatively good treatment of slaves he managed to include reports of irresponsible floggings and even stabbings of slaves. He gave considerable space to the history and development of the slave aristocracy of South Carolina, citing standard histories and newspapers. In his conclusion he stated that improvement and progress in the state was impossible under its present labor system, and he condemned the desperate expedient of reviving the African slave trade to provide more labor. "South Carolina," he said, "must meet her destiny: either be democratized or barbarianized." He was not much more optimistic about Georgia. A large part of the people, he felt, "still have the vagrant and hopeless habits and character of Oglethorpe's first colonists" but lacked Oglethorpe's democratic ideals since they were intent upon the extension of slavery.

The journey through Alabama from Savannah by the Macon road was not as fully recorded as his travels through Virginia and the Carolinas. He remarked that the rapid enlargement of slave plantations had the effect of driving the poor to move away into the frontier lands. Many of the planters, however, were also still living in log cabins. Few of the planters that Olmsted described in various parts of the South seemed to live in the palatial plantation mansions of architectural tradition. Much of the Deep South had emerged from the frontier stage only within the past few decades.

Louisiana, New Orleans in particular, fascinated him with its commerce on the Mississippi, the colorful "Cajun" population in the rural background, and the Spanish and French-speaking inhabitants of the city. He went so far as to render their mixed English speech into dialogue and to reproduce at length several songs of the Negro boathands. Like George Washington Cable of that city he felt the romantic quality of the unique quadroon society, described the racial aspects of their existence, particularly the liaisons of quadroon women with upper-class white men, and the two households—one with a white woman —that these men often supported. Outside of the city, he took detailed notes of the large semi-mechanized sugar plantations, conceded that some of their labor practices were enlightened, but insisted that the prevailing patriarchal system was no better than that of a Northern poorhouse. In Louisiana, as elsewhere, all slave occupations were considered degrading and assigned to the lower caste of the community.

Olmsted obviously had strong opinions on slavery, and he edited his report in such a way that only an antislavery conclusion was possible. But he made an effort to temper this by reporting proslavery arguments, although he never permitted this to disturb his general thesis regarding the unprofitableness of slavery. For example, he reported that many Virginians believed that slavery was to be justified on non-economic grounds because it protected the South from the class conflicts and "isms" of the North—the anti-rent riots, the strikes, immigrant unrest, "diseased" philanthropy, radical democracy, and the advance of socialistic ideas. One peculiar prejudice that occasionally emerged in his books was an inexplicable antisemitic bias concerning "the dirty, smelly German Jews" and their allegedly avaricious dealings with the Negroes. He was ready to credit the various anti-Jewish stories that were retailed to him.

A Journey in the Seaboard States, like the subsequent volumes, was enriched by scenic landscape descriptions, acute character portrayals, dialogue and all, and considerable social picturization, even apart from the impact of slavery. He angered James D. B. De Bow, editor of *De Bow's Review* of New Orleans, by his repeated strictures on Southern hospitality and the alleged planter's tendency to convert neighborliness into a business transaction. Also, too many slaveholders seemed to possess a morose disposition in the eyes of Olmsted.

Among his really excellent pictures of social life were the discussions of slave customs, such as their colorful religious practices. He described the intense emotional atmosphere of their religious services and their spontaneous responses and fine singing, but he concluded on the basis of interviews and observation that only a small proportion of slaves actually went to church. In Richmond and Charleston he was fascinated by the ceremonies of a slave funeral at night, but noted the presence of a white spy as required in the South for security reasons. He visited festive slave marriages, learned about the Negro clergy, and also watched religious services among the Crackers.

Unlike many writers on the South who insisted upon Negro backwardness, Olmsted was optimistic about the potentialities of the Negro. Like so many of the mid-nineteenth century reformers, he was a devout believer in the transforming power of a beneficial environment. To change the environment was indeed to change man. He even leaned on phrenology—which was then considered a science even by educated people—to refute the alleged backwardness of Negroes.

The second volume, *A Journey Through Texas* (1857), which was a somewhat smaller book of 516 pages, takes on special interest because of the propaganda use that Olmsted made of it in promoting a free soil colony in western Texas with the aid of the German colonists and the New England Emigrant Aid Company. The writing was entrusted to his brother John. "Owing to the pressure of other occupations," he stated in the preface, "the preparation of the volume from the author's journal has been committed with free scope of expression and personality, to his brother, Dr. J. H. Olmsted, his companion on this trip." Although the journal referred to has long since disappeared, possibly in a fire at Staten Island, the final result was not very different from Frederick's usual style, ideas, and the previous letters to the *Times*. A long introductory letter appeared at the beginning which was written by Frederick to "A Southern Friend" and reflected his emphatic opposition to any extension of slavery in the territories: "Any further extension or annexation of slavery, under whatever pretense or covering it is attempted, will only be effected in contemptuous defiance of the people of the Free States." This was written on December 29, 1856 in the midst of the Kansas crisis and the recent sensational showing of the new Republican Party, a purely sectional party, in the Frémont-Buchanan contest.

The first chapter, "Route to Texas," described a train trip from Baltimore to Wheeling, then a ride by steamer along the Ohio to Cincinnati. From there they took a stage coach to Lexington, a rail trip to Louisville, and another by steamer down the Ohio and the Mississippi to the Red River, and finally they traveled, by ferry, emigrant train, and horseback across eastern Texas. There were many adventures to report and diverse terrain quite different from the land of tobacco, rice, sugar, and cotton described in the first volume. Olmsted was almost as critical of Cincinnati as he had been of Richmond and Charleston, decrying its atmosphere of "bricks, hurry, a muddy roar, and

damp coal smoke," and its sanguine glories as "Porkopolis
with its vast slaughter yards." But things were far worse
on the other side of the Ohio. In slaveholding Kentucky
they noted a young man with a pistol projecting from his
pocket and learned that pistols and bowie-knives were
universal among such youth. They were surprised to find
a large iron works along the Cumberland River which
employed 700 slaves. The fact that white men would not
accept employment here was attributed by citizens not
only to the heavy tasks but also the competition with slave
labor.

With a knack for losing their way and stumbling upon
broken-down plantations, they stopped at such a place in
western Louisiana, a small square log cabin surrounded by
two rows of comfortable Negro cabins. In the main house
they shared the company of three hounds. a collection of
chickens, some cats, and children of both races. The
owner who could not "read writin'," was busy trying to
cure some ailing slaves with old patent medicines and
some common drugs heaped up in a drawer. Yet this man
had raised sixty bales of cotton in a season and sold it for
thirty thousand dollars which he used to buy more slaves
and cotton fields. This wealth did not prevent the planter
from charging heavily for his alleged hospitality. Frequently the travelers found deserted cabins marked
"Gone to Texas" and dilapidated slave quarters. They continued to find roadside stopping places which charged
high prices for a revolting meal of impossible black coffee,
salt pork, cold corn bread, and boiled sweet potatoes.
Frontier conditions were intensified in Texas where the
two turned for a time to hunting game and living in a tent
on the prairie.

They picked up conversation about slave treatment—it
was usually mistreatment—and visited Austin, the capital,
which offered them bad hotels and poor food. Here at
least people were not as dull as those they had been meeting whom the Olmsteds described to be as monotonous as
their pork and corn diet. They visited with a planter in
moderate circumstances, but noted the crude furniture
and the spectacle of men cursing their women and children. Throughout eastern Texas they saw general illiter-
acy or, among the better-educated, an indifference even
to reading a newspaper. The women were overworked as
soon as they married and showed thin faces, sallow com-

plexions, and sad (or sour) expressions. Prejudices against the Mexicans were strong indeed, quite in contrast with the attitude of the Olmsteds who found them most gracious and dignified.

Across the Colorado, they came to western Texas, which they described with real enthusiasm—a not very surprising circumstance considering their stake at the time of writing in establishing a free colony there. They even found a well-ordered plantation. Most of all, they enjoyed the German town of Neu-Braunfels, with its wide main street, its lines of neat comfortable, stucco houses, the attractive gardens, the numerous workshops, the excellent schools, and, above all, the use of free labor in raising cotton. Altogether, they thought so highly of the Germans that they included in their narrative a short history and description of the German colony which included about 3000 people in the vicinity of Neu-Braunfels.

These settlers had suffered considerably from the ineptitude of their founders as well as the hardships of the frontier, but their successful adjustment was evident. Perhaps it did not require a high level of literacy to find the native Texans dull: one settler observed in disgust, "They can only sit all round the fire and speet! Why, then they drink some whisky; or may be they play cards, or they make great row." In their turn, the Texans resented the antislavery sentiments of the Germans, even if few were actually abolitionists determined upon immediate action. Besides, the planters did not find the educated Forty Eighter among the colonists a very congenial element.

The Olmsteds were amused by the incongruity of meeting some of these "Latin-farmers." or educated Germans who had romantic notions about the American frontier:

> You are welcomed by a figure in blue flannel shirt and pendant beard, quoting Tacitus, having in one hand a long pipe, in the other a butcher's knife; Madonnas upon log-walls; coffee in tin cups upon Dresden saucers; barrels for seats to hear a Beethoven symphony on the grand piano; a book case half-filled with classics, half with sweet potatoes.

The visitors thought that the best newspaper in all Texas was the San Antonio *Zeitung* of Dr. Douai, an intimate friend with whom they were associated in the project for a free-soil Texas. Douai persisted for a long time in pushing the project despite threats of lynching by proslavery Texans. Altogether the spectacle of a large community raising cotton by free labor in the South offered a convincing lesson in the minds of the Olmsteds.

When the two returned to their plantation tours, the contrast between free and slave labor seemed most disagreeable. "We heard the master threaten his negroes with flogging, at least six times, before we went to bed," wrote Frederick on the way to the coast. Along the road they met a migrating Alabama slaveholding family talking about their chattel; further along, they heard the story of a runaway. They disliked the Indians that they met, but admired the new Colt revolver used by the mounted guard over the United States mail train and the efficient system of the Texas Rangers. But the Noble Savage was a legend. "We could not find even a man of dignity. The universal expression towards us was either a silly leer or a stupid indifference." They summarized their impression of an Indian camp by saying that there "was nothing but the most miserable squalor, foul obscenity, and disgusting brutishness . . ."

After crossing the Rio Grande briefly and visiting the Mexicans who impressed them favorably, they turned home beginning with western Louisiana where they spent several nights among the French Creoles and shared the historic recollections of Old Acadia. They managed to get a good interview with two slaves belonging to a Creole master, apparently a kindly owner. One told the Olmsteds indignantly of some free Negroes who owned slaves, and the speaker vowed that he would never serve a Negro.

The final chapters are badly organized, with discussions and impressions that are not always closely connected. They recurred to the project of organizing free labor colonies in the West and facts were cited to prove the success of the New England Emigrant Aid Company in Kansas. A detailed account was given of the relations between the Texans and the Germans. Most of this story had already been told in the earlier chapters. Finally, the book ended with a long appendix containing news clippings and editorials about the Texas German settlements and other aspects of Southern life.

A Journey in the Back Country (1860), last of the trilogy, told of Olmsted's tortuous path through unfrequented plantation and hill country beginning in lower Mississippi through the mountainous parts of Alabama,

Georgia, Tennessee, and North Carolina, and then by steamer from Richmond to New York City. He avoided duplication of previous topics by concentrating on the highlanders, the interior and piedmont cotton plantations, and a lengthy evaluation of the cause and remedies for the backwardness of the South. His preface referred to the current excitement over John Brown's raid on Harper's Ferry, but his proposals remained moderate, still aimed at converting the South. "The subjection of the negroes of the South to the mastership of the whites," he reassured the planter, "I still consider justifiable and necessary, and I fully share the general ill-will of the people of the North toward any suggestion of their interfering politically to accomplish an immediate abolition of slavery." But he spoiled the effect of this gesture of friendliness by going on to argue that the existing agitation was due to the attitude of the slaveholders, not the abolitionists.

He offered a long-range program for the abolition of slavery which would educate and train the Negroes in such a way as to raise their productivity so that they could earn and provide for their own freedom. He looked ahead to the future of the races after abolition and cautiously examined the prospects of their living together:

> Popular prejudice, if not popular instinct, points to a separation of black from white as a condition of the abolition of slavery. . . . I do not now say that it is, or is not, right or desirable, that this should be so, but taking men as they are, I think that a happy and peaceful association of a large negro with a large white population can not at present [1860] be calculated on as a permanent thing. I think that the emancipation from slavery of such part of the existing actual negro population as shall remain in the country until the white population is sufficiently christianized, and civilized, and properly educated to understand that its interests are identical with its duty will take place gradually, and only after an intermediate period of systematic pupilage, restraint, and encouragement . . .

This was the type of gradualism that one found in Henry Raymond's New York *Daily Times* or in the thinking of Lincoln. Olmsted was still a Free Soiler vigorously opposed to the extension of slavery but quite willing to wait indefinitely for emancipation.

In Mississippi he met and learned about the "cotton snobs," who were often absentee owners, their overseers, and the abandoned plantations in the midst of the exhausted lands. The parvenu planter in the recently won lands of the Southwest obviously lacked the polish and culture of the South Carolina aristocrat. The brisk demand for cotton, he reported, led owners to pay overseers high wages and to ask no questions about cruel treatment of slaves. This report seemed supported by lengthy quotations from Southern newspapers and magazines. The mechanization of the large estates left little room for humane impulses and it was difficult to discover the alleged educational influence of the peculiar institution upon the Negro. Enlightening contacts, including those between slaves and Northern travelers, and between field hands and educated whites, were negligible. Education for moral living did not interest Olmsted's informants among the overseers who interrupted the irregular marriage attachments or promiscuity of the slaves only when they led to quarrels which threatened to break down plantation routine. Symbolic of this regime of ignorance and routine punishments was the sight of unsheltered stocks with holes for the head and the ankles. "Heaps o' runaways, dis country, sah," explained an old Negro, "Yes, sah, heaps on 'em round here." In the piedmont cotton areas, the traveler learned about "nigger-hunting" and bloodhounds trained in the tradition of *Uncle Tom's Cabin*.

Moving along on horseback, Olmsted visited the interior cotton districts where he saw plantations of varying sizes. He interviewed a slaveholding abolitionist, observed some pious slaves conducting services, and studied a poor white family along the margins of a plantation area. The whites told him in their unique dialect about their early experience in Alabama and South Carolina with plots of slave insurrections and expressed apprehension that emancipation would expose the whites to danger. "Make 'em free and leave 'em here and they's steal everything we made," said one.

An unusual feature of *A Journey in the Back Country* was the extensive and perspicacious treatment of the highlander and his reaction to slavery. Occasionally a gifted Southern writer like Augustus B. Longstreet in *Georgia Scenes* (1835) would sketch the frontier types of the Deep South, but even he was content with poking fun at them. While Olmsted was far short of the stark naturalism of *Tobacco Road* or of Faulkner's *Sanctuary*, he did not make the sentimental mistakes of the Local Color School of the 1880's and 1890's. His single-track mind, however, tended to see the highlander largely as a tragic victim of the impact of slavery, although he did not ignore the effects of isolation and limited markets. Gifted with an expert eye for agricultural problems and landscapes, he easily conveyed the atmosphere of the Southern Appalachians with their valley lands, mountain forests, wild animals, and mixture of slave and non-slaveholding farms.

Amidst these small farms he learned, as he expected, that slaves were unprofitable, except for sale on the currently rising market. Supervision was so expensive that the slaves were allowed to mishandle valuable animals and tools. The level of literacy among the whites was very low compared with that of the lowest class of New England working people. Yet he claimed that books were more common among the nonslaveholding highlander than among the slaveowners and that they were fond of reading aloud, even if they generally preferred doleful religious subjects. Their ignorance of the outside world was astonishing, for they had difficulty in locating New York and were surprised that slavery did not exist there. One Tennessee family thought that Virginia lay to the South and was a cotton-growing state; another asked whether the war with Mexico was over. Although Olmsted saw hard-working tobacco-smoking women and simple spinning wheels and handlooms, he concluded that there was little real poverty among them. "Compared with the slaveholders," he exclaimed, "these people are more cheerful, more amiable, and more liberal."

People of this class usually disliked slavery because of Negro competition, their own mean status, and the monopolistic position of the slaveholder. One highlander appeared to be a strong believer in African colonization of as many slaves as could be freed and asserted that nine-tenths of the slaves would do anything to be free. In Southwestern Virginia, he spoke to a slaveholder, an excellent plantation manager, who knew most of the arguments against the profitableness of slavery, but believed that if the slaves were freed they would ruin the country.

Virginia, Olmsted believed, had slipped backward since the great days of Jefferson and seemed to be making excuses for its shortcomings. Virginians blamed the inefficiency of poor white labor upon the natural indolence of the poor whites, who seemed content to revert to old frontier habits of carelessness. The talk about slavery as a patriarchal institution seemed absurd to Olmsted, for the relation of father and son was wholly out of keeping with the nature of slavery. Besides, a patriarchal society was necessarily primitive and fit only for the indolent and the defenseless.

He feared that the inefficiency of slavery which had hastened soil exhaustion had now driven slaveholders, especially those in South Carolina, to seek the revival of African slave importations in order to seize fresh slave territories in the West. Such a policy spelled ruin for the South and could precipitate civil war. He pressed his point home by arguing that in such a war, superior Northern resources and the disloyalty or unreliability of the slaves would defeat the South. He recurred again to his earlier proposals for gradual abolition through a system of slave incentives that would increase productivity and enable the bondsmen to buy their freedom. This was the last hope to avert war.

In 1861, when the two-volume condensation of his trilogy appeared as *The Cotton Kingdom,* war was already a fact and Olmsted now concentrated on converting British opinion to see the justice of the Union cause. Save for a new introductory chapter and some relatively few pages inserted to insure continuity, the new edition added little to the story that he had told previously.[20] He was now wholeheartedly for a military victory. "It is said that the South can never be subjugated," he observed. "*It* must be or *we* must." This was restated in a "house-divided" antithesis: "One system or the other is to thrive and extend, and eventually possess and govern this whole land." The title itself referred to the fire-eating speech of Senator James Hammond of South Carolina after the panic of 1857 which had swept the commercial North but left the Cotton South relatively untouched! "No! You dare not make war upon cotton: no power on earth dares to make war upon it. Cotton is king. . . ." So Olmsted took up this challenge.

One hundred years after the publication of his books, Frederick Law Olmsted is more strongly entrenched than ever as the interpreter of the Old South.[21] The eminent historian, William E. Dodd, wrote one of his best books using the title, *The Cotton Kingdom*, (1919) employing many of the same facts and viewpoints. Historians leaned toward the Olmsted idea that slavery did not pay, although vigorous critics took issue with this. Kenneth Stampp in his book, *The Peculiar Institution* (1956) rejected many of Olmsted's arguments and even his facts. Slaveholders, he thought, did make the system pay through bonuses and prestige rewards to cooperative slaves. It is apparent to the modern historian that much of the backwardness of the South was due to many more factors besides slavery—as became apparent by the Twentieth Century—such as the uneconomic one-crop system, racial and class exploitation, rural backwardness, and the failure of regional leadership to exploit the South's rich potentialities fully. These were among the factors that led President Franklin D. Roosevelt to stigmatize the South as the nation's Number One economic problem during the mid-1930's. Olmsted had been acutely aware of the race factor in Southern life apart from slavery, for he recognized the role of race prejudice and the power of white supremacists, but he chose to concentrate on the social and economic costs of slavery, hoping to convince masters that they had everything to lose by perpetuating the peculiar institution. His failure could have been anticipated, for the tension of over fifty years and the complex race issue would not be easily overcome by a reasoned appeal to humanitarianism and self-interest.

—Harvey Wish

EDITOR'S NOTE

In order to avoid the changes in meaning and emphasis that came with the condensation of Olmsted's three books, the new text has been chosen from the original trilogy itself and from the informative preface to *The Cotton Kingdom*. Thus certain later omissions, such as the interesting and significant discussion of the Texas German colony, have been restored.

Since this edition consists of somewhat less than one-sixth of the pages in the lengthy trilogy, care has been taken to make them as representative as possible. In addition, Olmsted's varied views and beliefs on slavery and the South are presented with some effort at sufficient continuity to offer a unified edition of the entire work. The editor has given particular space to *A Journey in the Sea-board States* because of its unusually informative nature.

H.W.

FOOTNOTES

1. Chief biographic facts are in Frederick L. Olmsted Jr. and Theodora Kimball (eds.), *Frederick Law Olmsted, Landscape Architect, 1822-1903* (G. P. Putnam's Sons, New York, 1922); Broadus Mitchell, *Frederick Law Olmsted* (The Johns Hopkins University Press, Baltimore, 1924); M. G. Van Rensselaer, "Frederick Law Olmsted," *Century Magazine,* October, 1893; "Frederick Law Olmsted," *The National Cyclopedia,* II, 298-299; and "Frederick L. Olmsted," *Dictionary of American Biography.*

2. Frederick L. Olmsted, *A Journey in the Back Country* (New York, 1860), 287.

3. *Id., Walks and Talks of an American Farmer in England* (New York, 1852), 31; Emma Brace, *The Life of Charles Loring Brace* (London, 1894), 72-73, 89-97, 112, 142.

4. Augustus Maverick, *Henry J. Raymond and the New York Press* (New York, 1870), *passim.*

5. New York *Daily Times,* April 7, 1853; see praise of Olmsted's articles by "B" of New York in *Ibid.,* May 18, 1853.

6. *Ibid.,* June 6, 1853. Olmsted replied to "A Native Southerner," in *Ibid.,* June 21, 1853.

7. *Ibid.,* April 29, 1853.

8. *Ibid.,* April 8, 1853. Olmsted's letter to the *Times* included the following statement which was later deleted from *A Journey in the Seaboard Slave States:* "Oh, God! Who are we to condemn our brother? No slave ever killed its own offspring in cool calculation of earning money by it, as do English free women. No slave is forced to eat of corruption, as are Irish tenants. . . . Remember that, Mrs. Stowe."

9. Laura Wood Roper, "Frederick L. Olmsted and the Western Texas Free Soil Movement," *American Historical Review,* LVI (1950-51), 58-64.

10. Percy W. Bidwell (ed.), "The New England Emigrant Aid Company and the English Cotton Supply Association: Letters of Frederick L. Olmsted, 1857," *Ibid.*, XXIII (1917-18), 114-119.

11. Laura Wood Roper, "Frederick Law Olmsted in the Literary Republic," *Mississippi Valley Historical Review*, XXXIX (1952), 459-482.

12. *Ibid.;* Laura Roper estimates that the total sales did not exceed 25,000 copies during 1856-1861.

13. Letters of March 11 and April 6, 1862 in W. C. Ford (ed.), *A Cycle of Adams Letters, 1861-1865* (Houghton, Mifflin, 1920), I, 117, 127.

14. F. L. Olmsted Jr. and Theodora Kimball (eds.), *Frederick Law Olmsted, Landscape Architect, passim;* Charles J. Stille, *A History of the United States Sanitary Commission* (Lippincott, 1866), 75-78.

15. Letter of August 5, 1889 in Thomas H. Clark, "Frederick Law Olmsted on the South, 1889," *South Atlantic Quarterly*, III (Jan.-Oct. 1904), 11-15.

16. Olmsted Jr. and Kimball, *passim.*

17. Based on a forthcoming book in historiography for the Oxford University Press.

18. Harvey Wish, *George Fitzhugh, Propagandist of the Old South* (Louisiana State University Press, 1943), *passim.*

19. Summarized from Harvey Wish, *Society and Thought in Early America* (Longmans, Green, 1950), 506-507.

20. Arthur M. Schlesinger Sr. has carefully compared the original three volumes with *The Cotton Kingdom* (Knopf, 1953), xxvii-xxxvi.

21. Broadus Mitchell notes that James F. Rhodes makes more frequent use of Olmsted than of any other writer on slavery. Mitchell, *Olmsted*, xv note.

Note: the punctuation throughout has, in many cases, been silently modernized.

A

JOURNEY

IN THE

SEABOARD
SLAVE STATES,

WITH REMARKS ON THEIR ECONOMY

BY
FREDERICK LAW OLMSTED,
AUTHOR OF "WALKS AND TALKS OF AN AMERICAN
FARMER IN ENGLAND"

———

NEW YORK: DIX & EDWARDS.
LONDON: SAMPSON LOW, SON & CO.
1856

CHAPTER I

VIRGINIA

SLAVE LABOR.

THE labor of this farm was entirely performed by slaves. I did not inquire their number, but I judged there were from twenty to forty. Their "quarters" lined the approach-road to the mansion, and were well-made and comfortable log cabins, about thirty feet long by twenty wide, and eight feet tall, with a high loft and shingle roof. Each, divided in the middle, and having a brick chimney outside the wall at each end, was intended to be occupied by two families. There were square windows closed by wooden ports, having a single pane of glass in the center. The house-servants were neatly dressed, but the field-hands wore very coarse and ragged garments.

During three hours or more in which I was in company with the proprietor, I do not think there were ten consecutive minutes uninterrupted by some of the slaves requiring his personal direction or assistance. He was even obliged three times to leave the dinner-table.

"You see," said he, smiling, as he came in the last time, "a farmer's life, in this country, is no sinecure." This turning the conversation to Slavery, he observed, in answer to a remark of mine, "I only wish your philanthropists would contrive some satisfactory plan to relieve us of it; the trouble and the responsibility of properly taking care of our negroes, you may judge, from what you see yourself here, is anything but enviable. But what can we do that is better? Our free negroes—and, I believe it is the same at the North as it is here—are a miserable set of vagabonds, drunken, vicious, worse off, it is my honest opinion, than those who are retained in slavery. I am satisfied, too, that our slaves are better off as they are, than the majority of your free laboring classes at the North."

I expressed my doubts.

"Well, they certainly are better off than the English agricultural laborers or, I believe, those of any other Christian country. Free labor might be more profitable to us: I am inclined to think it would be. The slaves are excessively careless and wasteful, and, in various ways—which, without you lived among them, you could hardly be made to understand—subject us to very annoying losses.

"To make anything by farming here, a man has got to live a hard life. You see how constantly I am called upon —and often it is about as bad at night as by day. Last night I did not sleep a wink till near morning; I am quite worn out with it, and my wife's health is failing. But I cannot rid myself of it."

OVERSEERS.

I asked why he did not employ an overseer.

"Because I do not think it right to trust to such men as we have to use, if we use any, for overseers."

"Is the general character of overseers bad?"

"They are the curse of this country, sir; the worst men in the community. * * * * But lately, I had another sort of fellow offer—a fellow like a dancing-master, with kid gloves, and wrist-bands turned up over his coat-sleeves, and all so nice that I was almost ashamed to talk to him in my old coat and slouched hat. Half a bushel of recommendations he had with him, too. Well, he was not the man for me—not half the gentleman, with all his airs, that Ned here is"—(a black servant, who was bursting with suppressed laughter, behind his chair).

"Oh, they are interesting creatures, sir," he continued, "and, with all their faults, have many beautiful traits. I can't help being attached to them, and I am sure they love us." In his own case, at least, I did not doubt it; his manner towards them was paternal—familiar and kind; and they came to him like children who have been given some task and constantly are wanting to be encouraged and guided, simply and confidently. At dinner, he frequently addressed the servant familiarly and drew him into our conversation as if he were a family friend, better informed, on some local and domestic points, than himself.

He informed me that able-bodied field-hands were hired out, in this vicinity, at the rate of one hundred dollars a year and their board and clothing. Four able-bodied men that I have employed the last year on my farm in New York, I pay, on an average, one hundred and five dollars each, and board them; they clothe themselves at an expense, I think, of twenty dollars a year;—probably slaves' clothing costs twice that. They constitute all the force of my farm, hired by the year (except a boy, who goes to school in Winter), and, in my absence, have no overseer except one of themselves, whom I appoint. I pay the fair wages of the market, more than any of my neighbors, I believe, and these are no lower than the average of what I have paid for the last five years. It is difficult to measure the labor performed in a day by one with that of the other, on account of undefined differences in the soil and in the bulk and weight of articles operated upon. But, here, I am shown tools that no man in his senses, with us, would allow a laborer, to whom he was paying wages, to be encumbered with, and the excessive weight and clumsiness of which, I would judge, would make work at least ten per cent greater than those ordinarily used with us. And I am assured that, in the careless and clumsy way they must be used by the slaves, anything lighter or less rude could not be furnished them with good economy, and that such tools as we constantly give our laborers, and find our profit in giving them, would not last out a day in a Virginia corn-field—much lighter and more free from stones though it be than ours.

So, too, when I ask why mules are so universally substituted for horses on the farm, the first reason given, and confessedly the most conclusive one, is that horses cannot bear the treatment they always *must* get from negroes; horses are always soon foundered or crippled by them, while mules will bear cudgeling and lose a meal now and then and not be materially injured, and they do not take cold or get sick if neglected or overworked. But I do not need to go further than to the window of the room in which I am writing to see, at almost any time, treatment of cattle that would insure the immediate discharge of the driver by almost any farmer owning them at the North.

A COAL MINE—NEGRO AND ENGLISH MINERS.

Yesterday I visited a coal-pit: the majority of the mining laborers are slaves, and uncommonly athletic and fine-looking negroes, but a considerable number of white hands are also employed, and they occupy all the responsible posts. The slaves are, some of them, owned by the

Mining Company; but the most are hired of their owners at from $120 to $200 a year, the company boarding and clothing them. (I have the impression that I heard it was customary to give them a certain allowance of money and let them find their own board).

The white hands are mostly English or Welchmen. One of them with whom I conversed told me that he had been here several years; he had previously lived some years at the North. He got better wages here than he had earned at the North, but he was not contented, and did not intend to remain. On pressing him for the reason of his discontent, he said, after some hesitation, that he had rather live where he could be more free; a man had to be too *"discreet"* here: if one happened to say anything that gave offense, they thought no more of drawing a pistol or a knife upon him, than they would of kicking a dog that was in their way. Not long since, a young English fellow came to the pit, and was put to work along with a gang of negroes. One morning, about a week afterwards, twenty or thirty men called on him and told him that they would allow him fifteen minutes to get out of sight, and if they ever saw him in those parts again they would "give him hell." They were all armed, and there was nothing for the young fellow to do but to move "right off."

"What reason did they give him for it?"

"They did not give him any reason."

"But what had he done?"

"Why I believe they thought he had been too free with the niggers; he wasn't used to them, you see, sir, and he talked to 'em free like, and they thought he'd make 'em think too much of themselves."

He said the slaves were very well fed, and well treated —not worked over hard. They were employed night and day, in relays.

The coal from these beds is of special value for gas manufacture, and is shipped for that purpose to all the large towns on the Atlantic sea-board, even to beyond Boston. It is delivered to shipping at Richmond at fifteen cents a bushel: about thirty bushels go to a ton.

VALUABLE SERVANTS.

The hotel at which I am staying, "the American," Milberger Smith from New York, proprietor, is a very capital

one. I have never, this side the Atlantic, had my comforts
provided for better, in my private room, with so little
annoyance from the servants. The chamber-servants are
negroes, and are accomplished in their business; (the
dining-room servants are Irish). A man and a woman
attend together upon a few assigned rooms in the hall adjoining which they are constantly in waiting; your bell is
answered immediately, your orders are quickly and quietly followed, and your particular personal wants anticipated as much as possible and provided for, as well as the
usual offices performed, when you are out. The man becomes your servant while you are in your room; he asks,
at night, when he comes to request your boots, at what
time he shall come in the morning, and then, without being very exactly punctual, he comes quietly in, makes
your fire, sets the boots before it, brushes and arranges
your clothes, lays out your linen, arranges your washing
and dressing gear, asks if you want anything else of him
before breakfast, opens the shutters and goes off to the
next room. I took occasion to speak well of him to my
neighbor one day, that I might judge whether I was
particularly favored.

"Oh yes," he said, "Henry was a very good boy, very—
valuable servant—quite so—would be worth two thousand dollars if he was a little younger—easy."

At dinner, a respectable-looking, gray-headed man
asked another:

"Niggers are going high now, aint they?"

"Yes, sir."

"What would you consider a fair price for a woman
thirty years old, with a young-one two years old?"

"Depends altogether on her physical condition, you
know.—Has she any other children?"

"*Yes; four.*"

"——Well—I reckon about seven to eight hundred."

"I bought one yesterday—gave six hundred and fifty."

"Well, sir, if she's tolerable likely, you did well."

DRESS AND STYLE OF PEOPLE.

What is most remarkable in the appearance of the people of the better class, is their invariably *high-dressed*
condition; look down the opposite side of the table, even
at breakfast, and you will probably see thirty men drink-

ing coffee, all in full funeral dress, not an easy coat
amongst them. It is the same in the street, and the same
with ladies as with gentlemen; silk and satin, under um-
brellas, rustle along the side-walk, or skip across it between carriages and the shops, as if they were going to a
dinner-party, at eleven o'clock in the morning. The last
is only New York repeated, to be sure, but the gentlemen carry it further than in New York, and seem never to
indulge in undress.

I have rarely seen a finer assemblage of people than
filled the theatre one night, at the benefit of the Bateman
children, who are especial favorites of the public here. As
the Legislature is in session, I presume there was a fair
representation of the Virginians of all parts of the State.
A remarkable proportion of the men were very tall and of
animated expression—and of the women, fair, refined and
serene. The men, however, were very deficient in robust-
ness, and the women, though graceful and attractive, had
none of that dignity and stateliness for which the dames
of Virginia were formerly much distinguished.

In *manners*, I notice that between man and man more
ceremony and form is sustained in familiar conversation
than well-bred people commonly use at the North.

Among the people you see in the streets, full half, I
should think, are more or less of negro blood, and a very
decent, civil people these seem, in general, to be; more so
than the laboring class of whites, among which there are
many very ruffianly looking fellows. There is a considerable population of foreign origin, generally of the least
valuable class; very dirty German Jews, especially,
abound, and their characteristic shops (with their characteristic smells, quite as bad as in Cologne), are thickly
set in the narrowest and meanest streets, which seem to
be otherwise inhabited mainly by negroes.

STREET PEOPLE.

Immense wagons, drawn by six mules each, the teamster always riding on the back of the near-wheeler, are a
characteristic feature of the streets. Another is the wood-
carts; small trucks loaded with about a cord of pine
wood, drawn by three mules or horses, one in shafts, and
two others, abreast, before him; a negro always riding the
shaft-horse and guiding the leaders with a single rein, one

pull to turn them to the right and two to the left with a great deal of the whip whichever way they go. The same guiding apparatus, a single line, with branches to each bit, is used altogether upon the long wagon teams. On the canal, a long, narrow, canoe-like boat, perhaps fifty feet long and six wide, and drawing but a foot or two of water, is nearly as common as the ordinary large boats, such as are used on our canals. They come out of some of the small, narrow, crooked streams, connected with the canals, in which a difficult navigation is effected by poling. They are loaded with tobacco, flour and a great variety of raw country produce. The canal boatmen of Virginia seem to be quite as rude, insolent and riotous a class as those of New York, and every facility is evidently afforded them at Richmond for indulging their peculiar appetites and tastes. A great many low eating, and, I should think, drinking shops are frequented chiefly by the negroes. Dancing and other amusements are carried on in these at night.

From reading the comments of Southern statesmen and newspapers on the crime and misery which sometimes result from the accumulation of poor and ignorant people, with no intelligent masters to take care of them, in our Northern towns, one might get the impression that Southern towns—especially those not demoralized by foreign commerce—were comparatively free from a low and licentious population. From what I have seen, however, I should be now led to think that there was at least as much vice and of what we call rowdyism in Richmond as in any Northern town of its size.[*]

THE GREAT SOUTHERN ROUTE AND ITS FAST TRAIN.

The train was advertised to leave at 3.30 P.M. At that hour the cars were crowded with passengers, and the engineer, punctually at the minute, gave notice that he was at his post, by a long, loud whistle of the locomotive. Five minutes afterwards he gave us an impatient jerk; ten min-

---

[*] SAD PICTURE.—A gentleman informs the *Richmond* (Va.) *Dispatch* that, while taking a stroll on one of the islands in James river, not far from Mayo's Bridge last Sunday morning, he counted as many as twenty-two boys, from ten to fifteen years of age, engaged in gaming with cards and dice for money. In some of the parties he saw grown men and small boys playing bluff, and cursing, swearing and drinking.—*Southern Newspaper.*

utes afterwards we advanced three rods; twelve minutes
afterwards, returned to first position: continued "backing
and filling" upon the bridge over the rapids of the James
river for half an hour. At precisely four o'clock, crossed
the bridge and fairly started for Petersburg.

Ran twenty miles in exactly an hour and thirty minutes, (thirteen miles an hour; mail train, especially recommended by advertisement as "fast"). Brakes on, three
times, for cattle on the track; twenty minutes spent at
way-stations. Flat rail. Locomotive built at Philadelphia.
I am informed that most of those used on the road—
perhaps all those of the *slow* trains—are made at Petersburg.

At one of the stoppages, smoke was to be seen issuing
from the truck of a car. The conductor, on having his attention called to it, nodded his head sagely, took a morsel
of tobacco, put his hands in his pocket, looked at the truck
as if he would mesmerize it, spat upon it, and then stept
upon the platform and shouted "All right! Go ahead!" At
the next stoppage, the smoking was furious; conductor
bent himself over it with an evidently strong exercise of
his will, but not succeeding to tranquilize the subject at
all, he suddenly relinquished the attempt, and, deserting
Mesmer for Preisnitz, shouted, "Ho! boy! bring me some
water here." A negro soon brought a quart of water in
a tin vessel.

"Hain't got no oil, Columbus?"

"No, sir."

"Hum—go ask Mr. Smith for some: this yer's a screak-
ing so, I durstn't go on. You Scott! get some salt. And look
here, some of you boys, get me some more water. D'ye
hear?"

Salt, oil and water, were crowded into the box, and,
after five minutes longer delay, we went on, the truck
still smoking, and the water and oil boiling in the box,
until we reached Petersburg. The heat was the result,
I suppose, of a neglect of sufficient or timely oiling. While
waiting, in a carriage, for the driver to get my baggage,
I saw a negro oiling all the trucks of the train; as he proceeded from one to the other, he did not give himself the
trouble to elevate the outlet of his oiler, so that a stream
of oil costing probably a dollar and a half a gallon was
poured out upon the ground the whole length of the train.

ONE OF THE LAW-GIVERS.

While on the bridge at Richmond, the car in which I
was seated was over-full—several persons standing; among
them one considerably "excited" who informed the company that he was a Member of the House of Delegates,
and that he would take advantage of this opportune collection of the people to expose an atrocious attempt on
the part of the minority to jump a Bill through the Legislature which was not in accordance with true Democratic
principles. He continued for some time to address them
in most violent, absurd, profane and meaningless language; the main point of his oration being to demand the
popular gratitude for himself for having had the sagacity
and courage to prevent the accomplishment of the ne-
farious design. He afterwards attempted to pass into the
ladies' car, but was dissuaded from doing so by the conductor who prevailed on a young man to give him his seat.
Having taken it, he immediately lifted his feet upon the
back of the seat before him, resting them upon the shoulders of its occupant. This gentleman turning his head, he
begged his pardon; but, hoping it would not occasion
him inconvenience, he said he would prefer to keep them
there, and did so; soon afterwards falling alseep.

FREIGHT TAKEN—THE SLAVE TRADE.

There were in the train two first-class passenger cars and
two freight cars. The latter were occupied by about forty
negroes, most of them belonging to traders, who were
sending them to the cotton States to be sold. Such kind of
evidence of activity in the slave trade of Virginia is to be
seen every day; but particulars and statistics of it are not
to be obtained by a stranger here. Most gentlemen of
character seem to have a special disinclination to converse
on the subject; and it is denied, with feeling, that slaves
are often reared, as is supposed by the Abolitionists, with
the intention of selling them to the traders. It appears to
me evident, however, from the manner in which I hear
the traffic spoken of incidentally, that the cash value of a
slave for sale, above the cost of raising it from infancy to
the age at which it commands the highest price, is generally considered among the surest elements of a planter's

wealth. Such a nigger is worth such a price, and such another is too old to learn to pick cotton, and such another will bring so much, when it has grown a little more. I have frequently heard people say, in the street, or the public-houses. That a slave woman is commonly esteemed least for her laboring qualities, most for those qualities which give value to a brood-mare is also constantly made apparent.*

By comparing the average decennial ratio of slave increase in all the States with the difference in the number of the actual slave-population of the slave-breeding States, as ascertained by the census, it is apparent that the number of slaves exported to the cotton States is considerably more than twenty thousand a year.

While calling on a gentleman occupying an honorable official position at Richmond, I noticed upon his table a copy of Professor Johnson's Agricultural Tour in the United States. Referring to a paragraph in it, where some statistics of the value of the slaves raised and annually exported from Virginia were given, I asked if he knew how these had been obtained, and whether they were reliable. "No," he replied; "I don't know anything about it; but if they are anything unfavorable to the institution of slavery, you may be sure they are false." This is but an illustration, in extreme, of the manner in which I find a desire to obtain more correct but *definite* information on the subject of slavery is usually met, by gentlemen otherwise of enlarged mind and generous qualities.

A gentleman who was a member of the "Union Safety Committee" of New York during the excitement which attended the discussion of the Fugitive Slave Act of 1850, told me that, as he was passing through Virginia this winter, a man entered the car in which he was seated, leading in a negro girl, whose manner and expression of face indicated dread and grief. Thinking she was a criminal, he asked the man what she had done:

---

* A slaveholder writing to me with regard to my cautious statements on this subject, made in the *Daily Times*, says:—"In the States of Maryland, Virginia, North Carolina, Kentucky, Tennessee and Missouri, as much attention is paid to the breeding and growth of negroes as to that of horses and mules. Further south, we raise them both for use and for market. Planters command their girls and women (married or unmarried) to have children; and I have known a great many negro girls to be sold off, because they did not have children. A breeding woman is worth from one-sixth to one-fourth more than one that does not breed."

"Done? Nothing."

"What are you going to do with her?"

"I'm taking her down to Richmond, to be sold."

"Does she belong to you?"

"No; she belongs to———; he raised her."

"Why does he sell her—has she done anything wrong?"

"Done anything? No: she's no fault, I reckon."

"Then, what does he want to sell for?"

"Sell her for! Why shouldn't he sell her? He sells one or two every year; wants the money for 'em, I reckon."

The irritated tone and severe stare with which this was said, my friend took as a caution not to pursue his investigation.

A gentleman with whom I was conversing on the subject of the cost of slave labor in answer to an inquiry—what proportion of all the stock of slaves of an old plantation might be reckoned upon to do full work?—answered that he owned ninety-six negroes; of these, only thirty-five were field-hands, the rest being either too young or too old for hard work. He reckoned his whole force as only equal to twenty-one strong men, or *"prime* field-hands." But this proportion was somewhat smaller than usual, he added, "because his women were uncommonly good breeders; he did not suppose there was a lot of women anywhere that bred faster than his; he never heard of babies coming so fast as they did on his plantation; it was perfectly surprising; and every one of them, in his estimation, was worth two hundred dollars, as negroes were selling now, the moment it drew breath."

I asked what he thought might be the usual proportion of workers to slaves supported on plantations throughout the South. On the large cotton and sugar plantations of the more Southern States, it was very high, he replied; because their hands were nearly all bought and *picked for work;* he supposed, on those, it would be about one-half; but on any old plantation, where the stock of slaves had been an inheritance, and none had been bought or sold, he thought the working force would rarely be more than one-third, at most, of the whole number.

This gentleman was out of health, and told me, with frankness, that such was the trouble and annoyance his negroes occasioned him—although he had an overseer—and so wearisome did he find the lonely life he led on his plantation, that he could not remain upon it; and, as he knew everything would go to the dogs if he did not, he was seriously contemplating to sell out, retaining only his foster-mother and a body-servant. He thought of taking them to Louisiana and Texas, for sale; but, if he should learn that there was much probability that Lower California would be made a slave State, he supposed it would pay him to wait, as probably, if that should occur, he could take them there and sell them for twice as much as they would now bring in New Orleans. He knew very well, he said, that, as they were, raising corn and tobacco, they were paying nothing at all like a fair interest on their value.*

Some of his best hands he now rented out to work in a furnace, and for the best of these he had been offered, for next year, two hundred dollars. He did not know whether he ought to let them go, though. They were worked hard, and had too much liberty, and were acquiring bad habits. They earned money by overwork, and spent it for whisky, and got a habit of roaming about and *taking care of themselves;* because, when they were not at work in the furnace, nobody looked out for them.

I begin to suspect that the great trouble and anxiety of Southern gentlemen is:—How, without quite destroying the capabilities of the negro for any work at all, to prevent him from learning to take care of himself.

RURAL SCENERY AND RURAL LIFE IN VIRGINIA.

PETERSBURG, Dec. 28.—It was early in a fine, mild, bright morning, like the pleasantest we ever have in March, that I alighted from a train of cars at a country station. Besides the shanty that stood for a station-house there was a small, comfortable farm-house on the right and a country store on the left and around them perhaps fifty acres of cleared land, now much flooded with muddy water;—all environed by thick woods.

A few negro children, staring as fixedly and posed as lifelessly as if they were really figures "carved in ebony," stood, lay and lounged on the sunny side of the ranks of locomotive-firewood; a white man smoking a cigar looked out of the door of the store, and another chewing tobacco

---

* Mr. Wise is reported to have stated in his electioneering tour when candidate for Governor in 1855, that if slavery were permitted in California, negroes would sell for $5,000 apiece.

leaned against a gate-post in front of the farm-house; I advanced to the latter and asked him if I could hire a horse in the neighborhood.

"How d'ye do, sir?" he replied; "I have some horses— none on 'em very good ones, though—rather hard riders; reckon, perhaps, they wouldn't suit you very well."

"Thank you; do you think I could find anything better about here?"

"Colonel Gillin, over here to the store, 's got a right nice saddle-horse, if he'll let you take her. I'll go over there with you, and see if he will. . . . Mornin', Colonel;— here's a gentleman that wants to go to Thomas W.'s: couldn't you let him have your saddle-horse?"

"How do you do, sir; I suppose you'd come back to-night?"

"That's my intention, but I might be detained till to-morrow, unless it would be inconvenient to you to spare your horse."

"Well, yes, sir, I reckon you can have her;—Tom!— Tom!—*Tom!* Now, has that devilish nigger gone again! Tom! *Oh*, Tom! saddle the filly for this gentleman.—— Have you ever been to Mr. W.'s, sir?"

"No, I have not."

"It isn't a very easy place for strangers to go to from here; but I reckon I can direct you, so you'll have no difficulty."

He accordingly began to direct me; but, the way appeared so difficult to find, I asked him to let me make a written memorandum, and from this memorandum I now repeat the directions he gave me.

"You take this road here—you'll see where it's most traveled, and it's easy enough to keep on it for about a mile; then there's a fork, and you take the right; pretty soon, you'll cross a creek and turn to the right—the creek's been up a good deal lately, and there's some big trees fallen along there, and, if they ha'n't got them out of the way, you may have some difficulty in finding where the road is; but you keep bearing off to the right, where it's the most open [*i. e.*, the wood], and you'll see it again pretty soon. Then you go on, keeping along in the road— you'll see where folks have traveled before—for maybe quarter of a mile, and you'll find a cross-road; you must take that to the left; pretty soon you'll pass two cabins; one of 'em's old and all fallen in, the other one's new, and there's a white man lives into it: you can't mistake it. About a hundred yards beyond it, there's a fork, and you take the left—it turns square off, and it's fenced for a good bit; keep along by the fence, and you can't miss it. It's right straight beyond that till you come to a school-house, there's a gate opposite to it, and off there there's a big house—but I don't reckon you'll see it neither, for the woods. But somewhere, about three hundred yards beyond the school-house, you'll find a little road running off to the left through an old field; you take that and keep along in it, and in less than half a mile you'll find a path going square off to the right; you take that, and keep on it till you pass a little cabin in the woods; ain't nobody lives there now: then it turns to the left, and when you come to a fence and gate, you'll see a house there, that's Mr. George Rivers' plantation—it breaks in two, and you take the right, and when you come to the end of the fence, turn the corner—don't keep on, but turn there. Then it's straight, till you come to the creek again— there's a bridge there; don't go over the bridge, but turn to the left and keep along nigh the creek, and pretty soon you'll see a meeting-house in the woods; you go to that, and you'll see a path bearing off to the right—it looks as if it was going right away from the creek, but you take it, and pretty soon it'll bring you to a saw-mill on the creek, up higher a piece; you just cross the creek there, and you'll find some people at the mill, and they'll put you right straight on the road to Mr. W.'s."

"How far is it all, sir?"

"I reckon it's about two hours' ride, when the roads are good, to the saw-mill. Mr. W.'s gate is only a mile or so beyond that, and then you've got another mile, or better, after you get to the gate, but you'll see some nigger-quarters—the niggers belong to Mr. W., and I reckon ther'll be some of 'em round, and they'll show you just where to go."

After reading over my memorandum, and finding it correct, and agreeing with him that I should pay two dollars a day for the mare, we walked out and found her saddled and waiting for me.

I remarked that she was very good-looking.

"Yes, sir; she a'nt a bad filly; out of a mare that came of Lady Rackett by old Lord-knows-who, the best horse we ever had in this part of the country: I expect you have

heard of him. Oh! She's maybe a little playful, but you'll
find her a pleasant riding-horse."

The filly was just so pleasantly playful and full of well-
bred life as to create a joyful, healthy, sympathetic, frolic-
some heedlessness in her rider—walking rapidly, and with
a sometimes irresistible inclination to dance and bound;
making believe she was frightened at all the burnt stumps,
and flashes of sun-light on the ice, and, everytime a hog
lifted himself up before her, starting back in the most ridiculous manner, as if she had never seen a hog before;
bounding over the fallen trees as easily as a lifeboat over
a billow; and all the time gracefully playing tricks with
her feet, and her ears, and her tail, and evidently enjoying
herself just like any child in a half-holiday ramble through
the woods, yet never failing to answer to every motion of
my hand or my knees as if she were a part of myself. In
fact, there soon came to be a real good understanding, if
not even something like a merging of identity, between
Jane and me (the filly's name was Jane Gillin); if *her*
feet were not in the stirrups, I am sure I had all the sensation of tripping it on the ground with mine, half the time,
and we both entered into each other's feelings, and
moved, and were moved, together, in a way which a two
hours' lecture by a professor of psychology would be in-
sufficient satisfactorily to explain to people who never——
but all that's of no consequence, except that, of course,
we soon lost our way.

We were walking along slowly, quietly, musingly—I
was fondling her with my hand under her mane, when it
suddenly came into my mind: "Why, Jane! It's a long
time since I've thought anything about the road—I wonder where we've got to." We stopped and tried to work
up our dead-reckoning.

First, we picked our way from the store down to the
brook, through a deeply corrugated clay-road; then there
was the swamp, with the fallen trees and thick under-
wood, beaten down and barked in the miry parts by wagons, making a road for themselves, no traces of which
could we find in the harder, pebbly ground. At length
when we came on to drier land, and among pine trees, we
discovered a clear way cut through them, and a distinct
road before us again; and this brought us soon to an old
clearing, just beginning to be grown over with pines, in
which was the old cabin of rotten logs, one or two of them

falling out of rank on the door-side, and the whole concern having a dangerous lurch to one corner, as if too
much whisky had been drank in it: then a more recent
clearing, with a fenced field and another cabin, the residence of that white man we were told of probably. No
white people, however, were to be seen, but two negroes
sat in the mouth of a wigwam, husking maize, and a
couple of hungry hounds came bounding over the zig-
zag, gateless fence, as if they had agreed with each other
that they would wait no longer for the return of their
master, but would straight-way pull down the first traveler that passed, and have something to eat before they
were quite famished. They stopped short, however, when
they had got within a good cart-whip's length of us, and
contented themselves with dolefully *youping* as long as
we continued in sight. We turned the corner, following
some slight traces of a road, and shortly afterwards met a
curious vehicular establishment, probably belonging to
the master of the hounds. It consisted of an axle-tree and
wheels, and a pair of shafts made of unbarked saplings, in
which was harnessed, by attachments of raw-hide and
rope, a single small black ox. There was a bit, made of
telegraph-wire, in his mouth, by which he was guided,
through the mediation of a pair of much knotted rope-
reins, by a white man—a dignified sovereign, wearing a
brimless crown—who sat upon a two-bushel sack, (of
meal, I trust, for the hounds' sake,) balanced upon the
axle-tree, and who saluted me with a frank "How are
you?" as we came opposite each other.

Soon after this, we reached a small grove of much older
and larger pines than we had seen before, with long and
horizontally stretching branches, and duller and thinner
foliage. In the middle of it was another log-cabin, with a
door in one of the gable-ends, a stove-pipe, half-rusted
away, protruding from the other, and, in the middle of
one of the sides, a small square port-hole, closed by a
wooden shutter. This must have been the school-house,
but there were no children then about it, and no appearance of there having been any lately. Near it was a long
string of fence and a gate and lane, which gave entrance,
probably, to a large plantation, though there was no cultivated land within sight of the road.

I could remember hardly anything after this, except a
continuation of pine trees, big, little and medium in size,

and hogs, and a black, crooked, burnt sapling, that we had made believe was a snake springing at us and had jumped away from, and then we had gone on at a trot—it must have been some time ago, that—and then I was paying attentions to Jane, and finally my thoughts had gone wool-gathering, and we must have traveled some miles out of our way and—"never mind," said Jane, lifting her head, and turning in the direction we had been going, "I don't think it's any great matter if we are lost; such a fine day—so long since I've been out; if you don't care, I'd just as lief be lost as not; let's go on and see what we shall come to."

"Very well, my dear, you know the country better than I do; go where you like; if you'll risk your dinner, I'm quite ready to go anywhere in your company. It's quite certain we have not passed any meeting-house, or creek, or saw-mill, or negro-quarters, and, as we have been two hours on the road, it's evident we are not going straight to Mr. W.'s; I'll try at least to take note of what we do pass after this," and I stood up in the stirrups as we walked on, to see what the country around us was.

"Old fields"—a coarse, yellow, sandy soil, bearing scarce anything but pine trees and broom-sedge. In some places, for acres, the pines would not be above five feet high—that was land that had been in cultivation, used up and "turned out," not more than six or eight years before; then there were patches of every age; sometimes the trees were a hundred feet high. At long intervals, there were fields in which the pine was just beginning to spring in beautiful green plumes from the ground, and was yet hardly noticeable among the dead brown grass and sassafras bushes and blackberry-vines, which nature first sends to hide the nakedness of the impoverished earth.

Of living creatures, for miles, not one was to be seen (not even a crow or a snow-bird), except hogs. These—long, lank, bony, snake-headed, hairy, wild beasts—would come dashing across our path, in packs of from three to a dozen, with short, hasty grunts, almost always at a gallop, and looking neither to right nor left, as if they were in pursuit of a fox and were quite certain to catch him in the next hundred yards; or droves of little pigs would rise up suddenly in the sedge, and scamper off squealing into cover, while their heroic mothers would turn around and make a stand, looking fiercely at us as if they were quite ready to fight if we advanced any further, but always breaking as we came near with a loud *boosch!*

Once I saw a house, across a large, new old-field, but it was far off, and there was no distinct path leading towards it out of the wagon-track we were following; so we did not go to it, but continued walking steadily on through the old-fields and pine woods for more than an hour longer.

We then arrived at a grove of tall oak trees, in the midst of which ran a brook giving motion to a small gristmill. Back of the mill were two log cabins, and near these a number of negroes in holiday clothes were standing in groups among the trees. When we stopped one of them came towards us. He wore a battered old hat of the cylindrical fashion, stiffly starched shirt-collar cutting his ears, a red cravat and an old black dress coat, thread-bare and a little ragged, but adorned with new brass buttons. He knew Mr. Thomas W., certainly he did; and he reckoned I had come about four miles (he did not know but it might be eight, if I thought so) off the road I had been directed to follow. But that was of no consequence, because he could show me where to go by a straight road— a cross cut—from here, that would make it just as quick for me as if I had gone the way I had intended.

"How far is it from here?" I asked.

"Oh, 'taint far, sar."

"How far do you think?"

"Well, massa, I spec—I spec—(looking at my horse) I spec, massa, ef you goes de way, sar, dat I shows you, I reckon it'll take you—"

"How far is it—how many miles?"

"How many miles, sar? ha! masser, I don 'zactly reckon I ken tell ou—not 'cisely, sar—how many miles it is, not 'zactly, 'cisely, sar."

"How is that—you don't what?"

"I don't 'zactly reckon I can give you de drection excise about de miles, sar."

"Oh! but how many miles do you think it is; is it two miles?"

"Yes, sar; as de roads is now, I tink it is just about two miles. Dey's long ones, dough, I reckon."

"Long ones? You think it's more than two miles, don't you, then?"

"Yes, sar, I reckon its four or five miles."

"Four or five! four or five long ones or short ones do you mean?"

"I don' zactly know, sar, wedder dey is short ones or long ones, sar, but I reckon you find em middlin' long; I spec you'll be about two hours 'fore you be done gone all de way to mass W.'s."

He walked on with us a few rods upon a narrow path, until we came to a crossing of the stream; pointing to where it continued on the other side, he assured me that it went right straight to Mr. W.'s plantation. "You juss keep de straight road, master," he repeated several times, "and it'll take you right dar, sar."

He had been grinning and bowing, and constantly touching his hat, or holding it in his hand during our conversation, which I understood to mean that he would thank me for a dime. I gave it to him, upon which he repeated his contortions and his form of direction—"keep de straight road." I rode through the brook, and he called out again—"you keep dat road right straight and it'll take you right straight dar." I rode up the bank and entered the oak wood, and still again heard him enjoining me to "keep dat road right straight."

Within less than quarter of a mile, there was a fork in the road to the left, which seemed a good deal more traveled than the straight one; nevertheless I kept the latter, and was soon well satisfied that I had done so. It presently led me up a slope out of the oak woods into a dark evergreen forest; and though it was a mere bridle-path, it must have existed, I thought, before the trees began to grow, for it was free of stumps and smooth and clean as a garden walk, and the pines grew thickly up, about four feet apart, on each side of it, their branches meeting just clear of my head and making a dense shade. There was an agreeable, slightly balsamic odor in the air; the path was covered with a deep, elastic mat of pine leaves so that our footstep could hardly be heard; and for a time we greatly enjoyed going along at a lazy, pacing walk of Jane's. It was noon-day, and had been rather warmer than was quite agreeable on the open road, and I took my hat off and let the living pine leaves brush my hair. But after a while I felt slightly chilly; and when Jane, at the same time, gave a little sympathizing caper, I bent my head down, that the limbs might not hit me, until it nearly rested on her neck, dropped my hands and pressed my knees tightly against her. Away we bounded!

What a glorious gallop Jane had inherited from her noble grandfather!

Out of the cool, dark-green alley, at last, and soon with a more cautious step, down a steep, stony declivity, set with deciduous trees—beech, ash, oak, gum—"gum," beloved of the "minstrels." A brawling shallow brook at the bottom, into which our path descended, though on the opposite shore was a steep high bank, faced by an impenetrable brake of bush and briar.

Have we been following a path only leading to a watering-place, then? I see no continuance of it. Jane does not hesitate at all; but, as if it was the commonest thing here to take advantage of nature's engineering in this way, walking into the water, turns her head up stream.

For more than a mile we continued following up the brook, which was all the time walled in by insurmountable banks, overhung by large trees. Sometimes it swept strongly through a deep channel, contracted by boulders; sometimes purled and tinkled over a pebbly slope; and sometimes stood in broad, silent pools, around the edges of which remained a skirt of ice, held there by bushes and long, broken water-grasses. Across the end of one of these, barring our way, a dead trunk had lately fallen. Jane walked up to it and turned her head to the right. "No," said I, "let's go over." She turned, and made a step left— "No! over," said I, drawing her back, and touching her with my heels.

Over we went, landing with such a concussion that I was nearly thrown off. I fell forward upon Jane's neck; she threw up her head, spurning my involuntary embrace; and then, with swollen nostrils and flashing eyes, walked on rapidly.

"Hope you are satisfied," said she, as I pulled my coat down; "if not, you had better spur me again."

"Why, my dear girl, what's the matter? It was nothing but leather—calf-skin—that I touched you with. I have no spurs—don't you see?" for she was turning her head to bite my foot. "Now, don't be foolish."

"Well, well," said she, "I'm a good-tempered girl, if I *am* blood; let's stop and drink."

After this, we soon came to pine woods again. Jane was

now for leaving the brook. I let her have her own way, and she soon found a beaten track in the woods. It certainly was not the "straight road" we had been directed to follow; but its course was less crooked than that of the brook, and after some time it led us out into a more open country, with young pines and inclosed fields. Eventually we came to a gate and lane, which we followed till we came to another cross-lane, leading straight to a farm-house.

As soon as we turned into the cross-lane, half-a-dozen little negro boys and girls were seen running towards the house to give alarm. We passed a stable with a cattle-pen by its side, opposite which was a vegetable garden enclosed with split palings; then across a running stream of water; then by a small cabin on the right; and a corn-crib and large pen, with a number of fatting hogs in it, on the left; then into a large, irregular yard, in the midst of which was the farm-house, before which were now collected three white children, six black ones, two negro women and an old lady with spectacles.

"How dy do, sir?" said the old lady, as we reined up, bowed, and lifted our hat, and put our black foot foremost.

"Thank you, madam, quite well; but I have lost my way to Mr. Thomas W.'s, and will trouble you to tell me how to go from here to get to his house."

By this time a black man came cautiously walking in from the field back of the house, bringing an axe; a woman, who had been washing clothes in the brook, left her work and came up on the other side, and two more girls climbed up on to a heap of logs that had been thrown upon the ground, near the porch, for fuel. The swine were making a great noise in their pen, as if feeding-time had come; and a flock of turkeys were gobbling so incessantly and loudly that I was not heard. The old lady ordered the turkeys to be driven away, but nobody stirred to do it, and I rode nearer and repeated my request. No better success. "Can't you shew away them turkeys?" she asked again; but nobody "shewed." A third time I endeavored to make myself understood. "Will you please direct me how to go to Mr. W.'s?"

"No, sir—not here."

"Excuse me—I asked if you would direct me to Mr. W.'s."

A VIRGINIA FARM-HOUSE

"If some of you niggers don't shew them turkeys, I'll have you all whipped as soon as your mass John comes home," exclaimed the old lady, now quite excited. The man with the axe, without moving towards them at all, picked up a billet of wood and threw it at the biggest cock-turkey, who immediately collapsed; and the whole flock scattered, chased by the two girls who had been on the log-heap.

"An't dat Colonel Gillen's mare, master?" asked the black man, coming up on my left.

"You want to go to Thomas W.'s?" asked the old lady.

"Yes, madam."

"It's a good many years since I have been to Thomas W.'s, and I reckon I can't tell you how to go there now."

"If master'll go over to Missy Abler's, I reckon dey ken tell 'em dah, sar."

"And how shall I go to Mrs. Abler's?"

"You want to go to Missy Abler's; you take dat path right over 'yond dem bars, dar, by de hog-pen, dat runs along by dat fence into de woods, and dat'll take you right straight dar."

"Is you come from Colonel Gillin's, massa?" asked the wash-woman.

"Yes."

"Did you see a black man dar, day calls Tom, sar?"

"Yes."

"Tom's my husband, massa; if you's gwine back dah, wish you'd tell um, ef you please, sar, dat I wants to see him *particklar;* will ou, massa?"

"Yes."

"Tank you, massa."

I bowed to the old lady, and, in turning to ride off, saw two other negro boys who had come out of the woods, and were now leaning over the fence and staring at us as if I was a giant and Jane was a dragoness.

We trotted away, found the path, and in course of a mile had our choice of at least twenty forks to go "straight to Mrs. Abler's." At length, cleared land again, fences, stubble-fields and a lane, that took us to a little cabin, which fronted, much to my surprise, upon a broad and well-traveled road. Over the door of the cabin was a sign, done in black, upon a hogshead stave, showing that it was a "GROSERY," which in Virginia means the same thing as in Ireland—a dram-shop.

I hung the bridle over a rack before the door, and walked in. At one end of the interior was a range of shelves, on which were two decanters, some dirty tumblers, a box of crackers, a canister, and several packages in paper; under the shelves were a table and a barrel. At the other end of the room was a fireplace; near this, a chest, and another range of shelves, on which stood plates and cooking utensils: between these and the grocery end were a bed and a spinning-wheel. Near the spinning-wheel sat a tall, bony, sickly, sullen young woman, nursing a languishing infant. The faculty would not have discouraged either of them from trying hydropathic practice. In a corner of the fire-place sat a man, smoking a pipe. He rose as I entered, walked across to the grocery-shelves, turned a chair round at the table, and asked me to take a seat. I excused myself, and requested him to direct me to Mr. W.'s. He had heard of such a man living somewhere about there, but he did not know where. He repeated this, with an oath, when I declined to "take" anything, and added that he had not lived here long and he was sorry he had ever come here. It was the worst job for himself ever he did, when he came here, though all he wanted was to just get a living.

I rode on till I came to another house, a very pleasant little house, with a steep, gabled roof, curving at the bottom, and extending over a little gallery, which was entered, by steps, from the road; back of it were stables and negro-cabins, and by its side was a small garden, and beyond that a peach-orchard. As I approached it, a well-dressed young man, with an intelligent and pleasant face, came out into the gallery. I asked him if he could direct me to Mr. W.'s. "Thomas W.'s?" he inquired.

"Yes, sir."

"You are not going in the right direction to go to Mr. W.'s. The shortest way you can take to go there is, to go right back to the Court House."

I told him I had just come out of the lane by the grocery on to the road. "Ah! well, I'll tell you; you had better turn round, and keep right straight upon this road till you get to the Court House, and anybody can tell you, there, how to go."

"How far is it, sir?"

"To the Court House?—not above a mile."

"And to Mr. W.'s?"

"To Mr. W.'s, I should think it was as much as ten miles, and long ones, too."

I rode to the Court House, which was a plain brick building in the centre of a small square, around which there were twenty or thirty houses, two of them being occupied as stores, one as a saddler's shop, one had the sign of "Law Office" upon it, two were occupied by physicians, one other looked as if it might be a meeting-house or school-house, or the shop of any mechanic needing much light for his work, and two were "Hotels." At one of these we stopped, to dine; Jane had "corn and fodder" (they had no oats or hay in the stable), and I had ham and eggs (they had no fresh meat in the house). I had several other things, however, that were very good, besides the company of the landlady, who sat alone with me at the table in a long, dining hall, and was very pretty, amiable and talkative.

In a course of apologies, which came in the place of soup, she gave me the clue to the assemblage of negroes I had seen at the mill. It was Christmas week; all the servants thought they must go for at least one day to have a frolic, and to-day (as luck would have it, when I was coming,) her cook was off with some others; she did not suppose they'd be back till to-morrow, and then, likely as not, they'd be drunk. She did not think this custom, of letting servants go so at Christmas, was a good one; niggers were not fit to be let to take care of themselves anyhow. It was very bad for them, and she didn't think it was *right*. Providence had put the servants into our hands to be looked out for, and she didn't believe it was intended they should be let to do all sorts of wickedness, if Christmas didn't come but once a year. She wished for her part it did not come but once in ten years.

(The negroes that were husking maize near the cabin where the White-man lived were no doubt slaves who had hired themselves out by the day during the holiday-week to earn a little money on their own account.)

In regard to the size of the dining hall, and the extent of sheds in the stable-yard, the landlady told me that though at other times they very often did not have a single guest in a day, at "Court time" they always had more than they could comfortably accommodate. I judged also from her manners and the general appearance of the house, as well as from the charges, that at such times the company was of a rather respectable character. The appearance of the other public-house indicated that it expected a less select patronage.

When I left, my direction was to keep on the main road until I came to a fork, about four miles distant, then take the left and keep *the best traveled road* until I came to a certain house, which was so described that I should know it where I was advised to ask further directions.

The sky was now clouding over; it was growing cold; and we went on as fast as we conveniently could, until we reached the fork in the road. The direction, to keep the best traveled road, was unpleasantly prominent in my mind; it was near sunset, I reflected, and however jolly it might be at twelve o'clock at noon, it would be quite another thing to be knocking about among those fierce hogs in the pine-forest, if I should be lost, at twelve o'clock at night. Besides, as the landlady said about her negroes, I did not think it was *right* to expose Jane to this danger unnecessarily. A little beyond the fork there was a large, gray, old house, with a grove of tall poplars before it; a respectable, country-gentleman-of-the-old-school look it had.—These old Virginians are proverbially hospitable. —It's rather impudent; but I hate to go back to the Court House, and I am——I will ride on, and look it in the face, at any rate.

Zig-zag fences up to a large, square yard, growing full of Lombardy poplar sprouts, from the roots of eight or ten old trees, which were planted some fifty years ago, I suppose, in a double row on two sides of the house. At the further end of this yard, beyond the house, a gate opened on the road, and out of this was just then coming a black man.

I inquired of him if there was a house near by at which I could get accommodations for the night. Reckoned his master'd take me in, if I'd ask him. Where was his master? In the house: I could go right in here (at a place where a panel of the paling had fallen over) and see him, if I wanted to. I asked him to hold my horse, and went in.

It was a simple, two-story house, very much like those built by the wealthier class of people in New England villages from fifty to a hundred years ago, except that the chimneys were carried up outside the walls. There was a

porch at the front door, and a small wing at one end, in
the rear; from this wing to the other end extended a broad
gallery.

A dog had been barking at me after I dismounted; and
just as I reached the steps of the gallery, a vigorous, middle-aged man, with a rather sullen and suspicious expression of face, came out without any coat on to see what had
excited him.

Doubting whether he was the master of the house, I
told him that I had come in to inquire if it would be convenient to allow me to spend the night with them. He
asked where I came from, where I was going to, and various other questions, until I had given him an epitome of
my day's wonderings and adventures; at the conclusion
of which he walked to the end of the gallery to look at my
horse; then, without giving me any answer, but muttering
indistinctly something about servants, walked into the
house, shutting the door behind him!

Well, thought I, this is not very overwhelmingly hospitable. What can it mean?

While I was considering whether he expected me to go
without any further talk—his curiosity being, I judged,
satisfied—he came out again, and said, "Reckon you can
stay, sir, if you'll take what we'll give you." (The good
man had been in to consult his wife.) I replied that I
would do so, thankfully, and hoped they would not give
themselves any unnecessary trouble, or alter their usual
family arrangements. I was then invited to come in, but I
preferred to see my horse taken care of first. My host
called for "Sam," two or three times, and then said he
reckoned all his "people" had gone off, and he would attend to my horse himself. I offered to assist him, and we
walked out to the gate, where the negro, not being inclined to wait for my return, had left Jane fastened to a
post. Our host conducted us to an old square log-cabin,
which had formerly been used for curing tobacco, there
being no room for Jane, he said, in the stables proper.

The floor of the tobacco-house was covered with lumber,
old plows, scythes and cradles, a part of which had to be
removed to make room for the filly to stand. She was then
induced, with some difficulty, to enter it through a low,
square door-way; saddle and bridle were removed, and
she was fastened in a corner by a piece of old plow-line.
We then went to a fodder-stack, and pulled out from it

several small bundles of maize leaves. Additional feed and water were promised when "some of the niggers" came in; and, after righting up an old door that had fallen from one hinge, and setting a rail against it to keep it in its place, we returned to the house.

My host (whom I will call Mr. Newman) observed that his buildings and fences were a good deal out of order. He had owned the place but a few years and had not had time to make much improvement about the house yet.

Entering the mansion, he took me to a large room on the first floor, gave me a chair, went out and soon returned (now wearing a coat) with two negro girls, one bringing wood and the other some flaming brands. A fire was made with a great deal of trouble, scolding of the girls, bringing in more brands, and blowing with the mouth. When the room had been suffocatingly filled with smoke, and at length a strong bright blaze swept steadily up the chimney, Mr. Newman again went out with the girls, and I was left alone for nearly an hour, with one interruption, when he came in and threw some more wood upon the fire, and said he hoped I would make myself comfortable.

It was a square room, with a door from the hall on one side, and two windows on each of the other sides. The lower part of the walls was wainscoted, and the upper part, with the ceiling, plastered and white-washed. The fire-place and mantle-piece were somewhat carved and were painted black, all the other woodwork, lead color. Blue paper curtains covered the windows; the floor was uncarpeted, and the only furniture in the room was some strong plain chairs, painted yellow, and a Connecticut clock, which did not run. The house had evidently been built for a family of some wealth, and, after having been deserted by them, had been bought at a bargain by the present resident, who either had not the capital or the inclination to furnish and occupy it appropriately.

When my entertainer called again, he merely opened the door and said, in the words of an order, but in a tone of advice, "Come! get something to eat!" I followed him out into the gallery, and thence through a door at its end into a room in the wing—a family room, and a very comfortable, homely room. A most bountifully spread supper-table stood in the centre, at which was sitting a very neat, pretty little woman, of as silent habits as her husband, but neither bashful nor morose. A very nice little girl sat at

her right side, and a peevish, ill-behaved, whining glutton
of a boy at her left. I was requested to be seated adjoining
the little girl, and the master of the house sat opposite
me. The fourth side of the table was unoccupied, though
a plate and chair were placed there, as if some one else
had been expected.

The two negro girls waited at table, and a negro boy
was in the room, who, when I asked for a glass of water,
was sent to get it. An old negro woman also frequently
came in from the kitchen, with hot biscuit and corn-cake.
There was fried fowl, and fried bacon and eggs, and cold
ham; there were preserved peaches, and preserved
quinces and grapes; there was hot wheaten biscuit, and
hot short-cake, and hot corn-cake, and hot griddle cakes,
soaked in butter; there was coffee, and there was milk,
sour or sweet, whichever I preferred to drink. I really ate
more than I wanted, and extolled the corn-cake and the
peach preserve, and asked how they were made; but I
evidently disappointed my pretty hostess, who said she
was afraid there wasn't anything that suited me,—she
feared there wasn't anything on the table I could eat; and
she was sorry I couldn't make out a supper. And this
was about all she would say. I tried to get a free conversation started, but I have myself but poor endowments
for such a purpose, and I could obtain little more than
very laconic answers to my questions.

Except from the little girl at my side, whose confidence
I gained by taking an opportunity, when her mother was
engaged, with young hopeful t'other side the coffee-pot,
to give her a great lot of quince and grape, and by several
times pouring molasses very freely on her cakes and bacon; and finally by feeding Pink out of my hand. (Hopeful
had done this first, and then kicked him away, when he
came round to Martha and me.) She told me her name,
and that she had got a kitten, and that she hated Pink; and
that she went to a Sunday-school at the Court House, and
that she was going to go to an every-day school next winter—she wasn't big enough to walk so far now, but she
would be then. But Billy said he didn't mean to go, because he didn't like to, though Billy was bigger nor she
was, a heap. She reckoned when Billy saw Wash. Baker
going past every day, and heard how much fun he had
every day with the other boys at the school, he would
want to go too, wouldn't he? etc., etc. When supper was

ended, I set back my chair to the wall, and took her on my knee; but after she had been told twice not to trouble the gentleman, and I had testified that she didn't do it, and after several mild hints that I would perhaps find it pleasanter in the sitting-room—(the chairs in the supper-room were the easiest, being country-made, low, and seated with undressed calf-skin), she was called to, out of the kitchen, and Mr. Newman, in the form of advice, but with the tone of command, said—going to the door and opening it for me—"Reckon you'd better walk into the sittin'-room, sir."

I walked out at this, and said I would go and look at the filly. Mr. Newman called "Sam" again, and Sam, having at that moment arrived at the kitchen-door, was ordered to go and take care of this gentleman's horse. I followed Sam to the tobacco-house, and gave him to know that he would be properly remembered for any attentions he could give to Jane. He watered her, and brought her a large supply of oats in straw, and some maize on the cob; but he could get no litter, and declared there was no straw on the plantation, though the next morning I saw a large quantity in a heap (not a stack), at a little greater distance than he was willing to go for it, I suppose, at a barn on the opposite side of the road. Having seen her rubbed clean and apparently well contented with her quarters and her supper, I bade her good-night, and returned to the house.

I did not venture again into the supper-room, but went to the sitting-room, where I found Miss Martha Ann and her kitten; I was having a very good time with her, when her father came in and told her she was "troubling the gentleman"; I denied it, and he took a seat by the fire with us, and I soon succeeded in drawing him into a conversation on farming, and the differences in our methods of work at the North and those he was accustomed to.

WHITE LABORING PEOPLE.

I learned that there were no white laboring men here who hired themselves out by the month. The poor white people that had to labor for their living never would work steadily at any employment. "They mostly followed boating"—hiring as hands on the bateaus that navigate the small streams and canals, but never for a longer term

at once than a single trip of a boat, whether that might be
long or short. At the end of the trip they were paid by the
day. Their wages were from fifty cents to a dollar, varying
with the demand and individual capacities. They hardly
ever worked on farms except in harvest, when they usually received a dollar a day, sometimes more. In harvest-
time, most of the rural mechanics closed their shops and
hired out to the farmers at a dollar a day, which would
indicate that their ordinary earnings are considerably less
than this. At other than harvest-time, the poor white people, who had no trade, would sometimes work for the
farmers by the job, not often at any regular agricultural
labor, but at getting rails or shingles, or clearing land.

He did not know that they were particular about working with negroes, but no white man would ever do certain
kinds of work (such as taking care of cattle, or getting
water or wood to be used in the house), and if you should
ask a white man you had hired to do such things, he
would get mad and tell you he wasn't a nigger. Poor white
girls never hired out to do servants' work, but they would
come and help another white woman about her sewing or
quilting, and take wages for it. But these girls were not
very respectable generally, and it was not agreeable to
have them in your house, though there were some very
respectable ladies that would go out to sew. Farmers depended almost entirely upon their negroes; it was only
when they were hard pushed by their crops that they got
white hands to help them any.

Negroes had commanded such high wages lately, to
work on railroads and in tobacco-factories, that farmers
were tempted to hire out too many of their people, and to
undertake to do too much work with those they retained,
and thus they were often driven to employ white men,
and to give them very high wages by the day, when they
found themselves getting much behind-hand with their
crops. He had been driven very hard in this way this last
season; he had been so unfortunate as to lose one of his
best women, who died in child-bed just before harvest.
The loss of the woman and her child, for the child had
died also, just at that time, came very hard upon him. He
would not have taken a thousand dollars of any man's
money for them. He had had to hire white men to help
him, but they were poor sticks and would be half the time
drunk, and you never know what to depend upon with

them. One fellow that he had hired, who had agreed to work for him all through harvest, got him to pay him some wages in advance, (he said it was to buy him some clothes with, so he could go to meeting, Sunday, at the Court-House,) and went off the next day, right in the middle of harvest, and he never had seen him since. He had heard of him—he was on a boat—but he didn't reckon he should ever get his money again.

Of course, he did not see how white laborers were ever going to come into competition with negroes here, at all. You never could depend on white men, and you couldn't *drive* them any; they wouldn't stand it. Slaves were the only reliable laborers—you could command them and *make* them do what was right.

From the manner in which he always talked of the white laboring people, it was evident that, although he placed them in some sort on an equality with himself, and that in his intercourse with them he wouldn't think of asserting for himself any superior dignity, or even feel himself to be patronizing them in not doing so, yet he, all the time, recognized them as a distinct and a rather despicable class, and wanted to have as little to do with them as he conveniently could.

I have been once or twice told that the poor white people, meaning those, I suppose, who bring nothing to market to exchange for money but their labor, although they may own a cabin and a little furniture, and cultivate land enough to supply themselves with (maize) bread, are worse off in almost all respects than the slaves. They are said to be extremely ignorant and immoral, as well as indolent and unambitious. That their condition is not as unfortunate by any means as that of negroes, however, is most obvious, since from among them, men *sometimes* elevate themselves to positions and habits of usefulness, and respectability. They are said to "corrupt" the negroes, and to encourage them to steal, or to work for them at night and on Sundays, and to pay them with liquor, and also to constantly associate licentiously with them. They seem, nevertheless, more than any other portion of the community, to hate and despise the negroes.

BED-TIME.

In the midst of our conversation, one of the black girls had come into the room and stood still with her head dropped forward, staring at me from under her brows, without saying a word. When she had waited, in this way, perhaps two minutes, her master turned to her and asked what she wanted.

"Miss Matty says Marta Ann go to bed now."

But Martha Ann refused to budge; after being told once or twice by her father to go with Rose, she came to me and lifted up her hands, I supposed to kiss me and go, but when I reached down, she took hold of my shoulders and climbed up on to my knees. Her father seemed to take no notice of this proceeding, but continued talking about guano; Rose went to a corner of the fire-place, dropped down upon the floor and presently was asleep, leaning her head against the wall. In about half an hour, the other negro girl came to the door, when Mr. Newman abruptly called out, "girl! take that child to bed!" and immediately got up himself and walked out. Rose roused herself and lifted Martha Ann out of my arms, and carried her off fast asleep. Mr. Newman returned holding a small candle in his hand, and, without entering the room, stood at the door and said, "I'll show you your bed if you are ready, sir." As he evidently meant, "I am ready to show you to bed if you will not refuse to go," I followed him up stairs.

Into a large room, again, with six windows, with a fire-place, in which a few brands were smoking, with some wool spread thinly upon the floor in a corner; with a dozen small bundles of tobacco leaves; with a lady's saddle; with a deep feather-bed, covered with a bright patchwork quilt, on a maple bedstead, and without a single item of any other furniture whatever. Mr. Newman asked if I wanted the candle to undress by, I said yes, if he pleased, and waited a moment for him to set it down: as he did not do so I walked towards him, lifting my hand to take it. "No—I'll hold it," said he, and I then perceived that he had no candle-stick, but held the lean little dip in his hand: I remembered also that no candle had been brought into the "sitting-room," and that while we were at supper only one candle had stood upon the table, which had been immediately extinguished when we rose, the room being lighted only from the fire.

I very quickly undressed and hung my clothes upon a bed-post: Mr. Newman looked on in silence until I had got into bed, when, with an abrupt "good-night, sir," he went out and shut the door.

SETTLING.

It was not until after I had consulted Sam the next morning, that I ventured to consider that my entertainment might be taken as a mere business transaction, and not as "genuine planter's hospitality," though this had become rather a ridiculous view of it, after a repetition of the supper, in all respects, had been eaten for breakfast, with equal moroseness on the part of my host and equal quietness on the part of his kind-looking little wife. I was, nevertheless, amused at the promptness with which he replied to my rather hesitating inquiry—what I might pay him for the trouble I had given him—"I reckon a dollar and a quarter will be right, sir."

THE WILDERNESS.

I have described, perhaps with tedious prolixity, what adventures befell me, and what scenes I passed through in my first day's random riding, for the purpose of giving an idea of the uncultivated and unimproved—rather, sadly worn and misused—condition of some parts, and I judge, of a very large part, of all Eastern Virginia, and of the isolated, lonely and dissociable aspect of the dwelling places of a large part of the people.

Much the same general characteristics pervade the Slave States everywhere, except in certain rich regions, or on the banks of some rivers, or in the vicinity of some great routes of travel and transportation, which have occasioned closer settlement or stimulated public spirit. For hours and hours one has to ride through the unlimited, continual, all-shadowing, all-embracing forest, following roads in the making of which no more labor has been given than was necessary to remove the timber which would obstruct the passage of wagons; and even for days and days he may sometimes travel and see never two dwellings of mankind within sight of each other, only at long distances often several miles asunder these isolated plantation patriarchates. If a traveler leaves the main road to go any distance, it is not to be imagined how difficult it is for him to find his way from one house to any other in particular; his only safety is in the fact that, unless there are mountains or swamps in the way, he is not likely to go many miles upon any wagon or horse track without coming to some white man's habitation.

THE MEETING-HOUSE.

The country passed through, in the early part of my second day's ride, was very similar in general characteristics to that I have already described, only that a rather larger portion of it was cleared, and plantations were more frequent. About eleven o'clock I crossed a bridge and came to the meeting-house I had been expecting to reach by that hour the previous day. It was in the midst of the woods, and the small clearing around it was still dotted with the stumps of the trees out of whose trunks it had been built; for it was a log structure. In one end there was a single square port, closed by a sliding shutter; in the other end were two doors, both standing open. In front of the doors, a rude scaffolding had been made of poles and saplings, extending out twenty feet from the wall of the house, and this had been covered with boughs of trees, the leaves now withered; a few benches, made of split trunks of trees, slightly hewn with the axe, were arranged under this arbor, as if the religious service was sometimes conducted on the outside in preference to the interior of the edifice. Looking in, I saw that a gallery or loft extended from over the doors, across about one-third the length of the house, access to which was had by a ladder. At the opposite end was a square, unpainted pulpit, and on the floor were rows of rude benches. The house was sufficiently lighted by crevices between the upper-logs.

A TOBACCO PLANTATION.

Half an hour after this I arrived at the negro-quarters —a little hamlet of ten or twelve small and dilapidated cabins. Just beyond them was a plain farm-gate, at which several negroes were standing; one of them, a well-made man, with an intelligent countenance and prompt manner, directed me how to find my way to his owner's house. It was still nearly a mile distant; and yet, until I arrived in its immediate vicinity, I saw no cultivated field, and but one clearing. In the edge of this clearing, a number of negroes, male and female, lay stretched out upon the ground near a small smoking charcoal pit. Their master afterwards informed me that they were burning charcoal for the plantation blacksmith, using the time allowed them for holidays—from Christmas to New Year's—to earn a little money for themselves in this way. He paid them by the bushel for it. When I said that I supposed he allowed them to take what wood they chose for this purpose, he replied that he had five hundred acres covered with wood, which he would be very glad to have any one burn, or clear off in any way. Cannot some Yankee contrive a method of concentrating some of the valuable properties of this old-field pine, so that they may be profitably brought into use in more cultivated regions? Charcoal is now brought to New York from Virginia; but when made from pine it is not very valuable, and will only bear transportation from the banks of the navigable rivers, whence it can be shipped, at one movement, to New York. Turpentine does not flow in sufficient quantity from this variety of the pine to be profitably collected, and for lumber it is of very small value.

Mr. W.'s house was an old family mansion, which he had himself remodeled in the Grecian style, and furnished with a large wooden portico. An oak forest had originally occupied the ground where it stood; but this having been cleared and the soil worn out in cultivation by the previous proprietors, pine woods now surrounded it in every direction, a square of a few acres only being kept clear immediately about it. A number of the old oaks still stood in the rear of the house, and, until Mr. W. commenced his improvements, there had been some in its front. These, however, he had cut away, as interfering with the symmetry of his grounds, and in place of them had planted ailanthus trees in parallel rows.

On three sides of the outer part of the cleared square there was a row of large and comfortable-looking negro-quarters, stables, tobacco-houses, and other offices, built of logs.

Mr. W. was one of the few large planters, of his vicinity who still made the culture of tobacco their principal business. He said there was a general prejudice against tobacco in all the tidewater region of the State, because it was through the culture of tobacco that the once fertile soils had been impoverished; but he did not believe that, at the present value of negroes, their labor could be applied to the culture of grain with any profit, except under peculiarly favorable circumstances. Possibly, the use of guano might make wheat a paying crop, but he still doubted. He had not used it, himself. Tobacco required fresh land, and was rapidly exhausting, but it returned more money for the labor used upon it than anything else, enough more, in his opinion, to pay for the wearing out of the land. If he was well paid for it, he did not know why he should not wear out his land.

His tobacco-fields were nearly all in a distant and lower part of his plantation; land which had been neglected before his time in a great measure, because it had been sometimes flooded, and was, much of the year, too wet for cultivation. He was draining and clearing it, and it now brought good crops.

He had had an Irish gang draining for him, by contract. He thought a negro could do twice as much work in a day as an Irishman. He had not stood over them and seen them at work, but judged entirely from the amount they accomplished: he thought a good gang of negroes would have got on twice as fast. He was sure they must have "trifled" a great deal, or they would have accomplished more than they had. He complained much, also, of their sprees and quarrels. I asked why he should employ Irishmen, in preference to doing the work with his own hands. "It's dangerous work [unhealthy?], and a negro's life is too valuable to be risked at it. If a negro dies, it's a considerable loss, you know."

He afterwards said that his negroes never worked so hard as to tire themselves—always were lively, and ready to go off on a frolic at night. He did not think they ever did half a fair day's work. They could not be made to work hard: they never would lay out their strength freely, and it was impossible to make them do it.

This is just what I have thought when I have seen slaves at work—they seem to go through the motions of labor without putting strength into them. They keep their powers in reserve for their own use at night perhaps.

Mr. W. also said that he cultivated only the coarser and lower-priced sorts of tobacco, because the finer sorts required more pains-taking and discretion than it was possible to make a large gang of negroes use. "You can make a nigger work," he said, "*but you cannot make him think.*"

Although Mr. W. was very wealthy (or, at least, would

be considered so anywhere at the North), and was a gentleman of education, his style of living was very farmer-like, and thoroughly Southern. On their plantations, generally, the Virginia gentlemen seem to drop their full-dress and constrained town-habits, and to live a free, rustic, shooting-jacket life. We dined in a room that extended out, rearwardly, from the house, and which, in a Northern establishment, would have been the kitchen. The cooking was done in a detached log-cabin, and the dishes brought some distance, through the open air, by the servants. The outer door was left constantly open, though there was a fire in an enormous old fire-place, large enough, if it could have been distributed sufficiently, to have lasted a New York seamstress the best part of the winter. By the door, there was indiscriminate admittance to negro-children and fox-hounds, and, on an average, there were four of these, grinning or licking their chops, on either side of my chair, all the time I was at the table. A stout woman acted as head waitress, employing two handsome little mulatto boys as her aids in communicating with the kitchen, from which relays of hot corn-bread, of an excellence quite new to me, were brought at frequent intervals.* There was no other bread, and but one vegetable served—sweet potato, roasted in ashes, and this, I thought, was the best sweet potato, also, that I ever had eaten; but there were four preparations of swine's flesh, besides fried fowls, fried eggs, cold roast turkey, and opossum, cooked I know not how, but it somewhat resembled baked sucking-pig. The only beverages on the table were milk and whisky.

I was pressed to stay several days with Mr. W., and should have been glad to have accepted such hospitality, had not another engagement prevented. When I was about to leave, an old servant was directed to get a horse and go with me, as guide, to the railroad station at Col. Gillin's. He followed behind me, and I had great difficulty in inducing him to ride near enough to converse with me. I wished to ascertain from him how old the different

---

* There is probably some choice in the sort of corn used. The best corn-bread that I have eaten was made simply by wetting coarse meal with pure water, adding only a little salt, and baking in the form of a breakfast-roll. The addition of milk, butter, or eggs, damages it. I speak now from experience—having been, in my second journey in the South, often obliged to make my own bread. The only care required, except not to burn it, is to make sure, if possible—which it was not, generally, in Texas—that the corn is not mouldy.

stages of the old-field forest-growth, by the side of our
road, might be, but for a long time he was, or pretended
to be, unable to comprehend my questions. When he did
so, the most accurate information he could give me was,
that he reckoned such a field (in which the pines were
now some sixty feet high) had been planted with tobacco the year his old master bought him. He thought he
was about twenty years old then, and that now he was
forty. He had every appearance of being seventy.

He frequently told me there was no need for him to go
any further, and that it was a dead, straight road to the
station, without any forks. As he appeared very eager to
return, I was at length foolish enough to allow myself to
be prevailed upon to dispense with his guidance; gave
him a quarter of a dollar for his time that I had employed,
and went on alone. The road, which for a short distance
further was plain enough, soon began to ramify, and, in
half an hour, we were stumbling along a dark wood-path,
looking eagerly for a house. At length, seeing one across
a large clearing, we went through a long lane, opening
gates and letting down bars, until we met two negroes,
riding a mule, who were going to the plantation near the
school-house, which we had seen the day before. Following them thither, we knew the rest of the way (Jane gave
a bound and neighed, when we struck the old road, showing that she had been lost, as well as I, up to the moment).

It was twenty minutes after the hour given in the time-
table for the passage of the train, when I reached the station, but it had not arrived; nor did it make its appearance
for a quarter of an hour longer; so I had plenty of time to
deliver Tom's wife's message and take leave of Jane. I am
sorry to say she appeared very indifferent, and seemed to
think a good deal more of Tom than of me. Mr. W. had
told me that the train would, probably, be half an hour
behind its advertised time, and that I had no need to ride
with haste, to reach it. I asked Col. Gillin if it would be
safe to always calculate on the train being half an hour
late: he said it would not; for, although usually that much
behind the time-table, it was sometimes half an hour
ahead of it. So those who would be safe had commonly
to wait an hour. People, therefore, who wished to go not
more than twenty miles from home would find it more
convenient, and equally expeditious, taking all things into
account, to go in their own conveyances—there being

but few who lived so near the station that they would not have to employ a horse and servant to get to it.

A FREE-LABOR FARM.

I have been visiting a farm, cultivated entirely by free-labor. The proprietor told me that he was first led to disuse slave-labor, not from any economical considerations, but because he had become convinced that there was an essential wrong in holding men in forced servitude with any other purpose than to benefit them alone, and because he was not willing to allow his own children to be educated as slave-masters. His father had been a large slave-holder, and he felt very strongly the bad influence it had had on his own character. He wished me to be satisfied that Jefferson uttered a great truth when he asserted that slavery was more pernicious to the white race than the black. Although, therefore, a chief part of his inheritance had been in slaves, he had liberated them all.

Most of them had, by his advice, gone to Africa. These he had frequently heard from. Except a child that had been drowned, they were, at his last account, all alive, in general good health, and satisfactorily prospering. He had lately received a letter from one of them, who told him that he was "*trying* to preach the Gospel," and who had evidently greatly improved, both intellectually and morally, since he left here. With regard to those going North, and the common opinion that they encountered much misery, and would be much better off here, he said that it entirely depended on the general character and habits of the individual; it was true of those who were badly brought up, and who had acquired indolent and vicious habits, especially if they were drunkards, but, if of some intelligence and well-trained, they generally represented themselves to be successful and contented.

He mentioned two remarkable cases, that had come under his own observation, of this kind. One was that of a man who had been free, but, by some fraud and informality of his papers, was reënslaved. He ran away, and afterwards negotiated, by correspondence, with his master, and purchased his freedom. This man he had accidentally met, fifteen years afterwards, in a Northern city; he was engaged in profitable and increasing business, and showed him, by his books, that he was possessed of property to the amount of ten thousand dollars. He was living a great deal more comfortably and wisely than ever his old master had done. The other case was that of a colored woman, who had obtained her freedom, and who became apprehensive that she also was about to be fraudulently made a slave again. She fled to Philadelphia, where she was nearly starved, at first. A little girl, who heard her begging in the streets to be allowed to work for bread, told her that her mother was wanting some washing done, and she followed her home. The mother, not knowing her, was afraid to trust her with the articles to be washed. She prayed so earnestly for the job, however—suggesting that she might be locked into a room until she had completed it—that it was given her.

So she commenced life in Philadelphia. Ten years afterwards he had accidentally met her there; she recognized him immediately, recalled herself to his recollection, manifested the greatest joy at seeing him, and asked him to come to her house, which he found a handsome three-story building, furnished really with elegance; and she pointed out to him, from the window, three houses in the vicinity that she owned and rented. She showed great anxiety to have her children well educated, and was employing the best instructors for them which she could procure in Philadelphia.

This gentleman, notwithstanding his anti-slavery sentiments, by no means favors the running away of slaves, and thinks the Abolitionists have done immense harm to the cause they have at heart. He wishes Northerners would mind their business, and leave Slavery alone, say but little about it—nothing in the present condition of affairs at the South—and never speak of it but in a kind and calm manner. He would not think it right to return a fugitive slave; but he would never assist one to escape. He has several times purchased slaves, generally such as his neighbors were obliged to sell, and who would otherwise have been taken South. This he had been led to do by the solicitation of some of their relatives. He had retained them in his possession until their labor had in some degree returned their cost to him, and he could afford to provide them with the means of going to Africa or the North, and a small means of support after their arrival. Having received some suitable training in his family, they had, without exception, been successful, and had frequently sent him money to purchase the freedom of relatives or friends they had left in slavery.

He considered the condition of slaves to have much improved since the Revolution, and very perceptibly during the last twenty years. The original stock of slaves, the imported Africans, he observed, probably required to be governed with much greater severity, and very little humanity was exercised or thought of with regard to them. The slaves of the present day are of a higher character; in fact, he did not think more than half of them were full-blooded Africans. Public sentiment condemned the man who treated his slaves with cruelty. The owners were mainly men of some cultivation, and felt a family attachment to their slaves, many of whom had been the playmates of their boyhood. Nevertheless, they were frequently punished severely, under the impulse of temporary passion, often without deliberation, and on unfounded suspicion. This was especially the case where they were left to overseers, who, though sometimes men of intelligence and piety, were more often coarse, brutal, and licentious; drinking men, wholly unfitted for the responsibility imposed on them.

He had read "Uncle Tom's Cabin" [published in 1852]; mentioned several points in which he thought it wrong—that Uncle Tom was too highly painted, for instance; that such a character could not exist in, or spring out of Slavery, and that no gentleman of Kentucky or Virginia would have allowed himself to be in the position with a slave-dealer in which Mr. Shelby is represented— but he acknowledged that cases of cruelty and suffering, equal to any described in it, might be found. In his own neighborhood, some time ago, a man had been whipped to death; and he recollected several that had been maimed for life by harsh and hasty punishment; but the whole community were indignant when such things occurred, and any man guilty of them would be without associates, except of similar character.

The opinions of this gentleman must not, of course, be considered as representative of those of the South in general, by any means; but as to facts, he is a competent and, I believe, a wholly candid and unprejudiced witness. He is much respected and on terms of friendship with all his neighbors, though they do not like his views on this subject. He told me, however, that one of them, becoming

convinced of their correctness some time ago, freed his
slaves, and moved to Ohio. As to "Uncle Tom," it is generally criticised very severely and its representations of
Slavery indignantly denied. I observe that it is not pla-
carded outside the booksellers' stores, though the whole
fleet of gunboats that have been launched after it show
their colors bravely. It must, however, be a good deal
read here, as I judge from the frequent allusions I hear
made to it.

With regard to the value of slave-labor, this gentleman
is confident that, at present, he has the advantage in
employing freemen instead of it. It has not been so until
of late, the price of slaves having much advanced within
ten years, while immigration has made free white laborers
more easy to be procured.

He has heretofore had some difficulty in obtaining
hands when he needed them, and has suffered a good deal
from the demoralizing influence of adjacent slave-labor,
the men, after a few months' residence, inclining to follow
the customs of the slaves with regard to the amount of
work they should do in a day, or their careless mode of
operation. He has had white and black Virginians, sometimes Germans, and latterly Irish. Of all these, he has
found the Irish on the whole the best. The poorest have
been the native white Virginians; next, the free blacks:
and though there have been exceptions, he has not generally paid these as high as one hundred dollars a year,
and has thought them less worth their wages than any he
has had. At present, he has two white natives and two
free colored men, but both the latter were brought up in
his family, and are worth twenty dollars a year more
than the average. The free black, he thinks, is generally
worse than the slave, and so is the poor white man. He
also employs, at present, four Irish hands, and is expecting two more to arrive, who have been recommended to
him, and sent for by those he has. He pays the Irishmen
$120 a year, and boards them. He has had them for $100;
but these are all excellent men, and well worth their price.
They are less given to drinking than any men he has ever
had; and one of them first suggested improvements to him
in his farm, that he is now carrying out with prospects of
considerable advantage. House-maids, Irish girls, he pays
$3 and $6 a month.

He does not apprehend that in future he shall have any

difficulty in obtaining steady and reliable men, that will accomplish much more work than any slaves. There are some operations, such as carting and spreading dung, and all work with the fork, spade, or shovel, at which his Irishmen will do, he thinks, over fifty per cent. more in a day than any negroes he has ever known. On the whole, he is satisfied that at present free-labor is more profitable than slave-labor, though his success is not so evident that he would be willing to have attention particularly called to it. His farm, moreover, is now in a transition state from one system of husbandry to another, and appearances are temporarily more unfavorable on that account.

The wages paid for slaves, when they are hired for agricultural labor, do not differ at present, he says, from those which he pays for his free laborers. In both cases the hiring party boards the laborer, but, in addition to money and board, the slave-employer has to furnish clothing, and is subject, without redress, to any losses which may result from the carelessness or malevolence of the slave. He also has to lose his time if he is unwell, or when from any cause he is absent or unable to work.

The slave, if he is indisposed to work, and especially if he is not treated well, or does not like the master who has hired him, will sham sickness—even make himself sick or lame—that he need not work. But a more serious loss frequently arises, when the slave, thinking he is worked too hard, or being angered by punishment or unkind treatment, "getting the sulks," takes to "the swamp," and comes back when he has a mind to. Often this will not be till the year is up for which he is engaged, when he will return to his owner, who, glad to find his property safe, and that it has not died in the swamp, or gone to Canada, forgets to punish him, and immediately sends him for another year to a new master.

"But, meanwhile, how does the negro support life in the swamp?" I asked.

"Oh, he gets sheep and pigs and calves, and fowls and turkeys; sometimes they will kill a small cow. We have often seen the fires, where they were cooking them, through the woods, in the swamp yonder. If it is cold, he will crawl under a fodderstack, or go into the cabins with some of the other negroes, and in the same way, you see, he can get all the corn, or almost anything else he wants.

"He steals them from his master?"

"From any one; frequently from me. I have had many a sheep taken by them."

"It is a common thing, then?"

"Certainly it is, very common, and the loss is sometimes exceedingly provoking. One of my neighbors here was going to build, and hired two mechanics for a year. Just as he was ready to put his house up, the two men, taking offense at something, both ran away, and did not come back at all till their year was out, and then their owner immediately hired them out again to another man."

These negroes "in the swamp," he said, were often hunted after, but it was very difficult to find them, and, if caught, they would run again, and the other negroes would hide and assist them. Dogs to track them he had never known to be used in Virginia.

RECREATION AND LUXURY AMONG THE SLAVES.

SATURDAY, Dec. 25. From Christmas to New-Year's Day, most of the slaves, except house servants, enjoy a freedom from Labor; and Christmas is especially holiday, or Saturnalia, with them. The young ones began last night firing crackers, and I do not observe that they are engaged in any other amusement to-day; the older ones are generally getting drunk, and making business for the police. I have seen large gangs coming in from the country, and these contrast much in their general appearance with the town negroes. The latter are dressed expensively, and frequently more elegantly than the whites. They seem to be spending money freely, and I observe that they, and even the slaves that wait upon me at the hotel, often have watches, and other articles of value.

The slaves have a good many ways of obtaining "spending money," which, though in law belonging to their owner, as the property of a son under age does to his father, they are never dispossessed of, and use for their own gratification, with even less restraint than a wholesome regard for their health and more condition may be thought to require. A Richmond paper, complaining of the liberty allowed to slaves in this respect, as calculated to foster an insubordinate spirit, speaks of their "champagne suppers." The police broke into a gambling cellar a few nights since, and found about twenty negroes at "high play," with all the usual accessories of a first-class

"Hell." It is mentioned that, among the number taken to the watch-house, and treated with lashes the next morning, there were some who had previously enjoyed a high reputation for piety, and others of a very elegant or foppish appearance.

Passing two negroes in the street, I heard the following:

"——Workin' in a tobacco factory all de year roun', an' come Christmas, only twenty dollars! Workin' mighty hard, too—up to 12 o'clock o' night very often—an' then to hab a nigger oberseah!"

"A nigger!"

"Yes—dat's it, yer see. Wouldn't care if 'twarnt for dat. Nothin' but a dirty nigger! orderin' 'round, jes' as if he was a wite man!"

It is the custom of tobacco manufacturers to hire slaves and free negroes at a certain rate of wages per year. A task of 45 lbs. per day is given them to work up, and all that they choose to do more than this they are paid for—payment being made once a fortnight; and invariably this over-wages is used by the slave for himself, and is usually spent in drinking, licentiousness and gambling. The man was grumbling that he had saved but $20 to spend at the holidays. One of the manufacturers offered to show me, by his books, that nearly all gained by overwork $5 a month, many $20, and some as much as $28.

INGENUITY OF THE NEGRO.

Sitting with a company of smokers last night, one of them, to show me the manner in which a slave of any ingenuity or cunning would manage to avoid working for his master's profit, narrated the following anecdote. He was executor of an estate in which, among other negroes, there was one very smart man, who, he knew perfectly well, ought to be earning for the estate $150 a year, and who could do it if he chose, yet whose wages for a year, being let out by the day or job, had amounted to but $18, while he had paid for medical attendance upon him $45. Having failed in every other way to make him earn anything, he proposed to him that he should purchase his freedom and go to Philadelphia, where he had a brother. He told him if he would earn a certain sum ($400 I believe), and pay it over to the estate for himself, he would give him his free papers. The man agreed to the arrangement, and by his overwork in a tobacco factory, and some assistance from his free brother, soon paid the sum agreed upon, and was sent to Philadelphia. A few weeks afterwards he met him in the street, and asked him why he had returned. "Oh, I don't like dat Philadelphy, massa; ant no chance for colored folks dere; spec' if I'd been a runaway, de wite folks dere take care o' me; but I couldn't git anythin' to do, so I jiss borrow ten dollar of my broder, and cum back to old Virginny."

"But you know the law forbids your return. I wonder that you are not afraid to be seen here; I should think Mr.——(an officer of police) would take you up."

"Oh! I look out for dat, Massr, I juss hire myself out to Mr.——himself, ha! ha! He tink I your boy."

And so it proved, the officer, thinking that he was permitted to hire himself out, and tempted by the low wages at which he offered himself, had neglected to ask for his written permission, and had engaged him for a year. He still lived with the officer, and was an active, healthy, good servant to him.

QUALITIES AS A LABORER.

A well-informed capitalist and slave-holder remarked, that negroes could not be employed in cotton factories. I said that I understood they were so in Charleston, and some other places at the South.

"It may be so, *yet*," he answered, "but they will have to give it up."

The reason was, he said, that the negro could never be trained to exercise judgment; he cannot be made to use his mind; he always depends on machinery doing its own work, and cannot be made to watch it. He neglects it until something is broken or there is great waste. "We have tried reward and punishments, but it makes no difference. It's his nature and you cannot change it. All men are indolent and have a disinclination to labor, but this is a great deal stronger in the African race than in any other. In working niggers, we must always calculate that they will not labor at all except to avoid punishment, and they will never do more than just enough to save themselves from being punished, and no amount of punishment will prevent their working carelessly and indifferently. It always seems on the plantation as if they took pains to break all the tools and spoil all the cattle that they possibly can, even when they know they'll be directly punished for it."

As to rewards, he said, "They only want to support life, they will not work for anything more; and in this country it would be hard to prevent their getting that." I thought this opinion of the power of rewards was not exactly confirmed by the narrative we had just heard, but I said nothing. "If you could move," he continued, "all the white people from the whole seaboard district of Virginia and give it up to the negroes that are on it now, just leave them to themselves, in ten years time there would not be an acre of land cultivated, and nothing would be produced, except what grew spontaneously."

The Hon. Willoughby Newton, by the way, seems to think that if it had not been for the introduction of guano, a similar desolation would have soon occurred without the Africanization of the country. He is reported to have said:

"I look upon the introduction of guano, and the success attending its application to our barren lands, in the light of a special interposition of Divine Providence, to save the northern neck of Virginia from reverting entirely into its former state of wilderness and utter desolation. Until the discovery of guano—more valuable to us than the mines of California—I looked upon the possibility of renovating our soil, of ever bringing it to a point capable of producing remunerating crops, as utterly hopeless. Our up-lands were all worn out, and our bottom-lands fast failing, and if it had not been for guano to revive our last hope, a few years more and the whole country must have been deserted by all who desired to increase their own wealth, or advance the cause of civilization by a proper cultivation of the earth."

IMPROVEMENT OF THE NEGRO IN SLAVERY.

"But are they not *improving?*" said I; "that is a point in which I am much interested, and I should be glad to know what is your observation? Have they not, as a race, improved during the last hundred years, do you not think?"

"Oh, yes indeed, very greatly. During my time—I can

remember how they were forty years ago—they have improved *two thousand per cent!* Don't you think so?" he asked another gentleman.

"Yes; certainly."

"And you may find them now, on the isolated old plantations in the back country, just as I recollect them when I was a boy, stupid and moping, and with no more intelligence than when they first came from Africa. But all about where the country is much settled their condition is vastly ameliorated. They are treated much better, they are fed better, and they have much greater educational privileges."

EDUCATIONAL PRIVILEGES.

"Educational privileges?" I asked, in surprise.

"I mean by preaching and religious instruction. They have the Bible read to them a great deal, and there is preaching for them all over the country. They have preachers of their own; right smart ones they are, too, some of them."

"Do they?" said I. "I thought that was not allowed by law."

"Well, it is not—that is, they are not allowed to have meetings without some white man is present. They must not preach unless a white man hears what they say. However, they do. On my plantation, they always have a meeting on Sundays, and I have sometimes, when I have been there, told my overseer,—'You must go up there to the meeting, you know the law requires it;' and he would start as if he was going, but would just look in and go by; he wasn't going to wait for them.'"

A DISTINGUISHED DIVINE.

He then spoke of a minister, whom he owned, and described him as a very intelligent man. He knew almost the whole of the Bible by heart. He was a fine-looking man—a fine head and a very large frame. He had been a sailor, and had been in New Orleans and New York, and many foreign ports. "He could have left me at any time for twenty years, if he had wished to," he said. "I asked him once how he would like to live in New York? Oh, he did not like New York at all! niggers were not treated well there—there was more distinction made between them and white folks than there was here. 'Oh, dey ain't no place in de worl like Ole Virginny for niggers, massa,' says he.

Another gentleman gave similar testimony.

HOW THEY ARE FED.

I said I supposed that they were much better off, more improved intellectually, and more kindly treated in Virginia than further South. He said I was mistaken in both respects—that in Louisiana, especially, they were more intelligent, because the amalgamation of the races was much greater, and they were treated with more familiarity by the whites; besides which, the laws of Louisiana were much more favorable to them. For instance, they required the planter to give slaves 200 pounds of pork a year: and he gave a very apt anecdote showing the effect of this law, but which, at the same time, made it evident that a Virginian may be accustomed to neglect providing sufficient food for his force, and that they sometimes suffer greatly for want of it. I was assured, however, that this was very rare—that, generally, the slaves were well provided for—always allowed a sufficient quantity of meal, and, generally, of pork—were permitted to raise pigs and poultry, and in summer could always grow as many vegetables as they wanted. It was observed, however, that they frequently neglect to provide for themselves in this way, and live mainly on meal and bacon. If a man does not provide well for his slaves, it soon becomes known, he gets the name of a "nigger-killer," and loses the respect of the community.

The general allowance of food was thought to be a peck and a half of meal, and three pounds of bacon a week. This, it was observed, is as much meal as they can eat, but they would be glad to have more bacon; sometimes they receive four pounds, but it is oftener that they get less than three. It is distributed to them on Saturday nights; or, on the better-managed plantations, sometimes, on Wednesday, to prevent their using it extravagantly, or selling it for whisky on Sunday. This distribution is called the "drawing," and is made by the overseer to all the heads of families or single negroes. Except on the smallest plantations, where the cooking is done in the house of the proprietor, there is a cook-house, furnished with a large copper for boiling, and an oven. Every night the negroes take their "mess," for the next day's breakfast and dinner, to the cook, to be prepared for the next day. Custom varies as to the time it is served out to them; sometimes at morning and noon, at other times at noon and night. Each negro marks his meat by cuts, so that he shall know it from the rest, and they observe each other's rights with regard to this, punctiliously.

After breakfast has been eaten early in the cabins, at sunrise or a little before in winter, and perhaps a little later in summer, they go to the field. At noon dinner is brought to them, and, unless the work presses, they are allowed two hours' rest. Very punctually at sunset they stop work and are at liberty, except that a squad is detached once a week for shelling corn, to go to the mill for the next week's drawing of meal. Thus they work in the field about eleven hours a day on an average. Returning to the cabins, wood "ought to have been" carted for them; but if it has not been, they then go to the woods and "tote" it home for themselves. They then make a fire—a big, blazing fire at this season, for the supply of fuel is unlimited—and cook their own supper, which will be a bit of bacon fried, often with eggs, corn-bread baked in the spider after the bacon, to absorb the fat, and perhaps some sweet potatoes roasted in the ashes. Immediately after supper they go to sleep, often lying on the floor or a bench in preference to a bed. About two o'clock they very generally rouse up and cook and eat, or eat cold, what they call their "mornin' bit"; then sleep again till breakfast.

I think the slaves generally (no one denies that there are exceptions) have plenty to eat; probably are fed better than the proletarian class of any other part of the world. I think that they generally save from their ration of meal. My informant said that commonly as much as five bushels of meal was sent to town by his hands every week, to be sold for them. Upon inquiry, he almost always found that it belonged to only two or three individuals, who had traded for it with the rest; he added that too often the exchange was for whisky, which, against his rules, they obtained of some rascally white people in the neighborhood, and kept concealed. They were very fond of whisky, and sometimes much injured themselves with it.

To show me how well they were supplied with eggs, he said that once a vessel came to anchor, becalmed, off his place, and the captain came to him and asked leave to purchase some eggs of his people. He gave him permission, and called the cook to collect them for him. The cook asked how many she should bring. "Oh, all you can get," he answered—and she returned after a time, with several boys assisting her, bringing nearly two bushels, all the property of the slaves, and which they were willing to sell at four cents a dozen.

One of the smokers explained to me that it is very bad economy not to allow an abundant supply of food to "a man's force." The negroes are fond of good living, and, if not well provided for, know how to provide for themself. It is also but simple policy to have them well lodged and clothed. If they do not have comfortable cabins and sufficient clothing, they will take cold, and be laid up. He lost a very valuable negro, once, from having neglected to provide him with shoes.

LODGINGS.

The houses of the slaves are usually log-cabins, of various degrees of comfort and commodiousness. At one end there is a great open fire-place, which is exterior to the wall of the house, being made of clay in an inclosure, about eight feet square and high, of logs. The chimney is sometimes of brick, but more commonly of lath or split sticks, laid up like log-work and plastered with mud. They enjoy great roaring fires, and, as the common fuel is pitch pine, the cabin, at night when the door is open, seen from a distance, appears like a fierce furnace. The chimneys often catch fire, and the cabin is destroyed. Very little precaution can be taken against this danger.* Several cabins are placed near together, and they are called "the quarters." On a plantation of moderate size there will be

---

* "AN INGENIOUS NEGRO.—In Lafayette, Miss., a few days ago, a negro, who, with his wife and three children, occupied a hut upon the plantation of Col. Peques, was very much annoyed by fleas. Believing that they congregated in great numbers beneath his house, he resolved to destroy them by fire; and accordingly, one night when his family were asleep, he raised a plank in the floor of his cabin, and, procuring an armful of shucks, scattered them on the ground beneath and lighted them. The consequence was, that the cabin was consumed, and the whole family, with the exception of the man who lighted the fire, was burned to death."—*Journal of Commerce.*

but one "quarters." The situation chosen for it has reference to convenience of obtaining water from springs and fuel from the woods. On some of the James River plantations there are larger houses, boarded and made ornamental. In these eight families, each having a distinct sleeping-room and lock-up closets, and every two having a common kitchen or living-room, are accommodated.

CLOTHING.

As to the clothing of the slaves on the plantations, they are said to be usually furnished by their owners or masters, every year, each with a coat and trousers, of a coarse woolen or woolen and cotton stuff (mostly made, especially for this purpose, in Providence, R. I.), for Winter, trousers of cotton osnaburghs for Summer, sometimes with a jacket also of the same; two pairs of strong shoes, or one pair of strong boots and one of lighter shoes for harvest; three shirts; one blanket, and one felt hat.

The women have two dresses of striped cotton, three shifts, two pairs of shoes, etc. The women lying-in are kept at knitting short sacks, from cotton which, in Southern Virginia, is usually raised, for this purpose, on the farm, and these are also given to the negroes. They also purchase clothing for themselves, and, I notice especially, are well supplied with handkerchiefs which the men frequently, and the women nearly always, wear on their heads. On Sundays and holidays they usually look very smart, but when at work, very ragged and slovenly.

At the conclusion of our bar-room session, some time after midnight, as we were retiring to our rooms, our progress up stairs and along the corridors was several times impeded, by negroes lying fast asleep, in their usual clothes only, upon the floor. I asked why they were not abed, and was answered by a gentleman, that negroes never wanted to go to bed; they always preferred to sleep upon the floor.

CHAPTER II

NORTH CAROLINA

THE largest and best hotel in Norfolk had been closed, shortly before I was there, from want of sufficient patronage to sustain it, and I was obliged to go to another house which, though quite pretending, was very shamefully kept. The landlord paid scarcely the smallest attention to the wants of his guests, turned his back when inquiries were made of him, and replied insolently to complaints and requests. His slaves were far his superiors in manners and morals; but, not being one quarter in number what were needed, and consequently not being able to obey one quarter of the orders that were given them, their only study was to disregard, as far as they would be allowed to, all requisitions upon their time and labor. The smallest service could only be obtained by bullying or bribing. I had to make a bargain for every clean towel that I got during my stay.

I was first put in a very small room, in a corner of the house, next under the roof. The weather being stormy, and the roof leaky, water was frequently dripping from the ceiling upon the bed and driving in at the window, so as to stand in pools upon the floor. There was no fire-place in the room; the ladies' parlor was usually crowded by ladies and their friends, among whom I had no acquaintance, and as it was freezing cold, I was obliged to spend most of my time in the stinking bar-room, where the landlord all the time sat with his boon companions, smoking and chewing and talking obscenely.

This crew of old reprobates frequently exercised their indignation upon Mrs. Stowe, and other "Infidel abolitionists;" and on Sunday, having all attended church, afterwards mingled with their ordinary ribaldry laudations of the "evangelical" character of the sermons they had heard.

On the night I arrived, I was told that I would be provided, the next morning, with a room in which I could

have a fire, and a similar promise was given me every
twelve hours, for five days, before I obtained it; then, at
last, I had to share it with two strangers.

When I left, the same petty sponging operation was
practiced upon me as at Petersburg. The breakfast, for
which half a dollar had been paid, was not ready until an
hour after I had been called; and, when ready, consisted
of cold salt fish; dried slices of bread and tainted butter;
coffee, evidently made the day before and half re-warmed;
no milk, the milkman not arriving so early in the morning,
the servant said; and no sooner was I seated then the
choice was presented to me, by the agitated book-keeper,
of going without such as this, or of losing the train and so
being obliged to stay in the house twenty-four hours
longer.

Of course I dispensed with the breakfast, and hurried
off with the porter, who was to take my baggage on a
wheel-barrow to the station. The station was across the
harbor, in Portsmouth. Notwithstanding all the haste I
could communicate to him, we reached the ferry-landing
just as the boat left, too late by three seconds. I looked at
my watch; it lacked but twenty minutes of the time at
which the landlord and the book-keeper and the breakfast-
table waiter and the rail-road company's advertisements
had informed me that the train left. "Nebber mine, masser," said the porter, "dey wont go widout 'ou—Baltimore
boat haant ariv yet, dey doan go till dat come in, sueh."

Somewhat relieved by this assurance, and by the arrival
of others at the landing, who evidently expected to reach
the train, I went into the market and bought a breakfast
from the cake and fruit stalls of the negro-women.

In twenty minutes the ferry-boat returned, and after
waiting some time at the landing, put out again; but when
midway across the harbor, the wheels ceased to revolve,
and for fifteen minutes we drifted with the tide. The fire-
man had been asleep, the fires had got low, and the steam
given out. I observed that the crew, including the master
or pilot, and the engineer, were all negroes.

We reached the rail-road station about half an hour
after the time at which the train should have left. There
were several persons prepared for traveling, waiting about
it, but there was no sign of a departing train, and the
ticket-office was not open. I paid the porter, sent him
back, and was added to the number of the waiters.

The delay was for the Baltimore boat, which arrived in an hour after the time the train was advertised, unconditionally, to start, and the first forward movement was more than an hour and a half behind time. A brakeman told me this delay was not very unusual, and that an hour's waiting might be commonly calculated upon with safety.

The distance from Portsmouth to Weldon, N. C., eighty miles, was run in three hours and twenty minutes —twenty-five miles an hour. The road, which was formerly a very poor and unprofitable one, was bought up a few years ago, mainly, I believe, by Boston capital, and reconstructed in a substantial manner. The grades are light, and there are few curves. Fare 2¾ cents a mile.

At a way-station, a trader had ready a company of negroes intended to be shipped South; but the "servants' car" being quite full already, they were obliged to be left for another train. As we departed from the station, I stood upon the platform of the rear car with two other men. One said to the other:—

"That's a good lot of niggers."

"Damn'd good; I only wished they belonged to me."

I entered the car and took a seat, and presently they followed, and sat near me. Continuing their conversation thus commenced, they spoke of their bad luck in life. One appeared to have been a bar-keeper; the other an overseer. One said the highest wages he had ever been paid were two hundred dollars a year, and that year he hadn't laid up a cent. Soon after, the other, speaking with much energy and bitterness, said:

"I wish to God old Virginny was free of all the niggers."

"It would be a good thing if she was."

"Yes, sir; and, I tell you, it would be a damn'd good thing for us poor fellows."

"I reckon it would, myself."

When we stopped at Weldon, a man was shouting from a stage-coach, "passengers for Gaston! Hurry up! Stage is waiting!" As he repeated this the third time, I threw up to him my two valises, and proceeded to climb to the box, to take my seat.

"You are in a mighty hurry, aint ye!!"

"Didn't you say the stage was waiting?"

"If ye'r going ter get any dinner to-day, you'd better

get it here; won't have much other chance. Be right smart about it, too."

"Then you are not going yet?"

"You can get yer dinner, if ye want to."

"You'll call me, will you, when you are ready to go?"

"I shan't go without ye, ye needn't be afeard—go 'long and get yer dinner; this is the place, if anywar;—don't want to go without yer dinner, do ye?"

Before arriving at Weldon, a handbill, distributed by the proprietors of this inn, had been placed in my hands, from which I make the following extracts:

> "We pledge our word of honor as gentlemen, that if the fare at our table be inferior to that on the table of our enterprising competitor, we will not receive a cent from the traveler, but relinquish our claims to pay, as a merited forfeit, for what we would regard as a wanton imposition upon the rights and claims of the unsuspecting traveler.
>
> "We have too much respect for the Ladies of our House, to make even a remote allusion to their domestic duties in a public circular. It will not, however, be regarded indelicate in us to say, that the duties performed by them have been, and are satisfactory to us, and, as far as we know, to the public. And we will only add, in this connection, that we take much pleasure in superintending both our "Cook-House" and table in person, and in administering in person to the wants of our guests.
>
> "We have made considerable improvement in our House of late, and those who wish to remain over at Weldon, will find, with us, airy rooms, clean beds, brisk fires, and attentive and orderly servants, with abundance of FRESH OYSTERS during the season, and every necessary and luxury that money can procure.
>
> "It is not our wish to deceive strangers nor others; and if, on visiting our House, they do not find things as here represented, they can publish us to the world as impostors, and the ignominy will be ours."

Going in to the house, I found most of the passengers by the train at dinner, and the few negro boys and girls in too much of a hurry to pay attention to any one in particular. The only palatable viand within my reach was some cold sweet-potatoes; of these I made a slight repast, paid the landlord, who stood like a sentry in the doorway, half a dollar, and in fifteen minutes, by my watch, from the time I had entered, went out, anxious to make sure of

my seat on the box, for the coach was so small that but
one passenger could be conveniently carried outside. The
coach was gone.

"Oh, yes, sir," said the landlord, hardly disguising his
satisfaction; "gone—yes, sir, some time ago; you was in
to dinner, was you, sir—pity! you'll have to stay over
till to-morrow now, won't you?"

"I suppose so," said I, hardly willing to give up my intention to sleep in Raleigh that night, even to secure a
clean bed and fresh oysters. "Which road does the stage
go upon?"

"Along the county road."

"Which is that—this way through the woods?"

"Yes, sir.—Carried off your baggage, did he?—Pity!
Suppose he forgot you. Pity!"

"Thank you—yes, I suppose he did. Is it a pretty good
road?"

"No, sir, 'taint first-rate—good many pretty bad slews.
You might go round by the Petersburg Rail-road, tomorrow, you'd overtake your baggage at Gaston."

"Thank you; it was not a very fast team, I know. I'm
going to take a little run; and, if I shouldn't come back
before night, you needn't keep a bed for me. Good day,
sir."

I am pretty good on the legs for a short man, and it
didn't take me long, by the *pas gymnastique,* to overtake
the coach.

As I came up, the driver hailed me—

"Hallo! that you?"

"Why did not you wait for me, or call me when you
wanted to go, as you promised?"

"Reckoned ye was inside—didn't look in, coz I asked
if 'twas all right, and somebody—this 'ere gentleman,
here"—(who had got my seat) " 'Yes,' says he, 'all right';
so I reckoned 'twas, and driv along. Mustn't blame me.
Ortn't to be so long swallerin' yer dinner—mind, next
time!"

The road was as bad as anything under the name of road
can be conceived to be. Wherever the adjoining swamps,
fallen trees, stumps, and plantation fences would admit
of it, the coach was driven, with a great deal of dexterity,
out of the road. When the wheels sunk in the mud below
the hubs, we were sometimes requested to get out and
walk. An upset seemed every moment inevitable. At

length, it came; and the driver, climbing on to the upper
side, opened the door, and asked, with an irresistibly jolly
drawl—

"Got mixed up some in here then, didn't ye? Ladies,
hurt any? Well, come, get out here; don't want to
stay here all night, I reckon, do ye?—Ain't nothing
broke, as I see. We'll right her right up. Nary durn'd rail
within a thousan' mile, I don't s'pose; better be lookin'
roun'; got to get somethin' for a pry."

In four hours after I left the hotel at Weldon, the coach
reached the bank of the Roanoke, a distance of fourteen
miles and stopped. "Here we are," said the driver, opening the door.

"Where are we—not in Gaston?"

"Durned nigh it. That ere's Gaston, over thar; and you
just holler, and they'll come over arter you in the boat."

Gaston was a mile above us, and on the other side of
the river. Nearly opposite to where we were was a house,
and a scow drawn up on the beach; the distance across
the river was, perhaps, a quarter of a mile. When the
driver had got the luggage off, he gathered his reins, and
said:

"Seems to me them gol-durned lazy niggers ain't a
goin' to come over arter you now; if they won't, you'd
better go up to the rail-road bridge, some of ye, and get
a boat, or else go down here to Free-town; some of them
cussed free niggers'll be glad of the job, I no doubt."

"But, confound it, driver! you are not going to leave
us here, are you? we paid to be carried to Gaston."

"Can't help it; you are close to Gaston, any how, and
if any man thinks he's goin' to heve me drive him up to
the bridge tonight, he's damnably mistaken, he is, and I
ain't a goin' to do it, not for no man, I ain't."

And away he drove, leaving us, all strangers, in a
strange country, just at the edge of night, far from any
house, to "holler."

The only way to stop him was to shoot him; and, as we
were all good citizens, and traveled with faith in the
protection of the law, and not like knights-errant, armed
for adventure, we could not do that.

Good citizens? No, we were not; for we have all, to this
day, neglected to prosecute the fellow, or his employers.
It would, to be sure, have cost us ten times any damages
we should have been awarded; but, if we had been really

good citizens, we should have been as willing to sacrifice the necessary loss, as knights-errant of old were to risk life to fight bloody giants. And, until many of us can have the nobleness to give ourselves the trouble and expense of killing off these impudent highwaymen of our time, at law, we have all got to suffer in their traps and stratagems.

We soon saw the "gol-durned lazy niggers" come to their scow, and after a scrutiny of our numbers, and a consultation among themselves, which evidently resulted in the conclusion that the job wouldn't pay, go back.

When it began to grow dark, leaving me as a baggage-guard, the rest of the coach's company walked up the bank of the river, and crossed by a rail-road bridge to Gaston. One of them afterwards returned with a gang of negroes, whom he had hired, and a large freight-boat, into which, across the snags which lined the shore, we passed all the baggage. Among the rest, there were some very large and heavy chests, belonging to two pretty women, who were moving, with their effects; and, although they remained in our company all the next day, they not only neglected to pay their share of the boat and negro-hire, but forgot to thank us, or even gratefully to smile upon us, for our long toil in the darkness for them.

Working up the swollen stream of the Roanoke, with setting-poles and oars, we at length reached Gaston. When I bought my tickets at the station in Portsmouth, I said: "I will take tickets to any place this side of Raleigh at which I can arrive before night. I wish to avoid traveling after dark." "You can go straight through to Raleigh, before dark," said the clerk. "You are sure of that?" "Yes, sir." On reaching Gaston, I inquired at what time the train for Raleigh had passed: "At three o'clock." According to the advertisement, it should have passed at two o'clock; and, under the most favorable circumstances, it could not have been possible for us, leaving Portsmouth at the time we did, to reach Gaston before four o'clock, or Raleigh in less than twenty-eight hours after the time promised. The next day, I asked one of the railroad men how often the connection occurred, which is advertised in the Northern papers, as if it were a certain thing to take place at Gaston. "Not very often, sir; it hain't been once, in the last two weeks." Whenever the connection is not made, all passengers whom these railroad freebooters have drawn into their ambush, are obliged to remain over a day, at

Gaston; for, as is to be supposed, with such management the business of the road will support but one train a day.

The route by sea, from Baltimore to Portsmouth, and thence by these lines, is advertised as the surest, cheapest, and most expeditious route to Raleigh. Among my stage companions were some who lived beyond Raleigh. This was Friday. They would now not reach Raleigh till Saturday night, and such as could not conscientiously travel on Sunday, would be detained from home two days longer than if they had come the land route. One of them lived some eighty miles beyond Raleigh, and intended to proceed by a coach, which was to leave Saturday morning. He would probably be now detained till the following Wednesday, as the coach left Raleigh but twice a week.

CHAPTER III

———•—•———

SOUTH CAROLINA AND GEORGIA

PASSING through long stretches of cypress swamps, with occasional intervals of either pine-barrens, or clear water ponds, in about two hours we came, in the midst of the woods, to the end of the rails. In the vicinity could be seen a small tent, a shanty of loose boards, and a large, subdued fire, around which, upon the ground, there were a considerable number of men, stretched out asleep. This was the camp of the hands engaged in laying the rails, and who were thus daily extending the distance which the locomotive could run.

The conductor told me that there was here a break of about eighty miles in the rail, over which I should be transferred by a stage coach, which would come as soon as possible after the driver knew that the train had arrived. To inform him of this, the locomotive screamed loud and long.

The negro property, which had been brought up in a freight car, was immediately let out on the stoppage of the train. As it stepped on to the platform, its owner asked, "Are you all here?"

"Yes, massa, we is all heah," answered one; "Do dysef no harm, for we's all heah," added another, quoting Saint Peter, in an undertone.

The negroes immediately gathered some wood, and, taking a brand from the rail-road hands, made a fire for themselves; then, all but the woman, opening their bundles, wrapped themselves in their blankets and went to sleep. The woman, bare-headed, and very inadequately clothed as she was, stood for a long time alone, perfectly still, erect and statue-like, with her head bowed, gazing in the fire. She had taken no part in the light chat of the others, and had given them no assistance in making the fire. Her dress, too, was not the usual plantation apparel. It was all sadly suggestive.

The principal other freight of the train was one hun-

dred and twenty bales of northern hay. It belonged, as the
conductor told me, to a planter who lived some twenty
miles beyond here, and who had bought it in Wilmington
at a dollar and a half a hundred weight, to feed to his
mules. Including the steam-boat and rail-road freight, and
all the labor of getting it to his stables, its entire cost to
him would not be much less than two dollars a hundred.
This would be at least four times as much as it would have
cost to raise and make it in the interior of New York or
New England. Now, there are not only several forage
crops which can be raised in South Carolina that cannot
be grown on account of the severity of the winter in the
free States, but, on a farm near Fayetteville, a few days
before, I had seen a crop of natural grass growing in half-
cultivated land, dead upon the ground, which I think
would have made, if it had been cut and well treated in
the summer, three tons of hay to the acre. The owner of
the land said that there was no better hay than it would
have made, but he hadn't had time to attend to it. He had
as much as his hands could do of other work at the period
of the year when it should have been made.

Probably the case was similar with the planter who had
bought this northern hay at a price four times that which
it would have cost a northern farmer to make it. He had
preferred to employ his slaves at other business.

The inference must be either that there was most
improbably-foolish, bad management, or that the slaves
were more profitably employed in cultivating cotton,
than they could have been in cultivating maize, or other
forage crops.

I put the case, some days afterwards, to an English merchant, who had had good opportunities, and made it a
part of his business, to study such matters.

"I have no doubt," said he, "that, if hay cannot be
obtained here, other valuable forage can, with less labor
than anywhere at the North; and all the Southern agricultural journals sustain this opinion, and declare it to be
purely bad management that neglects these crops, and de-
votes labor to cotton, so exclusively. Probably, it is so—at
the present cost of forage. Nevertheless, the fact is also
true, as the planters assert, that they cannot afford to apply their labor to anything else but cotton. And yet, they
complain that the price of cotton is so low that there is no
profit in growing it; which is evidently false. You see

that they prefer buying hay to raising it, at, to say the least, three times what it costs your Northern farmers to raise it. Of course, if cotton could be grown in New York and Ohio, it could be afforded at one-third the cost it is here—say at three cents per pound. And that is my solution of the Slavery question. Bring cotton down to three cents a pound, and there would be more abolitionists in South Carolina than in Massachusetts. If that can be brought about in any way—and it is not impossible that we may live to see it, as our railways are extended in India, and the French enlarge their free-labor plantations in Algiers—there will be an end of Slavery."

It was just one o'clock when the stage-coach came for us. There was but one passenger beside myself—a Philadelphia gentleman, going to Columbia. We proceeded very slowly for about three miles, across a swamp, upon a "corduroy road"; then more rapidly, over rough ground, being tossed about in the coach most severely, for six or eight miles further. Besides the driver, there was on the box the agent or superintendent of the coach line, who now opened the doors, and we found ourselves before a log stable, in the midst of a forest of large pines. The driver took out a horse, and, mounting him, rode off, and we collected wood, splitting it with a hatchet that was carried on the coach, and, lighting it from the coach lamp, made a fire. It was very cold, ice half an inch thick, and a heavy hoar frost. We complained to the agent that there was no straw in the coach bottom, while there were large holes bored in it that kept our feet excessively cold. He said that there was no straw to be had in the country. They were obliged to bed their horses with pine leaves, which were damp, and would be of no service to us. The necessity for the holes he did not immediately explain, and we, in the exercise of our Yankee privilege, resolved that they were made with reference to the habit of expectoration, which we had observed in the car to be very general and excessive.

In about half an hour the driver of the new stage came to us on the horse that the first had ridden away. A new set of horses was brought out, and attached to the coach, and we were driven on again. An hour later, the sun rose; we were still in pine-barrens, once in several miles passing through a clearing with a log farm-house and a few negro huts about it, often through cypress swamps, and

long pools of water. At the end of ten miles we break-
fasted and changed horses and drivers at a steam saw-mill.
A few miles further on, we were asked to get on the top
of the coach while it was driven through a swamp, in
which the water was over the road, for a quarter of a mile,
to such a depth that it covered the foot-board. The
horses really groaned, as they pushed the thin ice away
with their necks, and were very near swimming. The holes
in the coach bottom, the agent now told us, were to allow
the water that would here enter the body to flow out. At
the end of these ten miles we changed again, at a cotton-
planter's house—a very neat, well-built house having pine
trees about it, but very poor, old negro quarters.

Since the long ford we had kept the top, the inside of
the coach being wet, and I had been greatly pleased with
the driving—the coachman, a steady, reliable sort of fellow, saying but little to his horses, and doing what swearing he thought necessary in English; driving, too, with
great judgment and skill. The coach was a fine, roomy,
old-fashioned, fragrant, leathery affair and the horses the
best I had seen this side of Virginia. I could not resist expressing my pleasure with the whole establishment. The
new team was admirable: four sleek, well-governed,
eager, sorrel cobs, and the driver, a staid, bronzed-faced
man, keeping them tight in hand, drove quietly and
neatly, his whip in the socket. After about fifteen minutes,
during which he had been engaged in hushing down their
too great impetuosity, he took out a large silver hunting-
watch, and asked what time it was.

"Quarter past eleven," said the agent.

"Twelve minutes past," said the Philadelphian.

"Well, fourteen, only, I am," said the agent.

"Thirteen," said I.

"Just thirteen, I am," said the driver, slipping back his
watch to its place, and then, to the agent, "ha'an't touched
a hand of her since I left old Lancaster."

Suddenly guessing the meaning of what had been for
some time astonishing me—"You are from the North?" I
asked.

"Yes, sir."

"And you, too, Mr. Agent?"

"Yes, sir."

"And the coach, and the cattle, and all?"

"All from Pennsylvania."

"How long have you been here?"

"We have been here about a fortnight, stocking the road. We commenced regular trips yesterday. You are the first passenger through, sir."

It was, in fact, merely a transfer from one of the old National Road lines, complete. After a little further conversation, I asked, "How do you like the country, here?"

"Very nice country," said the agent.

"Rather poor soil, I should say."

"It's the cussedest poor country God ever created," snapped out the driver.

"You have to keep your horses on——?"

"*Shucks,* damn it!"

NATURE IN EASTERN SOUTH CAROLINA.

The character of the scenery was novel to me, the surface very flat, the soil a fine-grained, silvery white sand, shaded by a continuous forest of large pines, which had shed their lower branches, so that we could see from the coach-top, to the distance of a quarter of a mile, everything upon the ground. In the swamps, which were frequent and extensive, and on their borders, the pines gave place to cypresses, with great pedestal trunks, and protuberant roots, throwing up an awkward dwarf progeny of shrub cypress, and curious bulbous-like stumps, called "cypress-knees." Mingled with these were a few of our common deciduous trees, the white-shafted sycamore, the gray beech, and the shrubby black-jack oak, with broad leaves, brown and dead, yet glossy, and reflecting the sun-beams. Somewhat rarely, the red cedar, and, more frequently than any other except the cypress, the beautiful holly. Added to these, there was often a thick undergrowth of evergreen shrubs. Vines and creepers of various kinds grew to the tops of the tallest trees, and dangled beneath and between their branches, in intricate network. The tylandria hung in festoons, sometimes several feet in length, and often completely clothed the trunks and every branch of the trees in the low ground. It is like a fringe of tangled hair, of a light gray pearly color, and sometimes produces exquisite effects when slightly veiling the dark green, purple and scarlet of the cedar, and the holly with their berries. The mistletoe also grew in large, vivid, green tufts, on the ends of the branches of

SOUTH CAROLINA LOG CABIN

the oldest and largest trees. A small, fine and wiry dead grass, hardly perceptible, even in the most open ground, from the coach tops, was the only sign of herbage. Large black buzzards were constantly in sight, sailing slowly, high above the tree-tops. Flocks of larks, quails, and robins were common, as were also doves, swiftly flying in small companies. The red-headed woodpecker could at any time be heard hammering the old tree-trunks, and would sometimes show himself, after his rat-tat, cocking his head archly, and listening to hear if the worm moved under the bark. The drivers told me that they had, on previous days, as they went over the road, seen deer, turkeys, and wild hogs.

THE PEOPLE.

At every tenth mile, or thereabout, we changed horses, and, generally, were allowed half an hour to stroll in the neighborhood of the stable—the agent observing that we could reach the end of the staging some hours before the cars should leave to take us further; and, as there were no good accommodations for sleeping there, we would pass the time quite as pleasantly on the road. We dined at "Marion County House," a pleasant little village (and the only village we saw during the day), with a fine pine-grove, a broad street, a court-house, a church or two, a school-house, and a dozen or twenty dwellings. Towards night, we crossed the Great Pedee of the maps, the *Big* Pedee of the natives, in a flat-boat. A large quantity of cotton, in bales, was upon the bank, ready for loading into a steam-boat—when one should arrive—for Charleston.

The country was very thinly peopled, lone houses often being several miles apart. The large majority of the dwellings were of logs, and even those of the white people were often without glass windows. In the better class of cabins, the roof is usually built with a curve, so as to project eight or ten feet beyond the log-wall; and a part of this space, exterior to the logs, is inclosed with boards, making an additional small room—the remainder forms an open porch. The whole cabin is often elevated on four corner-posts, two or three feet from the ground, so that the air may circulate under it. The fire-place is built at the end of the house, of sticks and clay, and the chimney is carried up outside, and often detached from the log-walls; but the roof is extended at the gable, until in a line with its outer side. The porch has a railing in front, and a wide shelf at the end, on which a bucket of water, a gourd, and hand-basin, are usually placed. There are chairs, or benches, in the porch, and you often see women sitting at work on it, as in Germany.

The logs are usually hewn but little; and, of course, as they are laid up, there will be wide interstices between them—which are increased by subsequent shrinking. These, very commonly, are not "chinked," or filled up in any way; nor is the wall lined on the inside. Through the chinks, as you pass along the road, you may often see all that is going on in the house; and, at night, the light of the fire shines brightly out on all sides.

Cabins, of this class, would almost always be flanked by two or three negro-huts. The cabins of the poorest class of whites were of a meaner sort—being mere square pens of logs, roofed over, provided with a chimney, and usually with a shed of boards, supported by rough posts, before the door.

Occasionally, where the silvery sand was darkened by a considerable intermixture of mould, there would be a large plantation, with negro-quarters and a cotton-press and gin-house. We passed half a dozen of these, perhaps, during the day. Where the owners resided in them, they would have comfortable-looking residences, not unlike the better class of New England farm-houses. On the largest one, however, there was no residence for the owner, at all, only a small cottage, or whitewashed cabin, for the overseer. It was a very large plantation, and all the buildings were substantial and commodious, except the negro-cabins, which were the smallest I had seen—I thought not more than twelve feet square interiorly. They stood in two rows, with a wide street between them. They were built of logs, with no windows—no opening at all, except the doorway, with a chimney of sticks and mud, with no trees about them, on porches, or shades, of any kind. Except for the chimney—the purpose of which I should not readily have guessed—if I had seen one of them in New England I should have conjectured that it had been built for a powder-house, or perhaps an ice-house—never for an animal to sleep in.

We stopped, for some time, on this plantation, near where some thirty men and women were at work, repair-

ROAD-REPAIRING IN SOUTH CAROLINA

ing the road. The women were in majority, and were engaged at exactly the same labor as the men; driving the carts, loading them with dirt, and dumping them upon the road; cutting down trees, and drawing wood by hand, to lay across the miry places; hoeing, and shoveling.

They were dressed in coarse gray gowns, generally very much burned, and very dirty; which, for greater convenience of working in the mud, were reefed up with a cord drawn tightly around the body, a little above the hips— the spare amount of skirt bagging out between this and the waist-proper. On their legs were loose leggins, or pieces of blanket or bagging wrapped about, and lashed with thongs; and they wore very heavy shoes. Most of them had handkerchiefs, only, tied around their heads; some wore men's caps, or old slouched hats, and several were bare-headed.

The overseer rode about among them, on a horse, carrying in his hand a raw-hide whip, constantly directing and encouraging them; but, as my companion and I, both, several times noticed as often as he visited one end of the line of operations, the hands at the other end would discontinue their labor until he turned to ride towards them again. Clumsy, awkward, gross, elephantine in all their movements; pouting, grinning, and leering at us; sly, sensual, and shameless, in all their expressions and demeanor; I never before had witnessed, I thought, anything more revolting than the whole scene.

At length, the overseer dismounted from his horse, and, giving him to a boy to take to the stables, got upon the coach, and rode with us several miles. From the conversation I had with him, as well as from what I saw of his conduct in the field, I judged that he was an uncommonly fit man for his duties; at least ordinarily amiable in disposition, and not passionate; but deliberate, watchful, and efficient. I thought he would be not only a good economist, but a firm and considerate officer or master.

If these women, and their children after them, were always naturally and necessarily to remain of the character and capacity stamped on their faces—as is probably the opinion of their owner, in common with most wealthy South Carolina planters—I don't know that they could be much less miserably situated, or guided more for their own good and that of the world, than they were. They were fat enough, and didn't look as if they were at all overworked, or harassed by cares, or oppressed by a consciousness of their degradation. If that is all—as some think.

Afterwards, while we were changing at a house near a crossing of roads, strolling off in the woods for a short distance, I came upon two small white-topped wagons, each with a pair of horses feeding at its pole; near them was a dull camp fire, with a bake-kettle and coffee-pot, some blankets and a chest upon the ground; and an old negro, sitting with his head bowed down over a meal sack, while a negro boy was combing his wool with a common horse-card. "Good evening, uncle," said I, approaching them. "Good evening, sar," he answered, without looking up.

"Where are you going?"

"Well, we ain't goin' nower, master; we's peddlin' tobacco roun'."

"Oh! peddling tobacco. Where did you come from?"

"From Rockingham County, Norf Car'lina, master."

"How long have you been coming from there?"

"'Twill be seven weeks, to-morrow, sar, since we left home."

"Have you most sold out?"

"We had a hundred and seventy-five boxes in both wagons, and we's sold all but sixty. Want to buy some tobacco, master?" (Looking up.)

"No, thank you; I am only waiting here, while the coach changes. How much tobacco is there in a box?"

"Seventy-five pound."

"Are these the boxes?"

"No, them is our provision boxes, master. Show de gemman some of der tobacco, dah." (To the boy.)

A couple of negroes here passed along near us; the old man hailed them:

"Ho dah, boys! Doan you want to buy some backey?"

"No." (Decidedly.)

"Well, I'm sorry for it." (Reproachfully.)

"Are you bound homeward, now?" I asked.

"No, massa; wish me was; got to sell all our tobackey fuss; you don't want none, master, does you? Doan you tink it pretty fair tobacco, sar, just try it: it's right sweet, reckon you'll find."

"I don't wish any, thank you; I never use it. Is your master with you?"

"No, sar; he's gone across to Marion, to-day."

"Do you like to be traveling about, in this way?"

"Yes, master; I likes it very well."

"Better than staying at home, eh?"

"Well, I likes my country better dan dis; must say dat, master, likes my country better dan dis. I'se a free nigger in my country, master."

"Oh, you are a free man, are you! North Carolina is a better country than this, for free men, I suppose."

"Yes, master, I likes my country de best; I gets five dollar a month for dat boy." (Hastily, to change the subject.)

"He is your son, is he?"

"Yes, sar; he drives dat wagon. I drives dis; and I haant seen him fore, master, for six weeks, till dis mornin'."

"How were you separated?"

"We separated six weeks ago, sar, and we agreed to meet here, last night. We didn', dough, till dis mornin'."

The old man's tone softened, and he regarded his son with earnestness.

"'Pears dough, we was bofe heah, last night; but I couldn't find dem till dis mornin'. Dis mornin' some niggars tole me dar war a niggar camped off yander in de wood; and I knew 'twas him, and I went an' found him right off."

"And what wages do you get for yourself?"

"Ten dollars a month, master."

"That's pretty good wages."

"Yes, master, any niggar can get good wages if he's a mind to be industrious, no matter wedder he's slave or free."

"So you don't like this country as well as North Carolina?"

"No, master. Fac is, master, 'pears like wite folks doan ginerally like niggers in dis country; day doan ginerally talk so to niggars like as do in my country; de niggars ain't so happy heah; 'pears like de wite folks was kind o' different, somehow. I doan like dis country so well; my country suits me very well."

"Well, I've been thinking, myself, the niggers did not look so well here as they did in North Carolina and Virginia; they are not so well clothed, and they don't appear so bright as they do there."

"Well, massa, Sundays dey is mighty well clothed, dis country; 'pears like dere an't nobody looks better Sundays dan dey do. But Lord! workin' days, seems like dey haden no close dey could keep on 'um at all, master. Dey is a'mos' naked, wen deys at work, some on 'em. Why, master, up in our country, de wite folks, why, some on 'em has ten or twelve niggers; dey doan' hev no real big plantation, like dey has heah, but some on 'em has ten or twelve niggers, may be, and dey juss lives and talks along wid 'em; and dey treats 'um most as if dem was dar own chile. Dey doan' keep no niggers dey can't treat so; dey wont keep 'em, wont be bodered wid 'em. If dey gets a nigger and he doan behave himself, dey wont keep him; dey juss tell him, sar, he must look up anudder master, and if he doan' find hisself one, I tell 'ou, when de trader cum along, dey sell him, and he totes him away. Dey allers sell off all de bad niggers out of our country; dat's de way de bad nigger and all dem no-account nigger keep a cumin' down heah; dat's de way on't, master."

"Yes, that's the way of it, I suppose; these big planta-tions are not just the best thing for niggers, I see that plainly."

"Master, you wan't raise in dis country, was 'ou?"

"No; I came from the North."

"I tort so, sar, I knew 'ou wan't one of dis country peo-ple, 'peared like 'ou was one o' my country people, way 'ou talks; and I loves dem kine of people. Won't you take some whiskey, sar? Heah, you boy! bring dat jug of whisky dah, out o' my wagon; in dah, in dat box under dem foddar."

"No, don't trouble yourself, I am very much obliged to you; but I don't like to drink whisky."

"Like to have you drink some, massa, if you'd like it. You's right welcome to it. 'Pears like I knew you was one of my country people. Ever been in Greensboro' massa? dat's in Guilford."

"No, I never was there. I came from New York, further North than your country."

"New York, did 'ou, massa? I heerd New York was what dey calls a Free State; all de niggars free dah."

"Yes, that is so."

"Not no slaves at all; well, I expec dat's a good ting, for all de niggars to be free. Greensboro' is a right comely town; tain't like dese heah Souf Car'lina towns."

"I have heard it spoken of as a very beautiful town, and there are some very nice people there."

"Yes, dere's Mr. —— ——, I knows him, he's a mighty good man."

"Do you know Mr. ——?

"O, yes sar, he's a mighty fine man, he is, massa; ain't no better kind of man dan him."

"Well, I must go, or the coach will be kept waiting for me. Good-by to you."

"Far'well, master, far'well, 'pears like it's done me good to see a man dat's cum out of my country again. Far'well, master."

We took supper at an exquisitely neat log-cabin, standing a short distance off the road, with a beautiful evergreen oak, the first I had observed, in front of it. There was no glass in the windows, but drapery of white muslin restrained the currents of air, and during the day would let in sufficient light, while a great blazing wood-fire both warmed and lighted the room by night. A rifle and powder-horn hung near the fire-place, and the master of the house, a fine, hearty, companionable fellow, said that he had lately shot three deer, and that there were plenty of cats, and foxes, as well as turkeys, hares, squirrels and other small game in the vicinity. It was a perfectly charming little backwoods farm-house, good wife, supper, and all; but one disagreeable blot darkened the otherwise most agreeable picture of rustic civilization—we were waited upon at table by two excessively dirty, slovenly-dressed negro girls. In the rear of the cabin were two hovels, each lighted by large fires and apparently crowded with other slaves belonging to the family.

Between nine and ten at night, we reached the end of the completed rail-road, coming up in search for that we had left the previous night. There was another camp and fire of the workmen, and in a little white frame-house we found a company of engineers. There were two trains and locomotives on the track, and a gang of negroes was loading cotton into one of them.

NEGRO *Jodling.* "THE CAROLINA YELL."

I strolled off until I reached an opening in the woods, in which was a cotton-field and some negro-cabins, and beyond it large girdled trees, among which were two negroes with dogs barking, yelping, hacking, shouting, and whistling, after 'coons and 'possums. Returning to the railroad, I found a comfortable, warm passenger-car, and, wrapped in my blanket, went to sleep. At midnight I was awakened by loud laughter, and, looking out, saw that the loading gang of negroes had made a fire, and were enjoying a right merry repast. Suddenly, one raised such a sound as I never heard before, a long, loud, musical shout, rising, and falling, and breaking into falsetto, his voice ringing through the woods in the clear, frosty night air, like a bugle call. As he finished, the melody was caught up by another, and then, another, and then by several in chorus. When there was silence again, one of them cried out, as if bursting with amusement: "Did yer see de dog?—when I began eeohing, he turn roun' an' look me straight into der face; ha! ha! ha!" and the whole party broke into the loudest peals of laughter, as if it was the very best joke they had ever heard.

After a few minutes I could hear one urging the rest to come to work again, and soon he stepped towards the cotton bales, saying, "Come, brederen, come; let's go at it; come now, eoho! roll away! eeoho-eeoho-weeioho-i!"— and the rest taking it up as before, in a few moments they all had their shoulders to a bale of cotton and were rolling it up the embankment.

———— · ◆ · ————

CHAPTER IV

LOUISIANA

"ACADIENS."

AT ONE corner of Mr. R.'s plantation, there was a hamlet of Acadians (descendants of the refugees of Acadia), about a dozen small houses or huts, built of wood or clay, in the old French peasant style. The residents owned small farms, on which they raised a little corn and rice; but Mr. R. described them as lazy vagabonds, doing but little work, and spending much time in shooting, fishing, and play. He wanted very much to buy all their land, and get them to move away. He had already bought out some of them, and had made arrangements to get hold of the land of some of the rest. He was willing to pay them two or three times as much as their property was actually worth, to get them to move off. As fast as he got possession, he destroyed their houses and gardens, removed their fences and trees, and brought all their land into his cane-plantation.

Some of them were mechanics. One was a very good mason, and he employed him in building his sugar-works and refinery; but he would be glad to get rid of them all, and should then depend entirely on slave mechanics—of these he had several already and he could buy more when he needed them.

Why did he so dislike to have these poor people living near him? Because, he said, they demoralized his negroes. The slaves seeing them living in apparent comfort, without much property and without steady labor, could not help thinking that it was not necessary for men to work so hard as they themselves were obliged to; that if they were free they would not need to work. Besides, the intercourse of these people with the negroes was not favorable to good discipline. They would get the negroes to do them little services, and would pay them with luxuries which he did not wish them to have. It was better that negroes never saw anybody off their own plantation; that they had no intercourse with other white men than their owner or overseer; especially, it was best that they should not see white men who did not command their respect, and whom they did not always feel to be superior to themselves, and able to command them.

"CHICKEN THIEVES."

The nuisance of petty traders dealing with the negroes and encouraging them to pilfer, which I found everywhere a great annoyance to planters, seems to be greater on the Mississippi "Coast" than anywhere else. The traders generally come on boats, which they moor at night on the shore, adjoining the negro-quarters, and float away whenever they have obtained any booty, with very small chance of detection. One day, during my visit at Mr. R.'s, a neighbor called to apprise him that one of these trading-boats was in the vicinity, that he might take precautions to prevent his negroes dealing with it. "The law," he observed, with much feeling, "is entirely inadequate to protect us against these rascals; it rather protects them than us. They easily evade detection in breaking it; and we can never get them punished, except we go beyond or against the law ourselves." To show me how vexatious the evil was, he mentioned that a large brass cock and some pipe had been lately stolen from his sugar-works, and that he had ascertained that one of his negroes had taken it and sold it on board one of these boats for seventy-five cents, and had immediately spent the money, chiefly for whisky, on the same boat. It had cost him thirty dollars to replace it. Mr. R. said that he had lately caught one of his own negroes going towards one of the "chicken thieves," (so the traders' boats are called) with a piece of machinery, that he had unscrewed from his sugar-works, which was worth eighty dollars, and which might very likely have been sold for a drink. If the negro had succeeded in reaching the boat, as he would if he had not been on the watch, he could never have recovered it. There would have been no witnesses to the sale; the stolen goods would have been hid on board until the boat reached New Orleans; or, if an officer came to search the boat, they would have been dropped into the river before he got on board.

This neighbor of Mr. R.'s was a Creole, and had been educated in France. Conversing on the inconveniences of Slavery, he acknowledged that it was not only an uneconomical system, but a morally wrong one; "but," he said, "it was not instituted by us—we are not responsible for it. It is unfortunately fixed upon us; we could not do away with it if we wished; our duty is only to make the best of a bad thing; to lessen its evils as much as we can, so far as we have to do with it individually."

Mr. R. himself also acknowledged Slavery to be a very great evil, morally and economically. It was a curse upon the South; he had no doubt at all about it: nothing would be more desirable than its removal, if it were possible to be accomplished. But he did not think it could be abolished without instituting greater evils than those sought to be remedied. Its influence on the character of the whites was what was most deplorable. He was sorry to think that his children would have to be subject to it. He thought that eventually, if he were able to afford it, he would free his slaves and send them to Africa.

A SLAVE ABOLITIONIST.

When I left Mr. R.'s, I was driven about twenty miles in a buggy, by one of his house servants. He was inclined to be talkative and communicative; and as he expressed great affection and respect for his owner, I felt at liberty to question him on some points upon which I had always previously avoided conversing with slaves. He spoke rapidly, garrulously; and it was only necessary for me to give a direction to his thoughts by my inquiries. I was careful to avoid leading questions, and not to show such an interest as would lead him to reply guardedly. I charged my memory as much as possible with his very words, when this was of consequence, and made the following record of the conversation, within half an hour after I left him.

He first said that he supposed that I would see that he was not a "Creole nigger"; he came from Virginia. He reckoned the Virginia negroes were better-looking than those who were raised here; there were no black people anywhere in the world who were so "well made" as those who were born in Virginia. He asked if I lived in New Orleans; and where? I told him that I lived at the North; he asked:

"Da's a great many brack folks dah, massa?"

"No; very few."

"Da's a great many in Virginia; more'n da is heah?"

"But I came from beyond Virginia—from New York."

He had heard there were a great many black folk in New York. I said there were a good many in the city; but few in the country. Did I live in the country? What people did I have for servants? Thought if I hired all my labor, it must be very dear. He inquired further about negroes there. I told him they were all free, and described their general condition; told him what led them to congregate in cities, and what the effect was. He said the negroes, both slave and free, who lived in New Orleans, were better off than those who lived in the country. Why? Because they make more money, and it is "gayer" there, and there is more "society." He then drew a contrast between Virginia—as he recollected it—and Louisiana. There is but one road in this country. In Virginia, there are roads running in every direction, and often crossing each other. You could see so much more "society," and there was so much more "variety" than here. He would not like now to go back to Virginia to live, because he had got used to this country, and had all his acquaintances here, and knew the ways of the people. He could speak French. He would like to go to New Orleans, though; would rather live in New Orleans than any other place in the world.

After a silence of some minutes, he said, abruptly;

"If I was free, I would go to Virginia, and see my old mudder." He had left her when he was thirteen years old. He reckoned he was now thirty-three. "I don't well know, dough, exactly, how old I is; but, I rec'lect, de day I was taken away, my ole mudder she tell me I was tirteen year old." He did not like to come away at all; he "felt dreadful bad"; but, now he was used to it, he liked living here. He came across the Blue Ridge, and he recollected that, when he first saw it, he thought it was a dark piece of sky, and he wondered what it would be like when they came close to it. He was brought, with a great many other negroes, in wagons, to Louisville; and then they were put on board a steam-boat, and brought down here. He was sold to a Creole, and was put on this plantation, and had been on it ever since. He had been twice sold, along with it. Folks didn't very often sell their servants here, as they did in Virginia. They were selling their servants, in Virginia, all the time; but, here, they did not very often sell them, except they run away. When a man would run away, and they could not do anything with

him, they always sold him off. The people were almost all
French. "Were there any French in New York?" he asked.
I told him there were; but not as many as in Louisiana. "I
s'pose dah is more of French people in Lusiana, dan dah is
anywhar else in all de world—a'nt dah, massa?"

"Except in France."

"Wa's dat, sar?"

"France is the country where all the Frenchmen came
from, in the first place."

"Wa's dat France, massa?"

"France is a country across the ocean, the big water,
beyond Virginia, where all the Frenchmen first came
from; just as the black people all came first from Africa,
you know."

"I've heered, massa, dat dey sell one anoder dah, in de
fus place. Does you know, sar, was dat so?" This was said
very gravely, and with some expression of emotion.

I explained the savage custom of making slaves of prisoners of war, and described the constant wars of the native Africans. I told him that they were better off here
than they would be to be the slaves of cruel savages, in
Africa. He turned, and looked me anxiously in the face,
like a child, and asked:

"*Is* de brack folks better off to be here, massa?"

I answered that I thought so; and described the hea-
thenish barbarism of the people of Africa. I made exception of Liberia, knowing that his master thought of some
time sending him there, and described it as a place that
was settled by negroes, who went back there from this
country. He said he had heard of it, and that they had
sent a great many free negroes from New Orleans there.

After a moment's pause, he inquired, very gravely,
again:

"Why is it, massa, when de brack people is free, dey
wants to send 'em away out of dis country?"

The question took me aback. After bungling a little—
for I did not like to tell him the white people were afraid
to have them stay here—I said that it was thought to be
a better place for them there. But, he should think, that,
when they had got used to this country, they would be
better off here. He would not like to go out of this country. He wouldn't like even to go to Virginia, though Virginia was such a pleasant country; he had been here so
long, seemed like this was the best place for him to live.

To avoid discussion of the point, I asked what he would do, if he was free?

"If I was free, massa; if I was free [with great animation], I would—well, sar, de fus thing I would do, if I was free, I would go to work for a year, and get some money for myself,—den—den—den, massa, dis is what I do—I buy me, fus place, a little house, and little lot land, and den—no; den—den—I would go to old Virginny, and see my old mudder. Yes, sar, I would like to do dat fus thing; den, when I com back, de fus thing I'd do, I'd get me a wife; den, I'd take her to my house, and I would live with her dar; and I would raise things in my garden, and take 'em to New Orleans, and sell 'em dar, in de market. Dat's de way I would live, if I was free."

He said, in answer to further inquiries, that there were many free negroes all about this region. Some of them were very rich. He pointed out to me three plantations, within twenty miles, which were owned by colored men. These bought black folks, he said, and had servants of their own. They were very bad masters, very hard and cruel—hadn't any feeling. "You might think master, dat dey would be good to dar own nation; but dey is not. I will tell you de truth, massa; I know I'se got to answer; and it's a fact, dey is very bad masters, sar. I'd rather be a servant to any man in de world, dan to a brack man. If I was sold to a brack man, I'd drown myself. I would dat— I'd drown myself!—dough I shouldn't like to do dat nudder; but I wouldn't be sold to a colored master for anyting."

If he had got to be sold, he would like best to have an American master buy him. The French people did not clothe their servants well; though they now did much better than when he first came to Louisiana. The French masters were very severe, and "dey whip dar niggers most to deff—dey whip de flesh off of 'em."

Nor did they feed them as well as the Americans did. "Why, sometimes, massa, dey only gives 'em dry corn— don't give out no meat at all." I told him this could not be so, for the law required that every master should serve out meat to his negroes. "Oh, but some on 'em don't mind Law, if he does say so, massa. Law never here; don't know anything about him. *Very often*, dey only gives 'em dry corn—I knows dat; I sees de niggers. Didn't you see de niggers on our plantation, sar? Well, you nebber

see such a good-looking lot of niggers as ours on any of
de French plantations, did you, massa? Why, dey all looks
fat, and dey's all got good clothes, and dey look as if dey
all had plenty to eat, and hadn't got no work to do, ha!
ha! ha! Don't dey? But dey does work, dough. Dey does a
heap of work. But dey don't work so hard as dey does on
some ob de French plantations. Oh, dey does work *too*
hard on dem, sometimes."

"You work hard, in the grinding season, don't you?"

"Oh, yes; den we works hard; we has to work hard
den: harder dan any oder time of year. But, I tell 'ou,
massa, I likes to hab de grinding season come; yes, I does
—rader dan any oder time of year, dough we works so
hard den. I wish it was grinding season all de year roun'—
only Sundays."

"Why?"

"Because—oh, because it's merry and lively. All de
brack people like it when we begin to grind."

"You have to keep grinding Sundays?"

"Yes, can't stop, when we begin to grind, till we get
tru."

"You don't often work Sundays, except then?"

"No, massa; nebber works Sundays, except when der
crap's weedy, and we want to get tru 'fore rain comes;
den, wen we work a Sunday, massa gives us some oder day
for holiday—Monday, if we get tru."

He said that, on the French plantations, they oftener
work Sundays than on the American. They used to work
almost always on Sundays, on the French plantations,
when he was first brought to Louisiana; but they did not
so much now.

We were passing a hamlet of cottages occupied by
Acadians, or what the planters call *habitans,* poor white,
French Creoles. The negroes had always been represented
to me to despise the habitans and to look upon them as
their own inferiors; but William spoke of them respect-
fully; and, when I tempted him to sneer at their indolence
and vagabond habits, refused to do so, but insisted very
strenuously that they were "very good people," orderly
and industrious. He assured me that I was mistaken in
supposing that the Creoles, who did not own slaves, did
not live comfortably, or that they did not work as hard as
they ought to for their living. There were no better sort
of people than they were, he thought.

Some of the cottagers were engaged in threshing rice, which they performed by the ancient process of treading with horses walking in a circle. There were five horses, and three men driving them. He explained this operation to me, and told me that the negroes beat out the rice with sticks. He asked if wheat was not threshed by engines. In answer to inquiries, he said that the negroes raised rice in considerable quantity in wet places on the edge of the swamp, in the rear of the plantation. They also raised corn, potatoes, and pumpkins. His master allowed them land for this, and they sold their crop, or consumed it themselves; generally they sold it. They worked at night, and on Sundays on their patches, and after the sugar and corncrops of the plantation were "laid by," his master allowed them to have Saturday afternoons to work their own crops in.

He again recurred to the fortunate condition of the negroes on his master's plantation. He thought it was the best plantation in the State, and he did not believe there was a better lot of negroes in the State; some few of them, whom his master had brought from his plantation, were old; but altogether, they were "as right good a lot of niggers" as could be found anywhere. They could do all the work that was necessary to be done on the plantation. On some old plantations they had not nearly so many negroes as they needed to make the crop, and they "drove 'em awful hard"; but it wasn't so on his master's: they could do all the work, and do it well, and it was the best worked plantation, and made the most sugar to the hand, of any plantation he knew of. All the niggers had enough to eat, and were well clothed; their quarters were good, and they got a good many presents.

"Well, now, wouldn't you rather live on such a plantation than to be free, William?"

"Oh! no, sir, I'd rather be free! Oh, yes, sir, I'd like it better to be free; I would dat, master."

"Why would you?"

"Why, you see, master, if I was free—if I was *free*, I'd have *all* my time to myself. I'd rather work for myself. I'd like dat better."

"But then, you know, you'd have to take care of yourself, and you'd get poor."

"No, sir, I would not get poor, I would get rich; for you see, master, then I'd work *all de time* for myself."

"Suppose all the black people on your plantation, or all the black people in the country were made free at once, what do you think would become of them?—what would they do, do you think? You don't suppose there would be much sugar raised, do you?"

"Why, yes, master, I do. Why not, sir? What *would* de brack people do? Wouldn't dey hab to work for dar libben? and de wite people own all de land—war dey goin' to work? Dey hire demself right out again, and work all de same as before. And den, wen dey work for demself, dey work *harder* dan dey do now to get more wages—a heap harder. I tink so, sir. *I* would do so, sir. I would work for hire. I don't own any land; I hab to work right away again for massa, to get some money."

Perceiving from the readiness of these answers that the subject had been a familiar one with him, I immediately asked: "The black people talk among themselves about this, do they; and they think so, generally?"

"Oh! yes, sir; dey talk so; dat's wat dey tink."

"Then they talk about being free a good deal, do they?"

"Yes, sir. Dey—dat is, dey say dey wish it was so; dat's all dey talk, master—dat's all, sir."

His caution was evidently excited, and I inquired no further. We were passing a large old plantation, the cabins of the negroes upon which were mere hovels—small, without windows, and dilapidated. A large gang of negroes were at work by the road-side, planting cane. Two white men were sitting on horseback, looking at them, and a negro-driver was walking among them, with a whip in his hand.

William said that this was an old Creole plantation, and the negroes on it were worked very hard. There was three times as much land in it as in his master's, and only about the same number of negroes to work it. I observed, however, that a good deal of land had been left uncultivated the previous year. The slaves appeared to be working hard; they were shabbily clothed, and had a cowed expression, looking on the ground, not even glancing at us, as we passed, and were perfectly silent.

"Dem's all Creole niggers," said William: "ain't no Virginny niggers dah. I reckon you didn't see no such looking niggers as dem on our plantation, did you, master?"

After answering some inquiries about the levee, close inside of which the road continually ran, he asked me

about the levee at New York; and when informed that we
had not any levee, asked me with a good deal of surprise,
how we kept the water out? I explained to him that the
land was higher than the water, and was not liable, as it
was in Louisiana, to be overflowed. I had much difficulty
in making him understand this. He seemed never to have
considered that it was not the natural order of things that
land should be lower than water, or that men should be
able to live on land, except by excluding water artifi-
cially. At length, when he got the idea, he made a curious
observation.

"I suppose dis State is de lowest State dar is in de world.
Dar ain't no odder State dat is so low as dis is. I s'pose it is
five thousand five hundred feet lower dan any odder
State."

"What?"

"I s'pose, master, dat dis heah State is *five thousand five
hundred feet* lower down dan any odder, ain't it, sir?"

"I don't understand you."

"I say dis heah is de lowest ob de States, master. I s'pose
its *five thousand five hundred feet* lower dan any odder;
lower *down*, ain't it, master?"

"Yes, it's very low."

This is a very good illustration of the child-like manner
and habits of the negroes, and which in him were particularly observable, notwithstanding the shrewdness of some
of his observations. Such a mingling of simplicity and
shrewdness, ingenuousness and slyness, detracted much
from the weight of his opinions and purposes in regard to freedom. I could not but have a strong doubt if he
would keep to his word, if the opportunity were allowed
him to try his ability to take care of himself.

JOURNEY THROUGH TEXAS;

OR, A

SADDLE-TRIP ON THE SOUTHWESTERN FRONTIER;

WITH A

STATISTICAL APPENDIX

BY

FREDERICK LAW OLMSTED,

AUTHOR OF "A JOURNEY IN THE SEABOARD SLAVE STATES,"
"WALKS AND TALKS OF AN AMERICAN FARMER
IN ENGLAND," ETC., ETC.

NEW YORK:
DIX, EDWARDS & CO., 321 BROADWAY
LONDON: SAMPSON LOW, SON & CO.
EDINBURG: THOS. CONSTABLE & CO.
1857.

CHAPTER I

ROUTE THROUGH WESTERN TEXAS

GERMAN FARMS.

THE country next morning continued the same in all respects as that of the day before. The first German settlers we saw, we knew at once. They lived in little log cabins, and had inclosures of ten acres of land about them. The cabins were very simple and cheap habitations, but there were many little conveniences about them and a care to secure comfort in small ways evident that was very agreeable to notice. So, also, the greater variety of the crops which had been grown upon their allotments, and the more clean and complete tillage they had received contrasted favorably with the patches of corn-stubble overgrown with crab-grass, which are usually the only gardens to be seen adjoining the cabins of the poor whites and slaves. The people themselves were also to be seen, men, women and children, busy at some work, and yet not so busy but that they could give a pleasant and respectful greeting to the passing traveler.

A few miles further on, we passed several much more comfortable houses, boarded over, and a good deal like the smaller class of farm-houses in New England, but some of them having exterior plaster-work or brick laid up between the timbers instead of boards nailed over them. About these were larger inclosures, from which extensive crops of corn had been taken; and it caused us a sensation to see a number of parallelograms of COTTON—FREE-LABOR COTTON. These were not often of more than an acre in extent. Most of them looked as if they had been judiciously cultivated and had yielded a fine crop, differing, however, from that we had noticed on the plantations the day before in this circumstance—the picking had been entirely completed, and that with care and exactness, so that none of the cotton which the labor of cultivation had produced had been left to waste. The cotton-stalks stood rather more closely and were of less extraordinary size but much more even or regular in their growth than on the plantations.

A FREE-MINDED BUTCHER.

We were entering the valley of the Guadalupe river, which is of the same general character as that of the San Marcos, and had passed a small brown house with a turret and cross upon it, which we learned was a Lutheran church, when we were overtaken by a good-natured butcher who lived in Neu-Braunfels, whence he had ridden out early in the morning to kill and dress the hogs of one of the large farmers. He had finished his job, and was returning.

He had been in this country eight years. He liked it very much; he did not wish to go back to Germany; he much preferred to remain here. The Germans, generally, were doing well, and were contented. They had had a hard time at first, but they were all doing well now— getting rich. He knew but one German who had bought a slave; they did not think well of slavery; they thought it better that all men should be free; besides, the negroes would not work so well as the Germans. They were improving their condition very rapidly, especially within the last two years. It was sickly on the coast, but here it was very healthy. He had been as well here as he was in Germany—never had been ill. There were Catholics and Protestants among them; as for himself, he was no friend to priests, whether Catholic or Protestant. He had had enough of them in Germany. They could not tell him anything new, and he never went to any church.

We forded, under his guidance, the Guadalupe, and after climbing its high bank, found ourselves upon the level plateau between the prairie hills and the river on which Neu-Braunfels is situated. We had still nearly a mile to ride before entering the town, and in this distance met eight or ten large wagons, each drawn by three or four pairs of mules, or five or six yokes of oxen, each carrying under its neck a brass bell. They were all driven by Germans, somewhat uncouthly but warmly and neatly dressed, all smoking and all good-humored, giving us "good morning" as we met. Noticing the strength of the wagons, I observed that they were made by Germans, probably.

"Yes," said the butcher, "the Germans make better wagons than the Americans; the Americans buy a great many of them. *There are seven wagon-manufactories in Braunfels.*"

NEU-BRAUNFELS.

The main street of the town, which we soon entered upon, was very wide—three times as wide, in effect, as Broadway in New York. The houses, with which it was thickly lined on each side for a mile, were small, low cottages, of no pretensions to elegance, yet generally looking neat and comfortable. Many were furnished with verandahs and gardens, and the greater part were either stuccoed or painted. There were many workshops of mechanics and small stores, with signs oftener in English than in German; and bare-headed women, and men in caps and short jackets, with pendent pipes, were everywhere seen at work.

AN EVENING FAR FROM TEXAS.

We had no acquaintance in the village and no means of introduction, but in hopes that we might better satisfy ourselves of the condition of the people we agreed to stop at an inn and get dinner, instead of eating a cold snack in the saddle without stopping at noon, as was our custom. "Here," said the butcher, "is my shop" (indicating a small house, at the door of which hung dressed meat and beef sausages) "and if you are going to stop, I will recommend you to my neighbor there, Mr. Schmitz." It was a small cottage of a single story, having the roof extended so as to form a verandah, with a sign swinging before it, "Guadalupe Hotel, J. Schmitz."

I never in my life, except, perhaps, in awakening from a dream, met with such a sudden and complete transfer of associations. Instead of loose boarded or hewn log walls with crevices stuffed with rags or daubed with mortar, which we have been accustomed to see during the last month on staving in a door, where we have found any to open; instead, even, of four bare, cheerless sides of whitewashed plaster, which we have found twice or thrice only in a more aristocratic American residence, we were—in short, we were in Germany.

There was nothing wanting; there was nothing too much, for one of those delightful little inns which the pedestrian who has tramped through the Rhine land will ever remember gratefully. A long room, extending across the whole front of the cottage, the walls pink, with stenciled panels, and scroll ornaments in crimson, and with neatly-framed and glazed pretty lithographic prints hanging on all sides; a long, thick, dark oak table, with rounded ends, oak benches at its sides; chiseled oak chairs; a sofa, covered with cheap pink calico, with a small vine pattern; a stove in the corner; a little mahogany cupboard in another corner, with pitcher and glasses upon it; a smoky atmosphere; and finally, four thick-bearded men, from whom the smoke proceeds, who all bow and say "Good morning," as we lift our hats in the doorway.

The landlady enters; she does not readily understand us, and one of the smokers rises immediately to assist us. Dinner we shall have immediately, and she spreads the white cloth at an end of the table before she leaves the room, and in two minutes' time, by which we have got off our coats and warmed our hands at the stove, we are asked to sit down. An excellent soup is set before us, and in succession there follow two courses of meat, neither of them pork, and neither of them fried, two dishes of vegetables, salad, compote of peaches, coffee with milk, wheat bread from the loaf, and beautiful and sweet butter—not only such butter as I have never tasted south of the Potomac before, but such as I have been told a hundred times it was impossible to make in a southern climate. What is the secret? I suppose it is extreme cleanliness, beginning far back of where cleanliness usually begins at the South, and careful and thorough *working*.

We then spent an hour in conversation with the gentlemen who were in the room. They were all educated, cultivated, well-bred, respectful, kind and affable men. All were natives of Germany and had been living several years in Texas. Some of them were travelers, their homes being in other German settlements; some of them had resided long at Braunfels.

It was so very agreeable to meet such men again, and the account they gave of the Germans in Texas was so interesting and gratifying that we were unwilling to immediately continue our journey. We went out to look at our horses; a man in cap and jacket was rubbing their legs

—the first time they had received such attention in Texas, except from ourselves, or by special and costly arrangement with a negro. They were pushing their noses into racks filled with fine mesquit hay—the first they had had in Texas. They seemed to look at us imploringly. We ought to spend the night. But there is evidently no sleeping-room for us in the little inn. They must be full. But then we could sleep with more comfort on the floor here, probably, than we have been accustomed to of late. We concluded to ask if they could accommodate us for the night. Yes, with pleasure—would we be pleased to look at the room they could afford us? Doubtless in the cockloft. No, it was in another little cottage in the rear. A little room it proved, with blue walls again, and oak furniture; two beds, one of them would be for each of us—the first time we had been offered the luxury of sleeping alone in Texas; two large windows with curtains, and evergreen roses trained over them on the outside—not a pane of glass missing or broken—the first sleeping-room we have had in Texas where this was the case; a sofa; a bureau, on which were a complete set of the *Conversations Lexicon;* Kendall's Santa Fe Expedition; a statuette in porcelain; plants in pots; a brass study lamp; a large ewer and basin for washing, and a couple of towels of thick stuff, full a yard and a quarter long. O, yes, it will do for us admirably; we will spend the night.

In the afternoon, we called upon the German Protestant clergyman, who received us kindly, and, though speaking little English, was very ready to give all the information he could about his people and the Germans in Texas generally. We visited some of the workshops, and called on a merchant to ascertain the quality and amount of the cotton grown by the Germans in the neighborhood. At supper, we met a dozen or more intelligent people, and spent the later evening with several others, at the residence of one of our accidental inn acquaintances.

I will simply remark here that the facts learned from these gentlemen confirmed the simple good accounts of the butcher.

As I was returning to the inn about ten o'clock, I stopped for a few moments at the gate of one of the little cottages, to listen to some of the best singing I have heard for a long time, several parts being sustained by very sweet and well-trained voices.

In the day time, I saw in the public street, at no great distance from a school-house, a tame doe, with a band on its neck, to distinguish it from the wild deer, lest it should be shot by sportsmen. It was exceedingly beautiful, and so tame that it allowed me to approach, and licked my hand. In what Texan town through which we have passed before could this have occurred?

In the morning we found that our horses had been bedded, for the first time in Texas.

As we rode out of town, it was delightful to meet again troops of children, with satchels and knapsacks of books and little kettles of dinner, all with ruddy, cheerful faces, the girls especially so, with their hair braided neatly, and without caps or bonnets, smiling and saluting us—"guten morgen"—as we met. Nothing so pleasant as that in Texas before, hardly in the South.

Such was our first encounter with the Germans in Texas. Chance afterwards threw us in the way of seeing much more of them; but I have preferred to preserve the order of time and give now simply these first notes, that the reader who follows us may receive our succession of impressions.

THE SAN ANTONIO ROAD.

We had hardly left the town, which is straggling thickly to the westward and merges, by degrees, its town-lots into ten-acre homesteads and small farms, when one of our table companions came up on the road behind us, also on his way to San Antonio. He joined us, by our invitation, and though we found some difficulty in mutual comprehension, added much to our pleasure and information.

The distance to San Antonio, by the shortest road, is about thirty miles. The old road follows up a creek bottom, and houses, sheltered by live-oaks, stand thick along it, each in the centre of a little farm, having a broad open range of pasture before it. We left these and the hills beyond them, to the right, and went in a straight course out upon the open prairies. The grass had, in many places, been recently burned, giving the country a desolated surface of dead black monotony.

The trees were live-oaks and even these very rare. The ground-swells were long, and so equal in height and similar in form as to bring to mind a tedious sea voyage, where you go plodding on, slow hour after slow hour, without raising a single object to attract the eye.

At noon we crossed the Cibolo (pronounced by Texans "Sewilla"), a creek which has the freak of here and there disappearing in its course for miles, leaving its bed dry, except during freshets. Here were several settlements, almost the only ones on the day's route. Not very far away, however, are, in several places, Germans, who have built neat stone houses out upon the prairie away from any running water, depending entirely upon wells.

Seven miles from San Antonio we passed the Salado, another smaller creek, and shortly after, rising a hill, saw the domes and white clustered dwellings of San Antonio below us. We stopped and gazed long on the sunny scene.

The city is closely-built and prominent, and lies basking on the edge of a vast plain through which the river winds slowly off beyond where the eye can reach. To the east are gentle slopes toward it; to the north a long gradual sweep upward to the mountain country, which comes down within five or six miles; to the south and west, the open prairies, extending almost level to the coast a hundred and fifty miles away.

There is little wood to be seen in this broad landscape. Along the course of the river a thin edging appears, especially around the head of the stream, a short ride above the city. Elsewhere, there is only limitless grass and thorny bushes.

These last, making *chapparal,* we saw as we went further on for the first time. A few specimens of *mesquit* (*Algarobbia glandulosa*) had been pointed out to us; but here the ground shortly became thickly covered with it. This shrub forms one of the prominent features of Texas west of San Antonio. It is a short thin tree of the locust tribe whose branches are thick set with thorns, and bears, except in this respect, a close resemblance to a straggling, neglected peach-tree. Mixed with other shrubs of a like prickly nature, as an undergrowth it frequently forms, over acres together, an impenetrable mass. When the tree is old, its trunk and roots make an excellent firewood; but for other purposes it is almost useless, owing to its bent and tortuous fibre. A great value is said to lie in its gum, which, if properly secured, has been pronounced equal to gum-arabic in utility.

By a wall of these thorns the road is soon closed in.

Almost all the roads of entrance are thus lined, and so the city bristles like the porcupine, with a natural defense. Reaching the level, we shortly came upon the first house, which had pushed out and conquered a bit of the chapparal. Its neighbor was opposite, and soon the street closed in.

The singular composite character of the town is palpable at the entrance. For five minutes the houses were evidently German, of fresh square-cut blocks of creamy-white limestone, mostly of a single story and humble proportions, but neat, and thoroughly roofed and finished. Some were furnished with the luxuries of little bow-windows, balconies, or galleries.

From these we enter the square of the Alamo. This is all Mexican. Windowless cabins of stakes, plastered with mud and roofed with river-grass, or "tula"; or low, windowless, but better thatched houses of adobes (gray, unburnt bricks), with groups of brown idlers lounging at their doors.

The principal part of the town lies within a sweep of the river upon the other side. We descend to the bridge, which is close down upon the water, as the river, owing to its peculiar source, never varies in height or temperature. We irresistibly stop to examine it, we are so struck with its beauty. It is of a rich blue and pure as crystal, flowing rapidly but noiselessly over pebbles and between reedy banks. One could lean for hours over the bridge-rail.

From the bridge we enter Commerce street, the narrow principal thoroughfare, and here are American houses, and the triple nationalities break out into the most amusing display, till we reach the main plaza. The sauntering Mexicans prevail on the pavements, but the bearded Germans and the sallow Yankees furnish their proportion. The signs are German by all odds, and perhaps the houses, trim-built, with pink window-blinds. The American dwellings stand back, with galleries and jalousies and a garden picket-fence against the walk, or rise, next door, in three-story brick to respectable city fronts. The Mexican buildings are stronger than those we saw before but still of all sorts, and now put to all sorts of new uses. They are all low, of adobe or stone, washed blue and yellow, with flat roofs close down upon their single story. Windows have been knocked in their blank walls, letting the sun into their dismal vaults, and most of them are stored with dry goods and groceries, which overflow around the door. Around the plaza are American hotels, and new glass-fronted stores, alternating with sturdy battlemented Spanish walls, and [these are] confronted by the dirty, grim, old stuccoed stone cathedral, whose cracked bell is now clunking for vespers in a tone that bids us no welcome, as more of the intruding race who have caused all this progress on which its traditions, like its imperturbable dome, frown down.

SAN ANTONIO.

We have no city except perhaps New Orleans that can vie, in point of the picturesque interest that attaches to odd and antiquated foreignness, with San Antonio. Its jumble of races, costumes, languages and buildings; its religious ruins, holding to an antiquity for us indistinct enough to breed an unaccustomed solemnity; its remote, isolated, outposted situation, and the vague conviction that it is the first of a new class of conquered cities into whose decaying streets our rattling life is to be infused, combine with the heroic touches in its history to enliven and satisfy your traveler's curiosity.

Not suspecting the leisure we were to have to examine it at our ease, we set out to receive its impressions while we had the opportunity.

After drawing, at the Post-office window, our personal share of the dear income of happiness divided by that department, we strolled, by moonlight, about the streets. They are laid out with tolerable regularity, parallel with the sides of the main plaza, and are pretty distinctly shared among the nations that use them. On the plaza and the busiest streets, a surprising number of old Mexican buildings are converted, by trowel, paintbrush, and gaudy carpentry, into drinking-places, always labeled "Exchange," and conducted on the New Orleans model. About these loitered a set of customers, sometimes rough, sometimes affecting an "exquisite" dress, by no means attracting to a nearer acquaintance with themselves or their haunts. Here and there was a restaurant of a quieter look, where the traditions of Paris are preserved under difficulties by the exiled Gaul.

The doors of the cabins of the real natives stood open wide, if indeed they exist at all, and many were the family pictures of jollity or sleepy comfort they displayed to us as we sauntered curious about. The favorite dress appeared to be a dishabille, and a free-and-easy, loloppy sort of life generally seemed to have been adopted as possessing, on the whole, the greatest advantages for a reasonable being. The larger part of each family appeared to be made up of black-eyed, olive girls, full of animation of tongue and glance, but sunk in a soft embonpoint, which added a somewhat extreme good-nature to their charms. Their dresses seemed lazily reluctant to cover their plump persons, and their attitudes were always expressive of the influences of a Southern sun upon national manners. The matrons, dark and wrinkled, formed a strong contrast to their daughters, though, here and there, a fine cast of feature and a figure erect with dignity, attracted the eye. The men lounged in roundabouts and cigaritos, as was to be expected, and in fact the whole picture lacked nothing that is Mexican.

Daylight walks about the town yielded little more to curiosity. The contrast of nationalities remained the chief interest. The local business is considerable, but carried on without subdivision of occupation. Each of a dozen stores offers all the articles you may ask for. A druggist or two, a saddler or two, a watchmaker and a gunsmith ply almost the only distinct trades. The country supplied from this centre is extensive but very thinly settled. The capital owned here is quite large. The principal accumulations date from the Mexican war, when no small part of the many millions expended by Government were disbursed here in payment to contractors. Some prime cuts were secured by residents, and no small portion of the lesser pickings remained in their hands. Since then the town has been well-to-do, and consequently accumulates a greater population than its position in other respects would justify.

The traffic, open and illicit, across the frontier with interior Mexico, has some importance and returns some bulky bags of silver. All the principal merchants have their agencies on the Rio Grande, and throw in goods and haul out dollars as opportunity serves. The transportation of their goods forms the principal support of the Mexican population. It is this trade, probably, which accounts for the large stocks which are kept, and the large transactions that result, beyond the strength of most similar towns.

All goods are brought from Matagorda Bay, a distance
of 150 miles, by ox-teams, moving with prodigious slowness and irregularity. In a favorable season, the freight-
price is one-and-a-quarter cents per lb., from Lavacca.
Prices are extremely high, and subject to great variations,
depending upon the actual supply and the state of the
roads.

Cash is sometimes extremely scarce in the town. The
Mexican dollars are sent forward to a good market. Government brings its army-stores direct from the coast. But
some hay, corn, and other supplies are contracted for in
the region, and from this source, and from the leavings of
casual travelers and new emigrants, the hard money for
circulation is derived. Investments at present are mostly
in lands. There are no home-exports of the least account.
Pecan-nuts, and a little coarse wool, are almost the only
items of the catalogue. The wealth and steady growth of
the town depend almost entirely upon the rapid settlement of the adjacent country.

A scanty congregation attends the services of the battered old cathedral. The Protestant church attendance
can almost be counted upon the fingers. Sunday is pretty
rigidly devoted to rest, though most of the stores are open
to all practical purposes, and the exchanges keep up a
brisk distribution of stimulants. The Germans and Mexicans have their dances. The Americans resort to fast horses
for their principal recreation.

We noticed, upon a ruined wall, the remains of a plac-
ard, which illustrates at the same time a Yankee shrewdness in devoting a day to grief, without actual loss of time,
and the social manners of the people:

"RESOLUTIONS *on the death of*
THE HON. DANIEL WEBSTER."

"Be it resolved by the Board of Aldermen of the city
of San Antonio, in Common Council assembled, that, by
the death of the late Daniel Webster, the people are
plunged in mourning, and in testimonial of our grief, we
sincerely join with other cities and towns of our country
in requesting a suspension of labor, and the closing of all
places of business, on Sunday, *the 10th inst.*, from 10
o'clock A.M. to 4 o'clock P.M., and that all the flags in the
city be displayed at half-mast, and minute guns fired
through the day."

The town of San Antonio was founded in 1730 by a colony of twelve families of pure Spanish blood, from the Canary islands. The names of the settlers are perpetuated to this day by existing families which have descended from each, such as Garcia, Flores, Navarro, Garza, Yturri, Rodriquez. The original mission and fort of San Antonio de Valero dates from 1715, when Spain established her occupancy of Texas.

THE MISSIONS.

Not far from the city, along the river, are these celebrated religious establishments. They are of a similar character to the many scattered here and there over the plains of Northern Mexico and California, and bear a solid testimony to the strangely patient courage and zeal of the old Spanish fathers. They pushed off alone into the heart of a savage and unknown country, converted the cruel brutes that occupied it, not only to nominal Christianity but to actual hard labor, and persuaded and compelled them to construct these ponderous but rudely splendid edifices, serving, at the same time, for the glory of the faith, and for the defense of the faithful.*

The Alamo was one of the earliest of these establishments. It is now within the town, and in extent, probably, a mere wreck of its former grandeur. It consists of a few irregular stuccoed buildings huddled against the old church, in a large court surrounded by a rude wall; the whole used as an arsenal by the U. S. quartermaster. The church-door opens on the square and is meagerly decorated by stucco mouldings, all hacked and battered in the battles it has seen. Since the heroic defense of Travis and his handful of men in '36, it has been a monument not so much to faith as to courage.

The Mission of Concepcion is not far from the town, upon the left of the river. Further down are three others, San Juan, San José and La Espada. On one of them is said to have been visible, not long ago, the date, "1725." They are in different stages of decay, but all are real ruins, beyond any connection with the present—weird remains out of the silent past.

---

* Good drawings of two of these missions may be seen in Bartlett's "Personal Narrative."

They are of various magnificence, but all upon a common model, and of the same materials—rough blocks of limestone, cemented with a strong gray stucco. Each has its church, its convent, or celled house for the fathers, and its farm-buildings, arranged around a large court, entered only at a single point. Surrounding each was a large farm, irrigated at a great outlay of labor by aqueducts from the river.

The decorations of the doors and windows may be still examined. They are of stucco, and are rude heads of saints, and mouldings, usually without grace, corresponding to those described as at present occupying similar positions in Mexican churches. One of the missions is a complete ruin, the others afford shelter to Mexican occupants, who ply their trades, and herd their cattle and sheep in the old cells and courts. Many is the picturesque sketch offered to the pencil by such intrusion upon falling dome, tower, and cloister.

THE ENVIRONS.

The system of aqueducts, for artificial irrigation, extends for many miles around San Antonio, and affords some justification for the Mexican tradition that the town not long ago contained a very much larger population. Most of these lived by agriculture, returning at evening to a crowded home in the city. These water-courses still retain their old Spanish name, "acequias." A large part of them are abandoned, but in the immediate neighborhood of the city they are still in use, so that every garden-patch may be flowed at will.

In the outskirts of the town are many good residences recently erected by Americans. They are mostly of the creamy limestone, which is found in abundance near by. It is of a very agreeable shade, readily sawed and cut, sufficiently durable, and can be procured at a moderate cost. When the grounds around them shall have been put in correspondence with the style of these houses, they will make enviable homes.

THE SAN ANTONIO SPRING.

There are, besides the missions, several pleasant points for excursions in the neighborhood, particularly those to the San Antonio and San Pedro Springs. The latter is a wooded spot of great beauty but a mile or two from the town, and boasts a restaurant and beer-garden beyond its natural attractions. The San Antonio Spring may be classed as of the first water among the gems of the natural world. The whole river gushes up in one sparkling burst from the earth. It has all the beautiful accompaniments of a smaller spring, moss, pebbles, seclusion, sparkling sunbeams, and dense overhanging luxuriant foliage. The effect is overpowering. It is beyond your possible conceptions of a spring. You cannot believe your eyes, and almost shrink from sudden metamorphosis by invaded nymphdom.

BATHING.

The temperature of the river is of just that agreeable elevation that makes you loth to leave a bath, and the color is the ideal blue. Few cities have such a luxury. It remains throughout the year without perceptible change of temperature, and never varies in height or volume. The streets are laid out in such a way that a great number of houses have a garden extending to the bank, and so a bathing-house, which is in constant use. The Mexicans seem half the time about the water. Their plump women especially are excellent swimmers, and fond of displaying their luxurious buoyancy. The fall of the river is such as to furnish abundant water-power, which is now used but for a single corn-mill. Several springs add their current to its volume above the town, and that from the San Pedro below. It unites, near the Gulf, with the Guadalupe, and empties into Espiritu Santo Bay, watering a rich, and, as yet, but little-settled country.

The soil in the neighborhood of the city is heavy and sometimes mixed with drifts of limestone pebbles and deposits of shell, but is everywhere black and appears of inexhaustible fertility if well cultivated and supplied with moisture. The market-gardens belonging to Germans, which we saw later in the season, are most luxuriant. The prices of milk, butter and vegetables are very high, and the gains of the small German market-farmers must be rapidly accumulating.

TOWN LIFE.

The street-life of San Antonio is more varied than might be supposed. Hardly a day passes without some noise. If there be no personal affray to arouse talk, there is some Government train to be seen, with its hundred of mules, on its way from the coast to a fort above; or a Mexican ox-train from the coast, with an interesting supply of ice, or flour, or matches, or of whatever the shops find themselves short. A Government express clatters off, or news arrives from some exposed outpost, or from New Mexico. An Indian in his finery appears on a shaggy horse, in search of blankets, powder and ball. Or at the least, a stagecoach with the "States," or the Austin, mail, rolls into the plaza and discharges its load of passengers and newspapers.

The street affrays are numerous and characteristic. I have seen for a year or more a San Antonio weekly, and hardly a number fails to have its fight or its murder. More often than otherwise, the parties meet upon the plaza by chance, and each, on catching sight of his enemy, draws a revolver and fires away. As the actors are under more or less excitement, their aim is not apt to be of the most careful and sure; consequently it is, not seldom, the passers-by who suffer. Sometimes it is a young man at a quiet dinner in a restaurant who receives a ball in the head, sometimes an old negro woman returning from market who gets winged. After disposing of all their lead, the parties close to try their steel, but as this species of metallic amusement is less popular, they generally contrive to be separated ("Hold me! Hold me!") by friends before the wounds are mortal. If neither is seriously injured, they are brought to drink together on the following day, and the town waits for the next excitement.

Where borderers and idle soldiers are hanging about drinking-places, and where different races mingle on unequal terms, assassinations must be expected. Murders, from avarice or revenge, are common here. Most are charged upon the Mexicans, whose passionate motives are not rare, and to whom escape over the border is easiest and most natural.

The town amusements of a less exciting character are not many. There is a permanent company of Mexican

mountebanks, who give performances of agility and buf-
foonery two or three times a week, parading before night
in their spangled tights with drum and trombone through
the principal streets. They draw a crowd of whatever little
Mexicans can get adrift, and this attracts a few sellers of
whisky, *tortillas* and *tamaules* (corn, slap-jacks and hashed
meat in corn-shucks), all by the light of torches making a
ruddily picturesque evening group.

The more grave Americans are served with tragedy by
a thin local company, who are death on horrors and de-
spair, long rapiers and well oiled hair, and for lack of a
better place to flirt with passing officers, the city belles
may sometimes be seen looking on. The national background of peanuts and yells is not, of course, wanting.

A day or two after our arrival, there was the hanging of
a Mexican. The whole population left the town to see.
Family parties, including the grandmother and the little
negroes, came from all the plantations and farms within
reach, and little ones were held up high to get their share
of warning. The Mexicans looked on imperturbable.

San Antonio, excluding Galveston,* is much the largest
city of Texas. After the Revolution, it was half deserted
by its Mexican population, who did not care to come
under Anglo-Saxon rule. Since then its growth has been
rapid and steady. At the census of 1850, it numbered
3,500; in 1853, its population was 6,000; and in 1856, it
is estimated at 10,500. Of these, about 4,000 are Mexicans,
3,000 Germans, and 3,500 Americans. The money-capital
is in the hands of the Americans, as well as the officers and
the Government. Most of the mechanics and the smaller
shopkeepers are German. The Mexicans appear to have
almost no other business than that of carting goods. Almost the entire transportation of the country is carried on
by them, with oxen and two-wheeled carts. Some of them
have small shops for the supply of their own countrymen,
and some live upon the produce of farms and cattle-
ranches owned in the neighborhood. Their livelihood is,
for the most part, exceedingly meagre, made up chiefly of
corn and beans.

---

* The two towns have nearly kept pace in growth. The yellow fever,
it is said, has now given San Antonio the advantage.

THE MEXICANS IN TEXAS.

We had before we left opportunities of visiting familiarly many of the Mexican dwellings. I have described their externals. Within, we found usually a single room, open to the roof and invariably having a floor of beaten clay a few inches below the level of the street. There was little furniture—huge beds being the universal pièce de résistance. These were used by day as sofa and table. Sometimes there were chairs and a table besides; but frequently only a bench, with a few earthen utensils for cooking, which is carried on outside. A dog or a cat appears on or under the bed or on the clothes-chest, a saint on the wall, and frequently a game-cock fastened in a corner, supplied with dishes of corn and water.

We were invariably received with the most gracious and beaming politeness and dignity. Their manner towards one another is engaging and that of children and parents most affectionate. This we always noticed in evening walks and in the groups about the doors, which were often singing in chorus—the attitudes expressive of confident affection. In one house, we were introduced to an old lady who was supposed by her grandchildren to be over one hundred years old. She had come from Mexico, in a rough cart, to make them a visit. Her face was strikingly Indian in feature, her hair, snow white, flowing thick over the shoulders, contrasting strongly with the olive skin. The complexion of the girls is clear and sometimes fair, usually a blushing olive. The variety of feature and color is very striking, and is naturally referred to three sources— the old Spanish, the Creole Mexican and the Indian, with sometimes a suspicion of Anglo-Saxon or Teuton. The hair is coarse but glossy, and very luxuriant; the eye, deep, dark, liquid and well set. Their modesty, though real, we heard, was not proof against a long courtship of flattering attentions and rich presents. The constancy of the married women was made very light of, not that their favors were purchasable, but that they are sometimes seized by a strong penchant for some other than their lord. There was testimony of this in the various shades and features of their children; in fact we thought the number of babies of European hair and feature exceeded the native olive in number. We noticed, in a group of Mexican and negro women, when an indelicate occurrence took place, that the former turned away in annoyed modesty, while the latter laughed broadly. Their constitutions, in general, are feeble, and very many of both sexes, we were informed, suffered from scrofulous disease. Nevertheless, with good stimulus, the men make admirable laborers.

The common dress was loose and slight, not to say slatternly. It was frequently but a chemise, as low as possible in the neck, sometimes even lower, with a calico petticoat. On holidays they dress in expensive finery, paying special attention to the shoes, of white satin, made by a native artist.

The houses of the rich differ little from those of the poor, and the difference in their style of living must be small, owing to the want of education and of all ambition. The majority are classed as laborers. Their wages are small, usually, upon farms near San Antonio, $6 or $8 a month, with corn and beans. That of the teamsters is in proportion to their energy. On being paid off, they hurry to their family and all come out in their best to spend the earnings, frequently quite at a loss for what to exchange them. They make excellent drovers and shepherds, and in work like this, with which they are acquainted, are reliable and adroit. A horse-drover just from the Rio Grande with whom we conversed called them untiring and faithful at their work, but untrustworthy in character. To his guide he paid $24 a month, to his "right bower" $15, and to his "left bower" $12 a month.

Their tools are of the rudest sort. The old Mexican wheel of hewn blocks of wood is still constantly in use, though supplanted to some extent by Yankee wheels sent in pairs from New York. The carts are always hewn of heavy wood, and are covered with white cotton stretched over hoops. In these they live on the road as independently as in their own house. The cattle are yoked by the horns with raw-hide thongs, of which they make a great use.

They consort freely with the negroes, making no distinction from pride of race. A few, of old Spanish blood, have purchased negro servants, but most of them regard slavery with abhorrence.

The Mexicans were treated for a while after annexation like a conquered people. Ignorant of their rights, and of the new language, they allowed themselves to be imposed upon by the new comers, who seized their lands and property without shadow of claim, and drove hundreds of them homeless across the Rio Grande. They now, as they get gradually better informed, come straggling back, and often their claims give rise to litigation, usually settled by a compromise.

A friend told us that, wishing when he built to square a corner of his lot, after making diligent inquiry he was unable to hear of any owner for the adjoining piece. He took the responsibility, and moved his fence over it. Not long after, he was waited upon by a Mexican woman, in a towering passion. He carried her to a Spanish acquaintance, and explained the transaction. She was immediately appeased, told him he was welcome to the land, and has since been on the most neighborly terms, calling him always her "amigo."

Most adult Mexicans are voters by the organic law; but few take measures to make use of the right. Should they do so, they might probably, in San Antonio, have elected a government of their own. Such a step would be followed, however, by a summary revolution. They are regarded by slaveholders with great contempt and suspicion for their intimacy with slaves and their competition with plantation labor.

Americans, in speaking of them, constantly distinguish themselves as "white folks." I once heard a new comer informing another American that he had seen a Mexican with a revolver. "I shouldn't think they ought to be allowed to carry fire-arms. It might be dangerous." "It would be difficult to prevent it," the other replied; "Oh, they think themselves just as good as white men."

From several counties they have been driven out altogether. At Austin, in the spring of 1853, a meeting was held, at which the citizens resolved, on the plea that Mexicans were *horse-thieves* that they must quit the county. About twenty families were thus driven from their homes, and dispersed over the western counties. Deprived of their means of livelihood, and rendered furious by such wholesale injustice, it is no wonder if they should take to the very crimes with which they are charged.

A similar occurrence took place at Seguin, in 1854; and in 1855, a few families, who had returned to Austin, were again driven out.

Even at San Antonio, there had been talk of such a razzia. A Mexican, caught in an attempt to steal a horse, had been hung by a Lynching party, on the spot, for an example. His friends happened to be numerous and were much excited, threatening violence in return. Under pretext of subduing an intended riot the sheriff issued a call for an armed posse of 500 men, with the idea of dispersing and driving from the neighborhood a large part of the Mexican population. But the Germans, who include among them the great majority of young men suitable for such duty, did not volunteer as had been expected, and the scheme was abandoned. They were of the opinion, one of them said to me, that this was not the right and republican way. If the laws were justly and energetically administered, no other remedy would be needed. One of them, who lived on the Medina in the vicinity of the place of the occurrence, told us he had no complaint to make of the Mexicans; they never stole his property or troubled him in any way.

The following is the most reliable estimate I can obtain of the actual Mexican population in Texas, (1856):—

San Antonio	4,000
Bexar Co.	2,000
Uvalde Co.	1,000
Laredo	1,500
El Paso, with Presidio	8,500
Lower Rio Grande Counties	3,000
Goliad and Nueces Counties	1,000
Other parts of State	1,000
Floating, say	3,000
	25,000

A PAUSE.

We had made it our first business, on arriving at San Antonio, to find what company was to be had for our Mexican trip, and we were somewhat dismayed, on delivering our letters, to find that communication with Mexico was thought to be infrequent and precarious. Merchants dispatched goods occasionally to different points on the Rio Grande; now and then a Government express, or an officer with escort, left for our military stations there; a post-rider, once a week, crossed the desert beyond the Nueces, riding rapidly and sleeping on the ground. But traveling parties such as we had thought to join, for the

interior cities of Mexico, were almost unheard of: in fact,
in the unsettled state of political affairs in that crazy Republic, it was considered highly dangerous for a party to
travel there whose numbers did not enable them, not only
to stand nightly guard, but to resist, if necessary, organized attacks upon the road.

A train for Chihuahua, via El Paso, was just about leaving, which, if we wished to go in that direction, would
afford us ample protection. We rode a mile or two out of
town to the spot where it was encamped. It was commanded, we found, by Julius Froebel, who escaped by so
slender a thread the republican martyrdom which his companion, Robert Blum actually suffered in Vienna, and
whose scientific contributions to the natural and human
history of the central parts of the continent have now and
then appeared in the *New York Tribune*. The train was a
very large one and equipped in the best style. There were
twenty-six wagons, drawn by 260 mules, with experienced
drivers, forage and provisions, besides professional hunt-
ers, to obtain fresh meat where possible. Mr. Froebel,
however, gave such an account of the slowness and
tedium of the travel-life of such a trip as quite discouraged us, especially as the train was to leave within twelve
hours. We were fortunate, the event proved, in not having joined it, as, though it reached its destination quite
safely it was detained for *some months,* in camp at the
frontier, near El Paso, while custom-house difficulties were
being arranged.

After a day or two, our friend B. announced that a
change in his business affairs at the north would compel
him to ask a discharge from his enlistment, which we un-
willingly granted. This more completely blocked our
wheels, and threw us quite upon chance for our route and
our company. We made inquiries on all sides without success. The officer in command of the station here could
give us no promise of company, within a short time, even
to the Rio Grande. We consulted many old border travelers, who strongly dissuaded us from attempting the trip by
ourselves. Finally, among the boarders at a German inn,
we heard of a scientific gentleman living at Braunfels who
was about to make the trip to the city of Mexico, and resolved on returning there to offer ourselves as companions.

On entering San Antonio, our fellow-traveler had taken

us with him to this German inn, the more willingly on our part, as we retained a vivid impression of the contrast between the hotel at Neu-Braunfels and every other hotel we had seen in Texas. We had been extremely interested in what we had seen of the Germans, too, and were glad of an excuse to see more of them. We found a miserable old Mexican house, and close quarters enough for sleeping, but most pleasant company, a hearty, hospitable, unremitting kindness, and a table which, with its refreshing salads and variety of vegetables, was like returning spring to our salt and husky palates. At each meal we met some twenty boarders, mostly clerks or men in business, but with a sprinkling of professional men, and, from first to last, gentlemen in manner, and full of such information as we wanted. We cannot too strongly recommend a quiet traveler to follow our example.

By their advice we called upon the editor of their German newspaper, who received us most politely, and was able, not only to give us the name of the gentleman who was intending to go to Mexico, but to give us a more accurate idea of the numbers and position of the Germans in Texas than we had before obtained.

A NORTHER.

The day before we left San Antonio was cold and foggy. The following morning was warm but still foggy, making our ride, with a light wind behind us, exceedingly oppressive. We threw off our coats, and soon stripped off vest and cravat; but this we found was not enough, and we were obliged to stop to take off our flannel. Our horses were reeking with sweat. At two o'clock the thermometer, in a cool, shady spot, stood at 79° [centigrade], and the sky was nearly clear. We were very tired and thirsty, and one of us suggested that this was the very country and the very weather for mirage. It was not long after we saw the edge of the horizon rising in the flickering heat and groups of trees standing free in the air, as an island or a point stretches off into the sky of a hot day on the sea-coast. Then the trees connected themselves with the land below upon each side and we saw a beautiful lake, the water rippling in the sunlight. It grew wider and longer and shortly was like the open sea, with a rich and shady shore, extending up at intervals like bays and rivers into the land. Soon the lakes were common here and there about us, calm of surface, trees with heavy foliage bending over their banks to rest in the water. Had we not been prepared by a knowledge of the country, we should have been strongly tempted to ride towards some of them for a drink of cool water.

Later in the day, the air became clearer, and a pleasant breeze played upon our backs. The mirage gradually disappeared, and we lost it in descending a swell of the prairie. It was near sunset, with a dull cloud bank in the north. We were still suffering with the heat, when one of us said—

"See this before us, what is it, fog again or smoke?"

"A prairie fire, I think," said the other.

"Probably it is; but what is this on the hill close by, this is fog, surely? It must be a norther coming. Yes, it is a norther; listen to that roar! We must get our clothing on or we shall be chilled through."

First, a chilly whiff, then a puff, the grass bends flat, and, bang, it is upon us—a blast that would have taken a top-gallant sail smack out of the bolt-ropes, and cold as if blowing across a sea of ice. We galloped to the nearest ravine and hurried on all the clothing we could muster. Fortunately, though our baggage was left behind, we had taken a supply, having strapped blankets, Guernsey shirts, and Canada leggins, behind our saddles.

At nine o'clock, the thermometer stood at thirty-three degrees, and, at seven next morning, at twenty-one degrees. A thermometer hanging in Neu-Braunfels showed a fall of sixty degrees in seven hours.

These northers upon the open prairies are exceedingly trying. The fierce wind that accompanies such a sudden change gives them triple effect, especially as they often interrupt warm, relaxing weather. Teamsters, herdsmen, and travelers, caught out far from habitations, not unfrequently perish, and very great suffering is caused to animals. Cattle instinctively make for the nearest shelter of trees; but, on the open prairies of the coast, they fall by thousands before a freezing rain, which is sometimes added.

The northers continue from one to three days, growing milder at the close, and occur once or twice a week during the winter months. But a tight house and a blazing fire make one quite independent of them, and such we found in the German inn.

NEU-BRAUNFELS—THE ORPHANS.

Our naturalist, we were told, lived adjacent to the Orphan Asylum at Neu-Wied, a hamlet some three miles from the town.

Thither, after breakfast next day, we went, with a note of introduction, on foot, and briskly, for it was too cold to ride.

The Orphan Asylum, as we approached it, had the appearance of being a small American farm-house, with a German rear erection of brick laid up in a timber framework. A large live-oak sheltered the stoop, but the whole establishment was very rough with a common rail-fence about it, and not the least indication of fashionable philanthropy. As we entered a large, dark, unpainted hall, a man came forward from an inner room, who, from his dress, might have been taken for a day-laborer. It was the gentleman, however, whom we wished to see—a courteous and cultivated professor.

It was a holiday and he had been engaged in preparing some botanical specimens, but immediately left them to ferry us over the Guadalupe which ran through his grounds, the probable traveler residing beyond.

Leaving the house, we passed through a garden in the rear where he showed us little plots of wheat from Egypt, Algiers, Arabia, and St. Helena, which he was growing to ascertain which was best adapted to the climate. Wheat-growing, of any sort, is a novelty here, but the Germans are not satisfied with corn, nor are they willing to pay for the transportation of flour from Ohio, like the Anglo-Americans. There has been, therefore, considerable wheat grown among them and that with satisfactory success.

From the garden we passed into a grove, where, in a circular opening of the trees, a rude theatre had been formed, which was used by musical parties from Neu-Braunfels and as a school or lecture-room in summer.

Not finding the gentleman of whom we were in search, we returned to the professor's house, and spent there, at his invitation, a delightful day.

He had come to this country in 1839. In the steerage of his ship there were about forty Norwegians with their families. They suffered much hardship, and he assisted and comforted them as much as was in his power. They were very grateful, and before reaching New York they unanimously requested him to continue with them as their pastor, and assist them in forming their settlement at the West. While the ship was detained at Quarantine, he went to the city with the captain to make arrangements for necessary stay in the city. Returning to Staten Island, he found the ship had gone up, and the ferry-boat had discontinued running for the night. It was not till late the next day that he succeeded in finding the ship at her wharf in New York, and then all the Norwegians had departed. He spent several days searching for them, but saw none of them until nearly two years afterwards. He was then in a crowd at Milwaukie, when his arm was suddenly seized with both hands by a little boy, who sprung up to kiss him, crying, "Oh! papa E.! oh, papa E.!" It was one of the children of the steerage.

He went with the boy to his father's house, who told him that some persons came on board the ship, while they were still at Quarantine, and represented that they had been engaged by some of their countrymen to advise and assist the emigrants. They were accordingly taken to a boarding-house as soon as the ship reached New York, and during the evening they were induced to purchase a considerable tract of land by the counsel of their disinterested friends, who also furnished them with cheap tickets to carry them through to Milwaukie by a steamboat that was to start the next morning. They had thus been led to leave the city almost immediately; but the lands they had purchased, and, in part, paid for, they never found. The deeds they had received were forgeries.

From Wisconsin he had come to Texas, and joining the first company of the settlers who established Neu-Braunfels, became their pastor. The following year several thousand were landed upon the coast, and, unprovided with food or shelter, perished like sheep. Slowly, droves of them found their way into Neu-Braunfels, haggard and almost dying, having lost all family affection or fellow-feeling in intense despairing personal suffering. Many children came whose parents had died, and he found them starving upon the river bank. He could not bear the sight, but collected sixty of them, and went to work upon this farm with them. He had no means of his own, but took what he could find belonging to the children, and has since sustained them. Working with his wife and the children in the field he has managed to raise corn and keep them alive, until now, in better times, they are mostly distributed as helps in various homes. Eighteen are with him still, all calling him papa. He had obtained from the Legislature an incorporation for a University at Braunfels, and himself, as yet, sole Professor, had given a classical education to a few pay scholars.

The whole narrative was exceedingly interesting, as we heard it at our simple farm-house dinner—the Professor, with his horny hands, and with his much-patched coat, telling us of his own noble conduct in the simplest manner, but sometimes glowing and flushing with a superb home eloquence.

HISTORY OF THE GERMAN SETTLEMENTS.

The most accurate and full published account of these German settlements is the report of a lecture, by FREDERICK KAPP, upon the Germans in Texas in the *New York Tribune* of January 20, 1855. From this, and from our notes of oral statements on the spot, I will concisely give the story. The experiment was a most interesting one: that of using associated capital for the transportation and settlement of emigrants on a large scale; in fact, the removal, in organized bodies, of the poor of an old country to the virgin soil of a new.

In the year 1842, among many schemes evolved in Germany by the social stir of the time, and patronized by certain princes from motives of policy, was one of real promise. It was an association of which Count Castel was the head, for the diminution of pauperism by the organized assistance and protection of emigrants. At this time, annexation being already almost a certainty, speculators who represented the owners of large tracts of Texas land appeared in Germany with glowing accounts of their cheapness and richness. They succeeded in gaining the attention of this association, whose leaders were pleased with the isolated situation, as offering a more tangible and durable connection with their emigrants, and opening a new source of wealth and possible power. A German dependency or new Teutonic nation might result. Palmerston, it is said, encouraged the idea,* the Texan political leaders then coquetting with an English Protectorate, to induce more rapid advances on the part of the United States.

In 1843, an agent of the association, Count Waldeck, visited Texas, but effected nothing else than to secure himself a slave plantation not far from the coast. He was dismissed. The following year the association commenced active operations. It obtained, under the title of the MAINZER ADELS VEREIN, a charter from the Duke of Nassau, who assumed the protectorate. It had the Prince of Leiningen as president; Count Castel as director; Prince Frederick of Prussia, the Duke of Coburg-Gotha, and some thirty other princes and nobles as associated members. A plan inviting emigrants was published, offering each adult subscribing $120 a free passage and forty acres of land, a family subscribing $240 a free passage and eighty acres. The association undertook to provide log-houses, stock and tools at fair prices and to construct public buildings and roads for the settlements.

Prince Solms of Braunfels was appointed General commissioner and proceeded to Texas. Had he procured from the State Legislature a direct grant of land for the colony, as he might have done, all would have been well. But, most unfortunately, the association were induced, without sufficient examination, to buy a grant of the previous year. It was held by Fisher and Miller, and the tract was described by them as a second paradise. In reality, it lay in the heart of a savage country, hundreds of miles beyond the remotest settlement, between the Upper Colorado and the great desert plains, a region, to this day, almost uninhabited. This wretched mistake was the ruin of the whole enterprise. The association lost its money and its character, and carried many emigrants only to beggary and a miserable death.

* According to the work of Mr. SIEMERING upon the Germans in Texas, now in the hands of the publisher, this encouragement went so far as to take the form of a contract between the Verein and the British Government. By it the former agreed to place 10,000 families in Texas, the latter to furnish armed protection to the colony. A new market with indefinite capacities; a new source of cotton; opposition to slavery and to the extension of the area of the United States; such were the sufficient motives for England. Prince Leiningen was the half-brother of the Queen of England. Prince Solms was an intimate friend of Prince Albert, with whom he was educated at Bonn. Copies of the correspondence still exist.

In the course of the year 180 subscribers were obtained, who landed with their families in the autumn upon the coast of Texas and marched towards their promised lands, with Prince Solms at their head. Finding the whole country a wilderness, and being harassed by the attacks of Indians on reaching the union of the Comal with the Guadalupe, they became disheartened, and there Prince Solms, following the good advice of a naturalist of the company, Mr. Lindheimer, encamped, and laid out the present town of Neu-Braunfels.

This settlement, receiving aid from home while it was needed, was a success, in spite of the Prince who appears to have been an amiable fool, aping among the log-cabins the nonsense of mediæval courts. In the course of a year he was laughed out of the country.

He was succeeded by C. Von Meusebach, who proved at least much better adapted to the work.

Had he not been reduced to inaction by home routine, and a want of funds, the misery that followed might, perhaps, have been prevented.*

In course of the next year, 1845, more than 2,000 families joined the association. The capital which had been sufficient for its first effort was totally inadequate to an undertaking of this magnitude. These poor people sailed from Germany in the fall of this year, and were landed in the winter and early spring on the flat coast of the Gulf, to the number of 5,200. Annexation had now taken place, and the war with Mexico was beginning. The country had been stripped of provisions and of the means of transportation by the army. Neither food nor shelter had been provided by the association. The consequences may be imagined. The detail is too horrible. The mass remained for months encamped in sand-holes, huts, or tents; the only food procurable was beef. The summer heats bred pestilence.

The world has hardly record of such suffering. Human nature could not endure it. Human beings became brutes. "Your child is dying." "What do I care?" Old parents were hurried into the ground before the breath of life had left

---

* It is here difficult to sift various statements to an exact appreciation. —A new company (at Bieberich) subsequently bought out the Verein, but Mr. Martin, their agent in Texas, has never entered possession, having been forced into the law by Spies, the successor of Meusebach. In 1855, the original Fisher make his re-appearance, with a scheme for "scaling" both claims, and securing what remains. This speculation nowise affects the actual colonists.

them. The Americans who saw the stragglers thought a
new race of savages was come. Haggard and desperate,
they roved inland by twos and threes, beyond all law or
religion. Many of the survivors reached the German settlements; many settled as laborers in American towns. With
some of them, Meusebach founded another town—Fred-
ericksburg—higher up than Braunfels. He also explored
the Fisher grant, and converted the surrounding Indians
from enemies into good-natured associates.

"It is but justice," says Mr. Kapp, "to throw the light of
truth upon all this misery. The members of the association,
although well-meaning, did not understand what they
were about to do. They fancied that their *high protection*,
alone, was sufficient to make all right. They had not the
remotest idea of the toil and hardship of settling a new
country. They permitted themselves to be humbugged by
speculators and adventurers; they entered into ruinous
bargains, and had not even funds enough to take the smallest number of those whom they had induced to join them
to the place of settlement. When money was most wanted,
they failed to send it, either from mistrust or neglect. To
perform the obligation imposed by the agreement with
Fisher, they induced the emigration to Texas by the most
enchanting and exaggerated statements. The least that
even the less sanguine ones expected was to find parrots
rocking on the boughs and monkeys playing on the palm-
trees."

This condemnation seems to fall justly.

Such was the unhappy beginning. But the wretched-
ness is already forgotten. Things soon mended. The soil,
climate, and the other realities found were genial and
good, if not Elysian. Now, after seven years, I do not know
a prettier picture of contented prosperity than we witnessed at Neu-Braunfels. A satisfied smile, in fact, beamed
on almost every German face we saw in Texas.

PRESENT APPEARANCES.

Of the general appearance of Neu-Braunfels I gave
some notion in describing the route to San Antonio. We
now took pains to obtain some definite facts with regard
to its condition. The dwellings in general are small and
humble in appearance but weather-tight, and generally
provided with galleries or verandahs and with glazed

casement windows. In the latter respect, they have the advantage over most houses we have seen in Texas, and, I have no doubt, the average comforts of life within are much greater than among the Anglo-Americans, generally, in the state.

The citizens are, however, nearly all men of very small capital. Of the original settlers scarcely any now remain, and their houses and lands are occupied by more recent emigrants. Those who have left have made enough money during their residence to enable them to buy farms or cattle-ranches in the mountains, to which they have removed.

Half the men now residing in Neu-Braunfels and its vicinity are probably agricultural laborers or farmers who themselves follow the plough. The majority of the latter do not, I think, own more than ten acres of land each. Within the town itself, there are of master-mechanics, at least, the following numbers, nearly all of whom employ several workmen:

Carpenters and Builders	20
Wagon-makers	7
Blacksmiths	8
Gun and Locksmiths	2
Coppersmiths	1
Tinsmiths	2
Machinists	1
Saddlers	3
Shoemakers	6
Turners	2
Tailors	5
Button and Fringe-makers	1
Tanners	3
Butchers	3
Bakers	4

There are four grist-mills, and a couple of New-England men are building a sash and blind factory and propose erecting a cotton factory.

A weekly newspaper is published—the *Neu-Braunfels Zeitung*. It is a paper of much higher character than most of the German-American papers, [and is] edited by the naturalist, Lindheimer.

There are ten or twelve stores and a small tradesmen's shops, two or three apothecaries, and as many physicians, lawyers, and clergymen. I do not think there is another town in the slave states in which the proportion to the whole population of mechanics, or of persons employed in the exercise of their own discretion in productive occupations, is one-quarter as large as in Neu-Braunfels, unless it be some other in which the Germans are the predominating race.

There are several organizations among the people which indicate an excellent spirit of social improvement: an Agricultural Society, a Mechanics' Institute, a Harmonic Society, a Society for Political Debates and a "Turners'" Society. A horticultural club has expended $1,200 in one year in introducing trees and plants.

These associations are the evidence of an active intellectual life and desire for knowledge and improvement among the masses of the people like that which distinguishes the New-Englanders and which is unknown wherever slavery degrades labor. Will this spirit resist the progress of slavery westward, or must it be gradually lost as the community in which it now exists becomes familiar with slavery?

In Neu-Braunfels and the surrounding German hamlets, there are five free schools for elementary education, one exclusive Roman Catholic school, a town free school of higher grade, and a private classical school. In *all* of these schools English is taught with German. The teacher of the higher department of the central town school is paid four hundred dollars a year; that of the primary department (a female), two hundred dollars.

The following were the prices current at the time of my visit: Maize, 35 cents a bushel; meal, 45 cents; wheat, none in market; flour, extra St. Louis, $12; soda crackers, 20 cents; beef, fresh, retail for households, 3 cents per pound; pork, 7 cents; bacon, sides, 15 cents; hams, sugar-cured, 20 cents; fowls, 25 cents each; turkeys, 50 cents; ditto, wild, 25 cents; ducks, 20 cents; venison, a whole deer, $1, a quarter, 20 cents, or about 1 cent a pound; mutton, 7 cents; sweet potatoes, 50 cents per bushel.

There are here two items which New York farmers will hardly credit when placed in connection. Maize, 35 cents a bushel; pork, 7 cents a pound; and, still more remarkable, hams, 20 cents! In New York, I suppose, corn was fully double that price, and pork no higher.

Pine boards, 50 cents a foot; cedar, 40 cents; bar iron, 8 to 9 cents per pound; nails, $8 per keg. These articles are brought in wagons from the coast, about one hundred and fifty miles. Transportation by teams (owned and driven altogether by Germans), usually one cent a pound from the coast. Stone and brick clay, lime, sand and water-power can be conveniently and cheaply obtained.

Money here, as everywhere else in Western Texas, is very scarce, and may be always loaned on perfectly trust-worthy securities, at fifteen per cent. and upwards. The law of Texas makes all above eight per cent. usurious. Master-mechanics with whom I conversed informed me that they had no lack of work, but that it was difficult to get payment in money.

Journeymen (late emigrants and rough hands) in-formed me that they were paid wages, $15 a month and upward, and found. Farm-laborers, $8 to $15, and found. Domestics (females), $5 to $8. It is very difficult to ob-tain the latter and still more difficult to keep them as but few girls emigrate in proportion to the men, and they gen-erally obtain situations for life within a few weeks after their arrival. This state of things is likely to continue for a long time, and, as the Germans grow wealthy and luxuri-ous, will, undoubtedly, lead to their occasionally purchas-ing slaves to relieve themselves from the annoyance of constant changes in their household.

In Neu-Braunfels and the immediate vicinity are living about three thousand Germans.* The Anglo-American population of the place does not exceed twenty. Just out of the town a wealthy planter has settled who holds one hundred negroes. He also owns a mill and water-power and a good deal of real estate. Another American living in the town owns a negro girl, and one negro girl is hired by one of the Germans as a domestic. There are no other negroes in town. The blacks of the plantation, we were told, had acquired the power of speaking German in an extremely short time after their arrival.

Sunday was observed more thoroughly as a day of rest from labor than we had seen in any town of Texas. The stores, except one kept by a New Englander, were closed during the day. The people who appeared in the streets were well dressed, quiet and orderly. We saw no drunk-enness. In the evening there were amusements, among

---

* Since our notes, the adjacent farming county has increased its population at the expense of the town. The county population is now estimated at 5,000, the town, 2,000.

them a ball, which the Lutheran pastor was expected to attend.

The health of the town is good. For several years there has been no epidemic illness. The greater part of those of whom I made inquiry assured me their health had been better here than in Germany.

The Lutheran clergyman informed us that he had registered but seven deaths, during the year, among his congregation. The pastoral record during the early years of the settlement tells a pathetic story. It is as follows:

	Deaths.	Births.		Deaths.	Births.
1845	27	9	1847	71	35
1846	304	34	1848	19	75

About one-half the people, if I am not mistaken, are nominal Catholics.

CHAPTER II

———◆———

ALONG THE EASTERN COAST

OUR road, as far as the Sabine, lay through a district of poorer and more sandy soil thickly wooded with pine, having small and unfrequent wet prairies. Although rain was much needed for crops, we estimated that one-eighth of the surface was covered by water in stagnant pools. We passed on both sides the Sabine many abandoned farms, and the country is but thinly settled. We found it impossible to obtain information about roads, and frequently went astray upon cattle-paths, once losing twenty miles in a day's journey. The people were still herdsmen, cultivating a little cotton upon river-banks, but ordinarily only corn, with a patch of cane to furnish household sugar. We tried in vain to purchase corn for our horses, and were told that "folks didn't make corn enough to bread them, and if anybody had corn to give his horse, he carried it in his hat and went out behind somewhere." The herds were in poor condition, and must in winter be reduced to the verge of starvation. We saw a few hogs converted by hardship to figures so unnatural that we at first took them for goats. Most of the people we met were old emigrants from Southern Louisiana and Mississippi and more disposed to gayety and cheer than the Texan planters. The houses showed a tendency to Louisiana forms and the table to a French style of serving the jerked beef which is the general dish of the country. The meat is dried in strips over smoky fires and, if untainted and well prepared, is a tolerably savory food. I hardly know whether to chronicle it as a border barbarism or a Creolism that we were several times, in this neighborhood, shown to a bed standing next to that occupied by the host and his wife, sometimes with the screen of a shawl, sometimes without.

We met with one specimen of the Virginia habit of "dipping," or snuff-chewing, in the person of a woman who was otherwise neat and agreeable, and observed that a young lady, well-dressed, and apparently engaged, while we were present, in reading, went afterward to light her pipe at the kitchen fire, and had a smoke behind the house.

The condition of the young men appeared to incline decidedly to barbarism. We stopped a night at a house in which a drover bringing mules from Mexico was staying; and, with the neighbors who had come to look at the drove, we were thirteen men at table. When speaking with us, all were polite and respectful, the women especially so; but among one another, their coarseness was incredible. The master of the house, a well-known gentleman of the county, came after supper upon the gallery and commenced cursing furiously because some one had taken his pipe. Seeing us, he stopped, and after lighting the pipe said, "Where are you from, gentlemen?"

"From Beaumont, sir, last."

"Been out West?"

"Yes, sir."

"Traveling?"

"Yes, sir."

After pausing a moment to make up his mind—

"Where do you live when you are at home, gentlemen, and what's your business in this country?"

"We live in New York, and are traveling to see the country."

"How do you like it?"

"Just here we find it flat and wet."

"What's your name?"

"Olmsted."

"And what's this gentleman's name?"

"Olmsted."

"Is it a Spanish name?"

"No, sir."

He then abruptly left us, and the young men entertained one another with stories of fights and horse-trades, and with vulgar obscenities.

Shortly he returned, saying—

"Show you to bed now, gentlemen, if you wish?"

"We are ready, sir, if you will be good enough to get a light."

"A light?"

"Yes, sir."

"*A light?*"

"Yes, sir."

"Get a light?"

"Yes, sir."

"Well, I'll get one."

On reaching the bed-room, which was in a building adjoining, he stood awaiting our pleasure. Thanking him, I turned to take the light, but found his fingers were the candlestick. He continued to hold it, and six young men, who had followed us, stood grouped around while we undressed, placing our clothes upon the floor. Judy advanced to lie down by them. One of the young men started forward, and said—

"I've got a right good knife."

"What?"

"I've got a right good knife, if you want it."

"What do you mean?"

"Nothing, only I've got a right good knife, and if you'd like to kill that dog, I'll lend it to you."

"Please to tell me what you mean?"

"Oh, nothing."

"Keep your dog quiet, or I'll kill her," I suppose was the interpretation. When we had covered ourselves in bed, the host said—

"I suppose you don't want the light no more?"

"No, sir"; and all bade us good-night, but, leaving the door open, commenced feats of prolonged dancing, or stamping upon the gallery, which were uproariously applauded. Then came more obscenities and profanities, apropos to fandango frolics described by the drovers. As we had barely got to sleep, several came to occupy other beds in our room. They had been drinking freely, and continued smoking in bed.

Upon the floor lay two boys of fourteen, who continued shouting and laughing after the others had at length become quiet. Some one soon said to one of them—

"You had better stop your noise; Frank says he'll be damn'd if he don't come in and give you a hiding."

Frank was trying to sleep upon the gallery.

"By God," the boy cried, raising himself, and drawing a coat from under the pillow, "if he comes in here, I'll be damn'd if I don't kill him. He dare not come in here. I would like to see him come in here," drawing from his coat pocket a revolver, and cocking it. "By God, you may come in here now. Come in here, come in here! Do you hear that?" revolving the pistol rapidly. "God damn me, if I don't kill you, if you come near the door."

This continued without remonstrance for some time, when he lay down, asking his companion for a light for his pipe, and continuing the noisy conversation until we fell asleep. The previous talk had been much of knife and pistol fights which had taken place in the county. The same boy was obliging and amiable next morning, assisting us to bring in and saddle the horses at our departure.

One of the men here was a Yankee, who had lived so long in the Slave States that he had added to his original ruralisms a very complete collection of Southernisms, some of which were of the richest we met with. He had been in the Texas Rangers, and, speaking of the West, said he had been round the head of the Guadalupe "heaps and cords of times," at the same time giving us a very picturesque account of the county. Speaking of wolves, he informed us that on the San Jacinto shore were "*any dimensions* of them." Obstinacy, in his vocabulary, was represented by "damnation cussedness." He was unable to conceive of us in any other light than as two peddlers who had mistaken their ground in coming here.

At another house where we stopped (in which, by the way, we ate our supper by the light of pine knots blazing in the chimney, with an apology for the absence of candles), we heard some conversation upon a negro of the neighborhood who had been sold to a free negro and who refused to live with him, saying he wouldn't be a servant to a nigger. All agreed that he was right, although the man was well known to be kind to his negroes and would always sell any of them who wished it. The slave had been sold because he wouldn't mind. "If I had a negro that wouldn't mind," said the woman of the house, "I'd break his head, or I'd sell him. I wouldn't have one about me." Her own servant was standing behind her. "I do think it would be better if there wasn't any niggers in the world, they do behave so bad, some of 'em. They steal just like hogs."

We inquired about the free negroes of whom they were speaking, and were told that there were a number in the county, all mulattoes, who had come from Louisiana. Some of them owned many negroes and large stocks. There were some white people, good-for-nothing people, that married in with them, but they couldn't live in Texas after it; all went over into Louisiana. They knew of no law excluding free negroes from the State; if there were any such law, no one here cared for it.

This county has been lately the scene of events which prove that it must have contained a much larger number of free negroes and persons of mixed blood than we were informed on the spot, in spite of the very severe statute forbidding their introduction, which has been backed by additional legislative penalties in 1856. Banded together, they have been able to resist the power, not only of the legal authorities, but of a local "Vigilance Committee," which gave them a certain number of hours to leave the State, and a guerrilla of skirmishes and murders has been carried on for many months upon the banks of the Sabine, with the revival of the old names of "Moderators and Regulators," of the early Texans.

The feud appears to have commenced with the condemnation, by a justice of the peace, of a free mulatto named Samuel Ashworth to receive twenty-five lashes on a charge of malicious killing of his neighbor's hogs and of impertinent talking. The Ashworths were a rich mulatto family, settled in Texas in the earliest days of the Republic, and exempted by special mention from the operation of the law forbidding residence to free negroes. They are now three and four generations removed from black blood, and have had a reputation for great hospitality, keeping open house for all who call. The member of the family who was condemned to the indignity of being publicly whipped, rose upon his guard while in the hands of the sheriff and escaped. In a few days after, he returned with a mulatto companion and shot the man on whose testimony he was condemned. Upon this the Vigilance Committee was organized, and the sheriff, who was suspected of connivance at the escape of Ashworth, and all the Ashworth family with their relatives and supporters, summoned to leave the county on pain of death. On the other hand, all free men of color on the border, to the number of one hundred and fifty, or more, joined with a few whites and Spaniards, formed an organized band and defied the Committee, and then ensued a series of assassinations, burnings of houses and saw-mills and open fights. The Moderators, or Committee-men, became strong enough to range the county and demand that every man

capable of bearing arms should join them or quit the
county on pain of death. This increased the resistance and
the bloody retaliation, and at the last accounts they were
laying regular siege to the house of a family who had refused to join them. Thirty families had been compelled to
leave the county, and murders were still occurring every
week. Among those killed were two strangers traveling
through the county; also the deputy sheriff, and the sheriff himself, who was found concealed under the floor of a
lonely house with a quantity of machinery for the issue
of false money, and instantly shot; the proprietor of the
house, defending himself revolver in hand, fell pierced
with many balls. The aid of the military power of the State
had been invoked by the legal authorities; but the issue
I have not seen in the newspapers.

A JOURNEY

IN THE

BACK COUNTRY.

BY

FREDERICK LAW OLMSTED,

AUTHOR OF "A JOURNEY IN THE SEABOARD SLAVE STATES,"
"A JOURNEY IN TEXAS," "WALKS AND TALKS OF
AN AMERICAN FARMER IN ENGLAND," ETC.

NEW YORK:
PUBLISHED BY MASON BROTHERS,
5 AND 7 MERCER STREET.
LONDON: SAMPSON LOW, SON & CO., 47 LUDGATE HILL
1860

PREFACE

THIS is the third volume of a work, the first of which was a narrative of a journey in the sea-board districts of the older slave States; the second, of a rapid tour west of the Alleghanies, and of a winter spent in Texas. This volume concludes and somewhat focalizes the observations of those, its narrative being, in part, of the hill-country people, and mainly of those who are engaged in, or are most directly affected by, the great business of the South—the production of cotton. The record of facts, except as regards the domestic life of the people, is less elaborate than in the other volumes, because, reference being made to previous observations, less detail is needed to give a full statement of that which was seen by the writer. Facts of general observation and conclusions of judgment form a larger part of this volume than of the others, because they are appropriately deduced from all preceding details. It was prepared for the press nearly in its present form and announced for publication three years ago. A chapter was then intended to be added upon the natural history of southern politics, before preparing which, I was interrupted by unanticipated duties. Upon recent examination it was found that the facts recorded had not lost significance, and that the volume might be published without revision or addition. As the topic of slave insurrection is considerably discussed, I will here observe that all its narrative portion had been printed, and that all the matter of the last chapter bearing upon that subject had been written, some time before the John Brown plot is supposed to have been formed.

The controlling considerations which now induce the publication of the volume are, first, that after publishing the former volumes, to leave untold what is reported in this, would be to leave my story untrue through incompleteness; secondly, that the agitation growing out of the condition of the South is now graver, and the truth more important to be known, than ever before. Before preparing this volume, I had given more than two years' careful study simply to the matter of fact of the condition of the people, especially the white people, living under a great variety of circumstances where slavery is not prohibited. There has been no publication of observations made with similar advantages, and extended over so large a field. I may add that few men could have been so little inclined to establish previously formed opinions as I was when I began my journey in the South. I left a farm in New York to examine farms in Virginia. The Fillmore compromises had just been accomplished; a reaction from a state of suspicion and unwholesome excitement was obvious in the public mind. Looking upon slavery as an unfortunate circumstance, for which the people of the South were in nowise to blame, and the abolition of which was no more immediately practicable than the abrogation of hospitals, penitentiaries, and boarding-schools, it was with the distinct hope of aiding in this reaction, and of aiding those disposed to consider the subject of slavery in a rational, philosophical, and conciliatory spirit, that I undertook, at the suggestion of the editor of the *New York Times,* to make a personal study of the ordinary condition and habits of the people of the South. I believed that much mischief had resulted from statements and descriptions of occurrences which were exceptional, as if they were ordinary phenomena attending slavery. I had the most unquestioning faith that while the fact of slavery imposed much unenviable duty upon the people of the South, and occasioned much inconvenience, the clear knowledge of which would lead to a disposition of forbearance, and encourage a respectful purpose of assistance (such as soon after this found an expression in the organization of the Southern Aid Society), there was at the same time a moral condition of the human race, in connection with slavery—that there was an expression of peculiar virtues in the South, too little known or considered, the setting forth of which would do good.

I will not here conceal for a moment that I was disappointed in the actual condition of the people of the South, citizen and slave; that the more thoroughly and the longer I was acquainted with that which is ordinary and general, the greater was my disappointment. In the present aspect of affairs, it would be an affectation of moderation if I refrained from expressing my conviction that the larger part of the people of the South are in a condition which can not be too much deplored, the extension and aggravation of the causes of which can not be too firmly and persistently guarded against.

The subjection of the negroes of the South to the mastership of the whites I still consider justifiable and necessary, and I fully share the general ill-will of the people of the North toward any suggestion of their interfering politically to accomplish an immediate abolition of slavery. This is not from idolatry of a parchment, or from a romantic attachment to the word Union; it certainly is not from a low estimation of the misfortune of slavery, or of the flagrant wrong of the laws and customs of the Slave States. It is from a fair consideration of the excellence of our confederate constitution when compared with other instruments of human association, and from a calculation of the chances of getting a better, after any sort of revolution at this time, together with the chances of thereby accomplishing a radical and satisfactory remedy for the evils which must result from slavery. I do not see that a mere setting free of the blacks, if it could be accomplished would surely remedy these evils. An extraction of the bullet does not at once remedy the injury of a gun-shot wound; it sometimes aggravates it.

It does not follow, however, that the evils of slavery must continue to be as great as at present. Nor does it follow that consideration of these evils at the North must be either futile or impertinent, for they are by no means limited in their action to the people of the Slave States, and there are matters in the discussion of which the people of the North have a constitutional right to be heard, the decision of which may greatly help to perpetuate or to limit them.

The emancipation of the negroes is evidently not a matter to be accomplished by this generation, but again it does not follow that even emancipation can not be anticipated, or the way of accomplishing it in some degree prepared. The determination that it shall not be is much more impracticable, fanatical, and dangerous than argument for immediate abolition. The present agitation of the country results less from the labors of abolitionists than from the conceit, avarice, and folly of wealthy owners of slaves. These constantly, and by organized action, endeavor to reverse the only line of policy by which safety and peace can, in the nature of things, be secured to the people of the South; for there are moral forces, as well as material, in nature, and there is the same folly in expecting to overcome the one as the other.

It would be presumptuous in any man to predict when,

or in what manner, slavery is to end, but, if the owners of slaves were so disposed, it appears to me that there would be no difficulty whatever, politically, financially, or socially, in diminishing the evil of slavery, and in preparing the way for an end to it. It is to be hoped that elements will, by-and-by, come into play, the nature of which we can not now imagine, which will make a peaceful end more practicable than it now appears. Whitney's invention has, to all appearance, strengthened the hold of slavery a thousand times more than all labors directly intended for that purpose. A botanical discovery, a new motive power, the decease of some popular fallacy, a physical, or mental, or moral epidemic, a theological reformation a religious revival, a war, or a great man fortunately placed, may, in a single year, do more to remove difficulties than has thus far been done in this century.

Popular prejudice, if not popular instinct, points to a separation of black from white as a condition of the abolition of slavery. It may be hoped that something will occur which will force, or encourage and facilitate, a voluntary and spontaneous separation. If this is to be considered as a contingency of emancipation, it is equally to be anticipated that an important emigration of whites to the slave districts will precede it.* I do not now say that it is, or is not, right or desirable, that this should be so, but, taking men as they are, I think a happy and peaceful association of a large negro, with a large white population, can not at present be calculated on as a permanent thing. I think that the emancipation from slavery of such part of the existing actual negro population as shall remain in the country until the white population is sufficiently christianized, and civilized, and properly educated to understand that its interests are identical with its duty, will take place gradually, and only after an intermediate period of systematic pupilage, restraint, and encouragement, of such a nature as is suggested in this volume.

To be more explicit: it seems to me to be possible that a method of finally emancipating the slaves and of immediately remedying many of the evils of slavery, without an annihilation of that which the State has made property,

---

* If gold fields as attractive as those of California should, for instance, be discovered and opened to adventurers in Mississippi, slavery would be practically abolished in the State within two years. Cotton culture would be more profitable work than gold digging, but not until something else had once drawn free laborers to a cotton district in large numbers.

or conceded to be held as property, may be eventually
based on these accepted facts: That a negro's capacities,
like a horse's, or a dog's, or a white man's, for all indus-
trial purposes, including cotton-growing and cotton-
picking, must be enlarged by a voluntary, self-restrained,
self-urged, and self-directed exercise of those capacities.
That a safely-conducted cultivation and education of the
capacities of the slaves will, of necessity, increase the
value of the slaves, and that the slaves may thus be made
to pay, year by year, for their own gradual emancipation.

I do not suppose that in one generation or two the effects of centuries of barbarism and slavery are to be extinguished. I do not think negroes are ever to become
Teutons or Celts, but I do suppose that negroes may become thoroughly civilized, thoroughly independent individuals, and thus of tenfold more value in the common-
wealth than they are. I know, for a certainty, that the
most dogged have a capacity for some improvement, even
within their own lives; that the most valuable cotton-
pickers are capable of being made yet more valuable; and
I do not believe that even ten years of careful, judicious,
and economical cultivation of this capacity, with all the
negroes of a large plantation, would fail to earn some
pecuniary as well as moral reward.

But a vain delusion possesses the South that slavery
carries with it certain defined advantages for the master
class. (I do believe, after a careful study, that there are
no such advantages.) Owing to this delusion, moral forces
in nature, as irresistible as the laws of climate, are blindly
disregarded, or held in contempt, and the hope lives that
a power, found paramount within the South itself, must
yet control the continent. This hope makes light of all
present evils growing out of slavery, or attributes them to
causes which it gives the purpose to remove. Not till it is
decisively and finally dispelled, can any general policy for
remedying the evils of slavery be initiated, or even an individual slaveholder be permitted to govern his property
in a manner consistent with what would otherwise be the
requirements of Christianity, civilization, and a sound and
far-seeing economy.

In the preparation of this book, my conscious first purpose has been to obtain and report facts of ordinary life at
the South, not to supply arguments. Lest it should be
thought I had some concealed purpose to advocate by my

selection of facts, I have here frankly set forth the inner plans and theories for which it might have been agreeable to me to have gained the approval of its readers. The facts of my personal observation fill the greater part of the book, though I have not neglected others obtained at second hand in the South. There are various theories and purposes for which these facts may be turned to account. Their influence need not be, and should not be, the same with all that it has been with me, but I believe that there are few who will chance to read to whom they will not afford some entertainment and instruction.

CHAPTER I

THE VALLEY OF THE LOWER MISSISSIPPI

A COTTON MAN.

A DEEP notch of sadness marks in my memory the morning of the May day on which I rode out of the chattering little town of Bayou Sara, and I recollect little of its suburbs but the sympathetic cloud-shadows slowly going before me over the hill of St. Francis. At the top is an old French hamlet, and a very American tavern.

One from among the gloomy, staring loungers at the door, as I pass, throws himself upon a horse, and overtaking me, checks his pace to keep by my side. I turn toward him, and full of aversion for the companionship of a stranger, nod, in such a manner as to say, "Your equality is acknowledged; go on." Not a nod; not the slightest deflection of a single line in the austere countenance; not a ripple of radiance in the sullen eyes, which wander slowly over, and, at distinct intervals, examine my horse, my saddle-bags, my spurs, lariat, gloves, finally my face, with such stern deliberation that at last I should not be sorry if he would speak. But he does not; does not make the smallest response to a further turning of my head, which acknowledges the reflex interest excited in my own mind; his eyes remain fixed upon me, as if they were dead. I can no longer endure it in silence, so I ask, in a voice attuned to his apparent humor.

"How far to Woodville?"

The only reply is a slight grunt, with an elevation of the chin.

"You don't know?"

"No."

"Never been there?"

"No."

"I can ride there before night, I suppose?"

No reply.

"Good walker, your horse?"

Not a nod.

"I thought mine pretty good."

Not a sneer, or a gleam of vanity, and Belshazzar and I warmed up together. Scott's man of leather occurred to my mind, and I felt sure that I could guess my man's chord. I touched it, and in a moment he became animated, civil; hospitable even. I was immediately informed that this was a famous cotton region; "when it was first settled up by 'Mericans, used to be reckoned the gardying of the world, the almightiest rich sile God Almighty ever shuck down; gettin' thinned down powerful fast now, though; nothin' to what it was. All on't owned by bigbugs." Finally he confided to me that he was an overseer for one of them, "one of the biggest sort." This greatest of the local hemipteras was not now on his plantation, but had "gone North to Paris or Saratogy, or some of them places."

Wearing no waistcoat, the overseer carried a pistol, without a thought of concealment, in the fob of his trowsers. The distance to Woodville, which, after he had exhausted his subject of cotton, I again tried to ascertain, he did not know, and would not attempt to guess. The ignorance of the more brutalized slaves is often described by saying of them that they can not count above twenty. I find many of the whites but little more intelligent. At all events, it is rarely that you meet, in the plantation districts, a man, whether white or black, who can give you any clear information about the roads, or the distances between places in his own vicinity. While in or near Bayou Sara and St. Francisville, I asked, at different times, ten men, black and white, the distance to Woodville (the next town to the northward on the map). None answered with any appearance of certainty, and those who ventured to give an opinion, differed in their estimates as much as ten miles. I found the actual distance to be, I think, about twenty-four miles. After riding by my side for a mile or two, the overseer suddenly parted from me at a fork in the road, with hardly more ceremony than he had used in joining me.

THE LANDSCAPE.—ROSE HEDGES.

For some miles about St. Francisville the landscape has an open, suburban character, with residences indicative of rapidly accumulating wealth, and advancement in luxury among the proprietors. For twenty miles to the north

of the town, there is on both sides a succession of large
sugar and cotton plantations. Much land still remains uncultivated, however. The roadside fences are generally
hedges of roses—Cherokee and sweet brier. These are
planted first by the side of a common rail fence, which,
while they are young, supports them in the manner of a
trellis; as they grow older they fall each way and mat
together, finally forming a confused, sprawling, slovenly
thicket often ten feet in breadth and four to six feet high.
Trumpet creepers, grapevines, green-briers, and in very
rich soil, cane, grow up through the mat of roses, and add
to its strength. It is not as pretty as a trimmer hedge, yet
very agreeable, and the road being sometimes narrow,
deep and lane-like, delightful memories of England were
often brought to mind.

There were frequent groves of magnolia grandiflora,
large trees, and every one in the glory of full blossom.
The magnolia does not, however, show well in masses,
and those groves, not unfrequently met, were much finer
where the beech, elm and liquid amber formed the body
and the magnolias stood singly out, magnificent chande-
liers of fragrance. The large-leafed magnolia, extremely
beautiful at this season of the year, was more rarely seen.

THE PLANTATIONS.

The soil seems generally rich, though much washed
off the higher ground. The cultivation is directed with
some care to prevent this. Young pine trees, however, and
other indications of impoverishing agriculture, are seen
on many plantations.

The soil is a sandy loam, so friable that the negroes,
always working in large gangs, superintended by a driver
with a whip, continued their hoeing in the midst of quite
smart showers, and when the road had become a poach-
ing mud.

Only once did I see a gang which had been allowed to
discontinue its work on account of the rain. This was after
a very heavy thunder-shower, and the appearance of the
negroes whom I met crossing the road in returning to the
field, from the gin-house to which they had retreated, was
remarkable.

First came, led by an old driver carrying a whip, forty
of the largest and strongest women I ever saw together;

they were all in a simple uniform dress of a bluish check stuff, the skirts reaching little below the knee; their legs and feet were bare; they carried themselves loftily, each having a hoe over the shoulder, and walking with a free, powerful swing, like *chasseurs* on the march. Behind them came the cavalry, thirty strong, mostly men, but a few of them women, two of whom rode astride on the plow mules. A lean and vigilant white overseer, on a brisk pony, brought up the rear. The men wore small blue Scotch bonnets, many of the women handkerchiefs, turban-fashion, and a few nothing at all on their heads.

The slaves generally of this district appear uncommonly well—doubtless, chiefly, because the wealth of their owners has enabled them to select the best from the yearly exportations of Virginia and Kentucky, but also because they are systematically well fed.

The plantation residences were of a cottage class, sometimes with extensive and tasteful grounds about them.

An old gentleman, sensible, polite, and communicative, and a favorable sample of the wealthy planters, who rode a short distance with me, said that many of the proprietors were absentees—some of the plantations had dwellings only for the negroes and the overseer. He called my attention to a field of cotton which, he said, had been ruined by his overseer's laziness. The negroes had been permitted at a critical time to be too careless in their hoeing, and it was now impossible to recover the ground thus lost. Grass grew so rampantly in this black soil that if it once got a good start ahead, you could never overtake it. That was the devil of a rainy season. Cotton could stand drouth better than it could grass.*

---

* "FINE PROSPECT FOR HAY.—While riding by a field the other day which looked as rich and green as a New England meadow, we observed to a man sitting on the fence, 'You have a fine prospect for hay, neighbor.' 'Hay! that's *cotton, sir,*' said he, with an emotion that betrayed an excitement which we cared to provoke no further; for we had as soon sport with a rattlesnake in the blind days of August as a farmer at this season of the year, badly in the grass.* * *

"All jesting aside, we have never known so poor a prospect for cotton in this region. In some instances the fields are clean and well worked, but the cotton is diminutive in size and sickly in appearance. We have seen some fields so foul that it was almost impossible to tell what had been planted.

"All this backwardness is attributable to the cold, wet weather that we have had almost constantly since the planting season commenced. When there was a warm spell, it was raining so that plows could not run to any advantage; so, between the cold and the rain, the cotton crop is very unpromising.* * *

"The low, flat lands this year have suffered particularly. Thoroughly

The inclosures are not often of less area than a hundred acres. Fewer than fifty negroes are seldom found on a plantation; many muster by the hundred. In general the fields are remarkably free from weeds and well tilled.

I arrived shortly after dusk at Woodville, a well-built and pleasant court-town, with a small but pretentious hotel. Court was in session, I fancy, for the house was filled with guests of somewhat remarkable character. The landlord was inattentive, and, when followed up, inclined to be uncivil. At the ordinary—supper and breakfast alike—there were twelve men beside myself, all of them wearing black cloth coats, black cravats and satin or embroidered silk waistcoats; all, too, sleek as if just from a barber's hands, and redolent of perfumes, which really had the best of it with exhalations of the kitchen. Perhaps it was because I was not in the regulation dress that I found no one ready to converse with me and could obtain not the slightest information about my road, even from the landlord.

I might have left Woodville with more respect for this decorum if I had not, when shown by a servant to my room, found two beds in it, each of which proved to be furnished with soiled sheets and greasy pillows, nor was it without reiterated demands and bribery of the servant that I succeeded in getting them changed on the one I selected. A gentleman of embroidered waistcoat took the other bed as it was with no apparent reluctance soon after I had effected my arrangements. One wash-bowl and a towel which had already been used was expected to answer for both of us, and would have done so but that I carried a private towel in my saddle-bags. Another requirement of a civilized household was wanting, and its only substitute unavailable with decency.

The bill was excessive and the hostler, who had left the mud of yesterday hanging all along the inside of Belshazzar's legs, and who had put the saddle on so awkwardly that I resaddled him myself after he had brought him to the door, grumbled in presence of the landlord at the smallness of the gratuity which I saw fit to give him.

saturated all the time, and often overflowed, the crops on them are small and sickly, while the weeds and grass are luxurious and rank.

"A week or two of dry hot weather will make a wonderful change in our agricultural prospects, but we have no idea that any sort of seasons could bring the cotton to more than an average crop."— *Hernando (Miss.) Advance, June 22, 1854.*

The country for some distance north of Woodville, is the most uneven, for a non-mountainous region, I ever saw. The road seems well-engineered, yet you are nearly all the time mounting or descending the sides of protuberances or basins, ribs or dikes. In one place it follows along the top of a crooked ridge as steep-sided and regular for nearly a quarter of a mile as a high railroad embankment. A man might jump off anywhere and land thirty feet below. The ground being too rough here for cultivation, the dense native forest remains intact.

"IMPORTANT TO BUSINESS MEN."

This ridge, a man told me, had been a famous place for robberies. It is not far from the Mississippi bottoms.

"Thar couldn't be," said he, "a better location for a feller that wanted to foller that business. There was one chap there a spell ago who built himself a cabin t'other side the river. He used to come over in a dug-out. He could paddle his dug-out up the swamp, you see, to within two mile of the ridge; then, when he stopped a man, he'd run through the woods to his dug-out, and before the man could get help, he'd be t'other side the Mississippi, a sittin' in his house as honest as you be."

The same man had another story of the ridge:

"Mr. Allen up here caught a runaway once, and started to take him down to Woodville to the jail. He put him in irons and carried him along in his waggin. The nigger was peaceable and submissive till they got along onto that yer ridge place. When they got thar, all of a sudden he gin a whoop like, and over he went twenty foot plum down the side of the ridge. 'Fore Allen could stop his hoss he'd tumbled and rolled himself 'way out of sight. He started right away arter him, but he never cotched a sight on him again."

HILL-SIDE COTTON CULTURE.

Not far north of the ridge plantations are found again, though the character of the surface changes but little. The hill-sides are so plowed that each furrow forms a narrow terrace. After the first plowing, thus scientifically directed, the lines are followed in subsequent cultivation, year in and year out, so long as enough soil remains to grow cotton with profit. On the hills recently brought into cultivation, broad, serpentine ditches, having a fall of from two to four inches in a rod, have been frequently constructed; these are intended to prevent the formation of more direct gullies during heavy rains. Of course, these precautions are not perfectly successful, the cultivated hills in spite of them losing soil every year in a melancholy manner.

ABANDONED PLANTATIONS.

I passed during the day four or five large plantations, the hill-sides gullied like icebergs, stables and negro quarters all abandoned, and given up to decay.

The virgin soil is in its natural state as rich as possible. At first it is expected to bear a bale and a half of cotton to the acre, making eight or ten bales for each able field-hand. But from the cause described its productiveness rapidly decreases.

Originally, much of this country was covered by a natural growth of cane, and by various nutritious grasses. A good northern farmer would deem it a crying shame and sin to attempt to grow any crops upon such steep slopes, except grasses or shrubs which do not require tillage. The waste of soil which attends the practice is much greater than it would be at the North, and, notwithstanding the unappeasable demand of the world for cotton, its bad economy, considering the subject nationally, can not be doubted.

If these slopes were thrown into permanent terraces, with turfed or stone-faced escarpments, the fertility of the soil might be preserved, even with constant tillage. In this way the hills would continue for ages to produce annual crops of greater value than those which are at present obtained from them at such destructive expense—from ten to twenty crops of cotton rendering them absolute deserts. But with negroes at $1000 a head and fresh land in Texas at $1 an acre, nothing of this sort can be thought of. The time will probably come when the soil now washing into the adjoining swamps will be brought back by our descendants, perhaps on their heads, in pots and baskets, in the manner Huc describes in China, which may be seen also in the Rhenish vineyards, to be relaid on the sunny slopes, to grow the luxurious cotton in.

The plantations are all large, but, except in their size and rather unusually good tillage, display few signs of wealthy proprietorship. The greater number have but small and mean residences upon them. No poor white people live upon the road, nor in all this country of rich soils are they seen, except en voyage. In a distance of seventy-five miles I saw no houses without negro-cabins attached, and I calculated that there were fifty slaves, on an average, to every white family resident in the country under my view. There is a small sandy region about Woodville, which I passed through after nightfall, and which of course my note does not include.

I called in the afternoon, at a house, almost the only one I had seen during the day which did not appear to be the residence of a planter or overseer, to obtain lodging. No one was at home but a negro woman and children. The woman said that her master never took in strangers; there was a man a few miles further on who did; it was the only place she knew of where I was likely to be entertained.

I found the place: probably the proprietor was the poorest white man whose house I had passed during the day, but he had several slaves; one of them, at least, a first-class man, worth $2,000.

Just before me, another traveler, a Mr. S., from beyond Natchez, had arrived. Learning that I was from Texas, he immediately addressed me with volubility:

"Ah! then you can tell us something about it, and I would be obliged to you if you would. Have you been out west about Antonio? Ranchering's a good business, eh, out west there, isn't it? Can a man make thirty per cent by it, eh? I hear so; should think that would be a good business. But how much capital ought a man to have to go into ranchering, good, eh? so as to make it a good business?"

He was a middle-aged, well-dressed man, devouring tobacco prodigiously, nervous and wavering in his manner, asking questions, a dozen at a breath, and paying no heed to the answers. He owned a plantation in the bottoms, and another on the upland; the latter was getting worn out, it was too unhealthy for him to live in the bottoms, and so, as he said, he had had "a good notion to go into ranchering, just for ease and pleasure."

"Fact is, though, I've got a family, and this is no country for children to be raised in. All the children get such foolish notions. I don't want my children to be brought up here—ruins everybody; does sir, sure—spoils 'em; too bad; 'tis so, too bad; can't make any thing of children here, sir—can't sir; fact."

He had been nearly persuaded to purchase a large tract of land at a point upon a certain creek where, he had been told, was a large court-house, an excellent school, etc. The waters of the creek he named are brackish, the neighboring country is a desert and the only inhabitants, savages. Some knavish speculator had nearly got a customer, but could not quite prevail on him to purchase until he examined the country personally. He gave me no time to tell him how false was the account he had had, but went on, after describing its beauties and advantages:

"But negro property isn't very secure there, I'm told. How is't? Know?"

"Not at all secure, sir; if it is disposed to go, it will go —the only way you could keep it would be to make it always contented to remain. The road would always be open to Mexico; it would go when it liked."

"So I hear. Only way is, to have young ones there and keep their mothers here, eh? negroes have such attachments, you know; don't you think that would fix 'em, eh? No? No, I suppose not; if they got mad at any thing, they'd forget their mothers, eh? Yes, I suppose they would; can't depend on niggers; but I reckon they'd come back; only be worse off in Mexico—eh?"

"Nothing but—"

"Being free, eh? get tired of that, I should think—nobody to take care of them. No, I suppose not; learn to take care of themselves."

Then he turned to our host and began to ask him about the neighbors, many of whom he had known when he was a boy, and been at school with. A sorry account he got of nearly all. Generally they had run through their property; their lands had passed into new hands; their negroes had been disposed of; two were now, he thought, "strikers" for gamblers in Natchez.

"What is a striker?" I asked the landlord at the first opportunity.

"Oh! to rope in fat fellows for the gamblers; they don't do that themselves, but get somebody else. I don't know as it is so; all I know is, they don't have no business, not till late at night; they never stir out till late at night, and nobody knows how they live, and that's what I expect they do. Fellows that come into town flush, you know—sold out their cotton and are flush—they always think they must see every thing, and try their hands at every thing—these fellows bring 'em in to the gamblers, and get 'em tight for 'em, you know."

"How's ——— got along since his father died?" asked Mr. S.

"Well, ———'s been unfortunate. Got mad with his overseer; thought he was lazy and packed him off; then he undertook to oversee for himself, and he was unfortunate. Had two bad crops. Finally the sheriff took about half his niggers. He tried to work the plantation with the rest, but they was old, used-up hands, and he got mad that they would not work more, and tired o' seein' 'em, and 'fore the end of the year he sold 'em all."

A MISSISSIPPI FAST MAN.

Another young man, of whom he spoke, had had his property managed for him by a relative till he came of age, and had been sent North to college. Two years previously he returned and got it into his own hands, and the first year he ran it in debt $16,000. He had now put it back into the hands of his relative to manage, but continued to live upon it. "I see," continued our host, "every time any of their teams are coming back from town they fetch a barrel or a demijohn. There is a parcel of fellows, who, when they can't liquor anywhere else, always go to him."

"But how did he manage to spend so much the first year—in gambling?"

"Well, he gambled some and he run horses. He don't know anything about a horse, and of course he thinks he knows every thing. Those fellows up at Natchez would sell him any kind of a tacky for four or five hundred dollars, and then after he'd had him a month, they'd ride out another and make a bet of five or six hundred dollars they'd beat him. Then he'd run with 'em, and of course he'd lose it."

"But sixteen thousand dollars is a large sum of money to be worked off even in that way in a year," I observed.

"Oh, he had plenty of other ways. He'd go into a barroom, and get tight and commence to break things. They'd let him go on, and the next morning hand him a bill for a hundred dollars. He thinks that's a smart thing, and just laughs and pays it, and then treats all around again."

By one and the other, many stories were then told of similar follies of young men. Among the rest, this:

A certain man had, as was said to be the custom when running for office, given an order at a grocery for all to be "treated" who applied in his name. The grocer, after the election, which resulted in the defeat of the treater, presented what was thought an exorbitant bill. He refused to pay it, and a lawsuit ensued. A gentleman in the witness box being asked if he thought it possible for the whole number of people taking part in the election to have consumed the quantity of liquor alleged, answered:

"Moy Goad! Judge" (reproachfully). "Yes, sir! Why, I've been charged for a hundred and fifty drinks 'fore *breakfast,* when I've stood treat, and I never thought o' disputin' it."

EDUCATION.

At supper, Mr. S., looking at the daughter of our host, said:

"What a pretty girl that is. My dear, do you find any schools to go to out here—eh? I reckon not. This isn't the country for schools. There'll not be a school in Mississippi 'fore long, I reckon; nothing but Institutes, eh? Ha! ha! ha! Institutes, humph! Don't believe there's a school between this and Natchez, is there?"

"No, sir."

"Of course there isn't." *

"What sort of a country is it, then, between here and Natchez?" I asked. "I should suppose it would be well settled."

---

* "Sectional excitement" has given a great impetus to educational projects in the South, and the Mississippi newspapers about this time contained numerous advertisements of a similar character to the following:

CALHOUN INSTITUTE—FOR YOUNG LADIES; MACON, NOXUBEE COUNTY, MISSISSIPPI.— W. R. POINDEXTER, A.M., Principal and Proprietor.— The above School, formerly known as the "Macon Female Institute," will be reopened on the first of October, 1855, with an entirely new corps of teachers from Principal down. Having purchased the property at public sale, and thus become *sole proprietor,* the Principal has determined to use all means he can now command, as well as he may realize for several years yet to come, in buildings, refitting and procuring such appurtenances as shall enable him to contribute his full quota, as a professional man, to the progress of the great cause of "SOUTHERN EDUCATION."

"SWELL-HEADS."

"Big plantations, sir, nothing else—aristocrats; swell-heads I call them, sir—nothing but swell-heads, and you can't get a night's lodging, sir. Beyond the ferry, I'll be bound, a man might die on the road 'fore he'd get a lodging with one of them, eh, Mr. N.? so, isn't it? 'Take a stranger in, and I'll clear you out!' That's the rule. That's what they tell their overseers, eh? Yes sir; just so inhospitable as that—swell-heads! swell-heads, sir, every plantation—can't get a meal of victuals or a night's lodging from one of them, I don't suppose, not if your life depended on it. Can you, Mr. N.?"

"Well, I believe Mr. ——, his place is right on the road, and it's half way to the ferry, and I believe he tells his overseer if a man comes and wants something to eat, he must give it to him, but he must not take any pay for it, because strangers must have something to eat. They start out of Natchez, thinking it's as 'tis in other countries; that there's houses along, where they can get a meal, and so they don't provide for themselves, and when they get along about there, they are sometimes desperate hungry. Had to be something done."

"Do the planters not live themselves on their plantations?"

"Why, a good many of them has two or three plantations, but they don't often live on any of them."

"Must have ice for their wine, you see," said Mr. S., "or they'd die; and so they have to live in Natchez or New Orleans; a good many of them live in New Orleans."

"And in summer they go up into Kentucky, do they not? I've seen country houses there which were said to belong to cotton-planters from Mississippi."

"No, sir; they go North, to New York, and Newport, and Saratoga, and Cape May, and Seneca Lake—somewhere that they can display themselves worse than they do here; Kentucky is no place for that. That's the sort of people, sir, all the way from here to Natchez, and all round Natchez, too, and in all this section of country where there's good land. Good God! I wouldn't have my children educated, sir, among them, not to have them as rich as Dr. ——, every one of them. You can know their children as far off as you can see them—young swell-

heads! You'll take note of 'em in Natchez. Why, you can
tell them by their walk; I noticed it yesterday at the Mansion House. They sort o' throw out their legs as if they
hadn't got strength enough to lift 'em and put them down
in any particular place. They do want so bad to look as if
they weren't made of the same clay as the rest of God's
creation."

Some allowance is of course to be made for the splenetic
temperament of this gentleman, but facts evidently afford
a justification of his sarcasms. And this is easily accounted
for. The farce of the vulgar-rich has its foundation in Mississippi, as in New York and in Manchester, in the rapidity
with which certain values have advanced, especially that
of cotton, and, simultaneously, that of cotton lands and
negroes.* Of course, there are men of refinement and cultivation among the rich planters of Mississippi, and many
highly estimable and intelligent persons outside of the
wealthy class, but the number of such is smaller in proportion to that of the immoral, vulgar, and ignorant
newly-rich, than in any other part of the United States.
And herein is a radical difference between the social condition of this region and that of the sea-board slave
States, where there are fewer wealthy families, but where,
among the people of wealth, refinement and education are
much more general.

I asked how rich the sort of men were of whom he
spoke.

"Why, sir, from a hundred thousand to ten million."

"Do you mean that between here and Natchez there
are none worth less than a hundred thousand dollars?"

"No, sir, not beyond the ferry. Why, any sort of a plantation is worth a hundred thousand dollars; the niggers
would sell for that."

"How many negroes are there on these plantations?"

"From fifty to a hundred."

"Never over one hundred?"

---

* As "a Southern lawyer," writing for *Harper's Weekly* (February,
1859) observes: "The sudden acquisition of wealth in the cotton-growing
region of the United States, in many instances by planters commencing
with very limited means, is almost miraculous. Patient, industrious,
frugal, and self-denying, nearly the entire amount of their cotton-crops
is devoted to the increase of their capital. The result is, in a few years
large estates, as if by magic, are accumulated. The fortunate proprietors
then build fine houses, and surround themselves with comforts and
luxuries to which they were strangers in their earlier years of care and
toil."

"No; when they've increased to a hundred they always divide them; stock another plantation. There are sometimes three or four plantations adjoining one another, with an overseer for each, belonging to the same man; but that isn't general—in general, they have to strike off for new land."

"How many acres will a hand tend here?"

"About fifteen—ten of cotton, and five of corn; some pretend to make them tend twenty."

"And what is the usual crop?"

"A bale and a half to the acre on fresh land and in the bottom. From four to eight bales to a hand they generally get; sometimes ten and better, when they are lucky."

"A bale and a half on fresh land? How much on old?"

"Well, you can't tell—depends on how much it's worn and what the season is, so much. Old land, after a while, isn't worth bothering with."

"Do most of these large planters who live so freely anticipate their crops as the sugar planters are said to—spend the money, I mean, before the crop is sold?"

"Yes, sir, and three and four crops ahead generally."

"Are most of them the sons of rich men? are they old estates?"

"No, sir; many of them were overseers themselves once."

"Well, have you noticed whether it is a fact that these large properties seldom continue long in the same family? Do the grandsons of wealthy planters often become poor men?"

"Generally the sons do; almost always their sons are fools, and soon go through with it."

"If they don't kill themselves before their fathers die," said the other.

"Yes; they drink hard and gamble, and of course that brings them into fights."

This was while they were smoking on the gallery after supper. I walked to the stable to see how my horse was provided for; when I returned they were talking of negroes who had died of yellow fever while confined in the jail at Natchez. Two of them were spoken of as having been thus "happily released," being under sentence of death, and unjustly so, in their opinion.

THE LOWER LAW.

A man living in this vicinity having taken a runaway while the fever was raging in the jail, a physician advised him not to send him there. He did not, and the negro escaped; was sometime afterward recaptured, and the owner learned from him that he had been once taken and not detained according to law. Being a patriotic man, he made a journey to inquire into the matter, and was very angry. He said, "Whenever you catch a nigger again, you send him to jail; no matter what's to be feared. If he dies in the jail, you are not responsible. You've done your duty, and you can leave the rest to Providence."

"That was right, too," said Mr. P. "Yes, he ought to a' minded the law; then if he'd died in jail, he'd know 'twasn't his fault.

Next morning, near the ferry house, I noticed a set of stocks, having holes for the head as well as the ankles; they stood unsheltered and unshaded in the open road. I asked an old negro what it was.

"Dat ting, massa?" grinning; "well, sah, we calls dat a ting to put black people, niggers, in, when dey misbehaves bad, and to put runaways in, sah. Heaps o' runaways, dis country, sah. Yes, sah, heaps on 'em round here."

Mr. S. and I slept in the same room. I went to bed some time before him; he sat up late, to smoke, he said. He woke me when he came in, by his efforts to barricade the door with our rather limited furniture. The room being small, and without a window, I expostulated. He acknowledged it would probably make us rather too warm, but he shouldn't feel safe if the door were left open. "You don't know," said he; "there may be runaways around."

He then drew two small revolvers, hitherto concealed under his clothing, and began to examine the caps. He was certainly a nervous man, perhaps a madman. I suppose he saw some expression of this in my face, for he said, placing them so they could be easily taken up as he lay in bed, "Sometimes a man has a use for them when he least expects it. There was a gentleman on this road a few days ago; he was going to Natchez. He overtook a runaway, and he says to him, 'bad company's better'n none, boy, and I reckon I'll keep you along with me into

Natchez.' The nigger appeared to be pleased to have company, and went along, talking with him, very well, till they came to a thicket place about six miles from Natchez, and then he told him he reckoned he would not go any further with him. 'What! you black rascal,' says he; 'you mean you won't go in with me; you step out and go straight ahead, and if you turn your face till you get into Natchez, I'll shoot you.' 'Aha! massa,' says the nigger, mighty good-natured, 'I reckon you haint got no shootin' irons,' and he bolted off into the thicket, and got away from him."

The carpentry of the house, as usual, was so bad that we did not suffer at all perceptibly for ventilation.

At breakfast, Mr. S. came rather late. He bowed his head as he took his seat, and closed his eyes for a second or two; then, withdrawing his quid of tobacco and throwing it in the fireplace, he looked round with a smile, and said:

"I always think it a good plan to thank the Lord for His mercies. I'm afraid some people'll think I'm a member of the church. I aint, and never was. Wish I was. I am a Son, though [of Temperance?] Give me some water, girl; coffee first—never too soon for coffee. And never too late, I say. Wait for any thing but coffee. These swell-heads drink their coffee after they've eaten all their dinner. I want it with dinner, eh? Don't nothing taste good without coffee, I reckon."

Before he left, he invited me to visit his plantations, giving me careful directions to find them, and saying that if he should not have returned before I reached them, his wife and his overseer would give me every attention if I would tell them he told me to visit them. He said again, and in this connection, that he believed this was the most inhospitable country in the world, and asked, "as I had been a good deal of a traveler, didn't I think so myself?" I answered that my experience was much too small to permit me to form an opinion so contrary to that generally held.

If they had a reputation for hospitality, he said, it could only be among their own sort. They made great swell-head parties; and when they were on their plantation places, they made it a point to have a great deal of company; they would not have any thing to do if they didn't. But they were all swell-heads, I might be sure; they'd never ask anybody but a regular swell-head to see them.

His own family, however, seemed not to be excluded from the swell-head society.

Among numerous anecdotes illustrative of the folly of his neighbors, or his own prejudices and jealousy, I remember none which it would be proper to publish but the following:

REFUSING A NOBLE TITLE.

"Do you remember a place you passed [describing the locality]?"

"Yes," said I; "a nice house, with a large garden, and a lawn with some statues or vases in it."

"I think it likely; got a foreign gardener, I expect; that's all the fashion with them; a nigger isn't good enough for them. Well, that belongs to Mr. A. J. Clayborn. He's got to be a very rich man; I suppose he's got as many as five hundred people on all his places. He went out to Europe a few years ago, and sometime after he came back, he came up to Natchez. I was there with my wife at the same time, and as she and Mrs. Clayborn came from the same section of the country, and used to know each other when they were girls, she thought she must go and see her. Mrs. Clayborn could not talk about any thing but the great people they had seen in Europe. She was telling of some great nobleman's castle they went to, and the splendid park there was to it, and how grandly they lived. For her part, she admired it so much, and they made so many friends among the people of quality, she said, she didn't care if they always staid there; in fact, she really wanted Mr. Clayborn to buy one of the castles, and be a nobleman himself; 'but he wouldn't,' says she; 'he's such a strong Democrat, you know.' Ha! ha! ha! I wonder what old Tom Jeff would have said to these swell-head Democrats."

WHERE ARE ALL THE PEOPLE?

I asked him if there were no poor people in this country. I could see no houses which seemed to belong to poor people.

"Of course not, sir—every inch of the land bought up by the swell-heads on purpose to keep them away. But you go back on to the pine ridge. Good Lord! I've heard a heap about the poor folks at the North; but if you ever saw any poorer people than them, I should like to know what they live on. Must be a miracle if they live at all. I don't see how these people live, and I've wondered how they do a great many times. Don't raise corn enough, great many of them, to keep a shoat alive through the winter. There's no way they can live, 'less they steal."

EXPERIENCE OF A FOREIGN TOURIST.

At the ferry of the Homochitto I fell in with a German, originally from Dusseldorf, whence he came seventeen years ago, first to New York; afterward he had resided successively in Baltimore, Cincinnati, New Orleans, Pensacola, Mobile and Natchez. By the time he reached the last place he had lost all his money. Going to work as a laborer in the town, he soon earned enough again to set him up as a trinket peddler; and a few months afterward he was able to buy "a leetle coach-dray." Then, he said, he made money fast; for he would go back into the country, among the poor people, and sell them trinkets, and calico, and handkerchiefs, and patent medicines. They never had any money. "All poor folks," he said; "dam poor; got no money; oh no; but I say, dat too bad, I don't like to balk you, my friend; may be so, you got some egg, some fedder, some cheeken, some rag, some sass, or some skin vot you kill. I takes dem dings vot they have, and ven I gets my load I cums to Natchez back and sells dem, always dwo or dree times so much as dey coss me; and den I buys some more goods. Not bad beesness—no. Oh, dese poor people dey deenk me is von fool ven I buy some dime deir rag vat dey bin vear; dey calls me de ole Dutch cuss. But dey don't know nottin' vot it is vorth. I deenk dey neever see no money; may be so dey geev all de cheeken vot dey been got for a leetle breastpin vot cost me not so much as von beet. Sometime dey be dam crazy fool; dey know not how do make de count at all. Yees, I makes some money, a heap."

NATCHEZ.

From the Homochitto to the suburbs of Natchez, a good half day's ride, I found the country beautiful; fewer hills than before, the soil very rich, and the land almost all inclosed in plantations, the roadside boundaries of which are old rose-hedges. The road is well constructed; often, in passing through the hills, with high banks on each side, coped with thick and dark, but free and sportive hedges, out of which avenues of trees growing carelessly and bending angel-like over the traveler, the sentiment of the most charming Herefordshire lanes is reproduced. There are also frequent woods, of a park-like character in their openness; the trees chiefly oak, and of great height. Sometimes they have been inclosed with neat palings, and slightly and tastily thinned out, so as to form noble grounds around the residences of the planters, which are always cottages or very simple and unostentatious mansions. Near two of these are unusually good ranges of negro-houses. On many of the plantations, perhaps most, no residence is visible from the road, and the negro-quarters, when seen, are the usual comfortless cabins.

Within three miles of the town the country is entirely occupied by houses and grounds of a villa character; the grounds usually exhibiting a paltry taste, with miniature terraces, and trees and shrubs planted and trimmed with no regard to architectural and landscape considerations. There is, however, an abundance of good trees, much beautiful shrubbery, and the best hedges and screens of evergreen shrubs that I have seen in America. The houses are not remarkable.

I was amused to recognize specimens of the "swell-head" fraternity, as described by my nervous friend, as soon as I got into the villa district. First came two boys in a skeleton wagon, pitching along with a racking pony, which ran over Jude; she yelped, I wheeled round, and they pulled up and looked apologetic. She was only slightly hurt, but thereafter gave a quicker and broader sheer to approaching vehicles than her Texas experience had taught her to do.

Then came four indistinct beards and two old roué-looking men, all trotting horses; the young fellows screaming, breaking up, and swearing. After them cantered a mulatto groom, white-gloved and neatly dressed, who, I noticed, bowed politely, lifting his hat and smiling to a ragged old negro with a wheelbarrow and shovel, on the footpath.

Next came—and it was a swelteringly hot afternoon—
an open carriage with two ladies taking an airing. Mr. S.
had said the swell-heads had "got to think that their old
mammy niggers were not good enough for their young
ones"; and here, on the front seat of the carriage, was a
white and veritable French bonne, holding a richly-
belaced baby. The ladies sat back, good-looking women
enough, and prettily dressed, but marble-like in propriety,
looking stealthily from the corners of their eyes without
turning their heads. But the dignity of the turn-out chiefly
reposed in the coachman, an obese old black man, who
should have been a manufacturer of iced root-beer in a
cool cellar, but who had by some means been set high up
in the sun's face on the bed-like cushion of the box, to
display a great livery top-coat, with the wonted capes and
velvet, buttoned brightly and tightly to the chin, of
course, and crowned by the proper narrow brimmed hat,
with broad band and buckle; his elbows squared, the
reins and whip in his hands, the sweat in globules all over
his ruefully-decorous face, and his eyes fast closed in
sleep.

The houses and shops within the town itself are generally small, and always inelegant. A majority of the names
on the signs are German; the hotel is unusually clean, and
the servants attentive; and the stable at which I left Belshazzar is excellent, and contains several fine horses. Indeed, I never saw such a large number of fine horses as
there is here, in any other town of the size. In the stable
and the hotel there is a remarkable number of young men,
extraordinarily dressed, like New York clerks on their
Sunday excursions, all lounging or sauntering, and often
calling at the bar; all smoking, all twisting lithe walking-
sticks, all "talking horse."

THE BLUFF.

But the grand feature of Natchez is the bluff, terminat-
ing in an abrupt precipice over the river, with the public
garden upon it. Of this I never had heard, and when, after
seeing my horse dried off and eating his oats with great
satisfaction—the first time he has ever tasted oats, I suppose—I strolled off to see the town, I came upon it by surprise. I entered a gate and walked up a slope, supposing
that I was approaching the ridge or summit of a hill, and

expecting to see beyond it a corresponding slope and the
town again, continuing in terraced streets to the river.
I found myself, almost at the moment I discovered that it
was not so, on the very edge of a stupendous cliff, and
before me an indescribably vast expanse of forest, extending on every hand to a hazy horizon, in which, directly in front of me, swung the round, red, setting sun.

Through the otherwise unbroken forest the Mississippi
had, opened a passage for itself forming a perfect arc, the
hither shore of the middle of the curve being hidden under the crest of the cliff, and the two ends lost in the vast
obscurity of the Great West. Overlooked from such an
eminence, the size of the Mississippi can be realized—a
thing difficult under ordinary circumstances; but though
the fret of a swelling torrent is not wanting, it is perceptible only as the most delicate chasing upon the broad,
gleaming expanse of polished steel, which at once shamed
all my previous conceptions of the appearance of the
greatest of rivers. Coming closer to the edge and looking downward, you see the lower town, its roofs with
water flowing all around them, and its pigmy people wad-
ing, and laboring to carry upward their goods and furniture, in danger from a rising movement of the great water.
Poor people, emigrants and niggers only.

I laid down, and would have reposed my mind in the
infinite vision westward, but was presently disturbed by a
hog which came grunting near me, rooting in the poor
turf of this wonderful garden. I rose and walked its length.
Little more has been done than to inclose a space along
the edge, which would have been dangerous to build
upon, to cut out some curving alleys now recaptured by
the grass and weeds, and to plant a few succulent trees. A
road to the lower town, cutting through it, is crossed by
slight wooden foot-bridges, and there are some rough
plank benches, adorned with stenciled "medical" advertisements. Some shrubs are planted on the crumbling face
of the cliff, so near the top that the swine can obtain access to them. A man, bearded and smoking, and a woman
with him, sitting at the extreme end, were the only visitors except myself and the swine.

As I am writing there is a bustle in the street. A young
man is being lifted up and carried into the bar-room. He

is insensible. A beautiful mare, from which he has evidently been thrown, is led back from around the corner quivering with excitement.

I could find no reading-room; no recent newspapers except *The Natchez Free Trader*, which has nothing but cotton and river news, and steamboat puffs; no magazines but aged Harpers; and no recent publications of any sort are for sale or to be seen at the booksellers'; so, after supper, I went to the cliff again, and most exquisite and solemn was the scene: the young moon shining through rents in the clouds, the great gleaming crescent of water below, the dim, ungapped horizon—the earth sensibly a mere swinging globe.

Of all the town, only five Germans, sitting together, but smoking in silence, had gathered here for evening worship.

As I returned up the main street, I stopped opposite a house from which there came the sound of excellent music—a violin and piano. I had heard no music since I was in Western Texas, and I leaned upon a lamp-post for an hour, listening. Many stopped near me for a few minutes, and went on. At length, a man who had remained some time addressed me, speaking in a foreign tongue. "Can't you speak English?" said I.

"You are not an American?"

"Yes."

"I should tzink it not."

"I am; I am a New Yorker."

"So?—O yes, perhaps, but not zis country."

"What are you?"

"Italian."

"Do you live here?"

"Yes."

"Are there many Italians in Natchez?"

"Yes—some many—seven. All big dam rascaal. Yes. Ha! ha! ha! True. Dam rascaal all of us."

"What do you do for a living here?"

"For me it is a cigar-store; fruit; confectionery."

"And the rest?"

"Oh, everytzing. I don't expect dem be here so much long now."

"Why—what will they do?"

"Dey all go to Cuba. Be vawr zair soon now. All go. All dam rascaal go, can go, ven ze vawr is. Good ting dat for Natchez, eh? Yes, I tzink."

He told me the names of the players; the violinist, an Italian, he asserted to be the best in America. He resided in Natchez, I understood, as a teacher; and, I presume, the town has metropolitan advantages for instruction in all fashionable accomplishments. Yet, with a population of 18,601, the number of children registered for the public schools and academies, or "Institutes," of the county seat, is but 1,015; and among these must be included many sent from other parts of the State, and from Arkansas and Louisiana; the public libraries contain but 2,000 volumes, and the churches seat but 7,700.*

Franklin, the next county in the rear of the county in which Natchez is situated (Adams), has a population of 6,000, and but 132 children attending school.

Mr. Russell (*North America: its Agriculture and Climate,* page 258) states that he had been led to believe that "as refined society was to be found at Natchez as in any other part of the United States," but his personal observation was, that "the chief frequenters of the best hotel were low, drunken fellows."

LABOR AND WAGES.—TOWN AND COUNTRY.

The first night after leaving Natchez I found lodging with a German, who, when I inquired if he could accommodate me, at once said, "Yes, sir, I make it *a business* to lodge travelers."

He had a little farm, and owned four strong negro men and a woman and children. All his men, however, he hired out as porters or servants in Natchez, employing a white man, a native of the country, to work with him on his farm.

To explain the economy of this arrangement, he said that one of his men earned in Natchez $30 a month clear of all expenses, and the others much more than he could ever make their labor worth to him. A negro of moderate intelligence would hire, as a house-servant, for $200 a year and his board, which was worth $8 a month; whereas

---

* This may be compared with the town of Springfield, county of Sangamon, Illinois, in which, with a population of 19,228 (nearer to that of Natchez than any other town I observe in the free States), the number of registered school children is 3,300, the public libraries contain 20,000 volumes, and the churches can accommodate 28,000 sitters.

he hired this white fellow, who was strong and able, for $10 a month; and he believed he got as much work out of him as he could out of a negro. If labor were worth so much as he got for that of his negroes, why did the white man not demand more? Well—he kept him in whiskey and tobacco beside his wages, and he was content. Most folks here do not like white laborers. They had only been used to have niggers do their work, and they did not know how to manage with white laborers; but he had no difficulty.

FOOD OF THE SLAVES.

I asked if $8 would cover the cost of a man's board? He supposed it might cost him rather more than that to keep the white man; $8 was what it was generally reckoned in town to cost to keep a negro; niggers living in town or near it were expected to have "extras"; out on the plantations, where they did not get any thing but bacon and meal, of course, it did not cost so much. Did he know what it cost to keep a negro generally upon the plantations? It was generally reckoned, he said, that a nigger ought to have a peck of meal and three pounds of bacon a week; some didn't give so much meat, but he thought it would be better to give them more.

"You are getting rich," I said. "Are the Germans generally, hereabouts, doing well? I see there are a good many in Natchez."

"Oh yes; anybody who is not too proud to work can get rich here."

The next day, having ridden thirty tedious miles, about six o'clock I called at the first house standing upon or near the road which I had seen for some time, and solicited a lodging. It was refused, by a woman. How far was it to the next house? I asked her. Two miles and a half. So I found it to be, but it was a deserted house, falling to decay, on an abandoned plantation. I rode several miles further, and it was growing dark and threatening rain before I came in sight of another. It was a short distance off the road, and approached by a private lane, from which it was separated by a grass plot. A well-dressed man stood between the gate and the house. I stopped and bowed to him, but he turned his back upon me and walked to the house. I opened a gate and rode in. Two men were upon the gallery, but as they paid no attention to my presence when I stopped near them, I doubted if either were the master of the house. I asked, "Could I obtain a lodging here to-night, gentlemen?" One of them answered, surlily and decidedly, "No." I paused a moment that they might observe me—evidently a stranger benighted, with a fatigued horse, and then asked, "Can you tell me, sir, how far it is to a public house?" "I don't know," answered the same man. I again remained silent a moment. "No public houses in this section of the country, I reckon, sir," said the other. "Do you know how far it is to the next house on the road, north of this?" "No," answered one. "You'll find one about two miles or two miles and a half from here," said the other. "Is it a house in which I shall be likely to get a lodging, do you know?" "I don't know, I'm sure."

"Good night, gentlemen; you'll excuse me for troubling you. I am entirely a stranger in this region."

A grunt, or inarticulate monosyllable, from one of them, was the only reply, and I rode away, glad that I had not been fated to spend an evening in such company.

Soon afterward I came to a house and stables close upon the road. There was a man on the gallery playing the fiddle. I asked, "Could you accommodate me here to-night, sir?" He stopped fiddling, and turned his head toward an open door, asking, "Wants to know if you can accommodate him?" "Accommodate him with what?" demanded a harsh-toned woman's voice. "With a bed, of course—what do you s'pose—ho! ho! ho!" and he went on fiddling again. I had, during this conversation, observed ranges of negro huts behind the stables, and perceived that it must be the overseer's house of the plantation at which I had previously called. "Like master, like man," I thought, and rode on, my inquiry not having been even answered.

I met a negro boy on the road, who told me it was about two miles to the next house, but he did not reckon that I would get in there. "How far to the next house beyond that?" "About four miles, sir, and I reckon you can get in there, master; I've heard they did take in travelers to that place."

Soon after this it began to rain and grow dark; so dark that I could not keep the road, for soon finding Belshazzar in difficulty, I got off and discovered that we were following up the dry bed of a small stream. In trying to get back I probably crossed the road, as I did not find it again, and wandered cautiously among trees for nearly an hour, at length coming to open country and a fence. Keeping this in sight, I rode on until I found a gate, entering at which I followed a nearly straight and tolerably good road full an hour, at last coming to a large negro-"settlement."

AN OVERSEER AT HOME.

I passed through it to the end of the rows, where was a cabin larger than the rest, facing on the space between the two lines of huts. A shout here brought out the overseer. I begged for a nights lodging; he was silent; I said that I had traveled far, was much fatigued and hungry; my horse was nearly knocked up; and I was a stranger in the country; I had lost my road, and only by good fortune had found my way here. At length, as I continued urging my need, he said:

"Well, I suppose you must stop. Ho, Byron! Here, Byron, take this man's horse, and put him in *my* stable. 'Light, sir, and come in."

Within I found his wife, a young woman, showily dressed—a caricature of the fashions of the day. Apparently, they had both been making a visit to neighbors, and but just come home. I was not received very kindly, but at the request of her husband she brought out and set before me some cold corn-bread and fat bacon.

Before I had finished eating my supper, however, they both quite changed their manner, and the woman apologized for not having made coffee. The cook had gone to bed and the fire was out, she said. She presently ordered Byron, as he brought my saddle in, to get some "lightwood" and make a fire; said she was afraid I had made a poor supper, and set a chair by the fire-place for me as I drew away from the table.

I plied the man with inquiries about his business, got him interested in points of difference between Northern and Southern agriculture, and soon had him in a very sociable and communicative humor. He gave me much overseer's lore about cotton culture, nigger and cattle maladies, the proper mode of keeping sweet potatoes, etc.; and when I proposed to ride over the plantation with him in the morning, he said he "would be very thankful of my company."

I think they gave up their own bed to me, for it was double, and had been slept in since the sheets were last changed; the room was garnished with pistols and other arms and ammunition, rolls of negro-cloth, shoes and hats, handcuffs, a large medicine chest and several books on medical and surgical subjects and farriery; while articles of both men's and women's wearing apparel hung against the walls, which were also decorated with some large patent-medicine posters. One of them is characteristic of the place and the times.°

REVIEW OF A FIRST-RATE COTTON PLANTATION.

We had a good breakfast in the morning, and immediately afterward mounted and rode to a very large cotton-field, where the whole field-force of the plantation was engaged.

It was a first-rate plantation. On the highest ground stood a large and handsome mansion, but it had not been occupied for several years, and it was more than two years since the overseer had seen the owner. He lived several hundred miles away, and the overseer would not believe that I did not know him, for he was a rich man and an honorable, and had several times been where I came from —New York.

° THE WASHINGTON REMEDIES—TO PLANTERS AND OTHERS—These Remedies, now offered to the public under the title of the Washington Remedies, are composed of ingredients, many of which are not even known to Botany. No apothecary has them for sale; they are supplied to the subscriber by the native red-men of Louisiana. The recipes by which they are compounded have descended to the present possessor, M. A. MICKLEJOHN, from ancestors who obtained them from the friendly Indian tribes, prior to and during the Revolution, and they are now offered to the public with that confidence which has been gained from a knowledge of the fact that during so long a series of years there has never been known an instance in which they have failed to perform a speedy and permanent cure. The subscribers do not profess these remedies will cure *every* disarrangement of the human system, but in such as are enumerated below they feel they can not fail. The directions for use have only to be strictly followed, and however despairing the patient may have been, he will find cause for blissful *hope* and renewed *life.*

These preparations are no Northern patent humbug, but are manufactured in New Orleans by a Creole, who has long used them in private practice, rescuing many unfortunate victims of disease from the grave, after they have been given up by their physicians as incurable, or have been tortured beyond endurance by laceration and painful operations.

The whole plantation, including the swamp land around it, and owned with it, covered several square miles. It was four miles from the settlement to the nearest neighbor's house. There were between thirteen and fourteen hundred acres under cultivation with cotton, corn, and other hoed crops, and two hundred hogs running at large in the swamp. It was the intention that corn and pork enough should be raised to keep the slaves and cattle. This year, however, it has been found necessary to purchase largely, and such was probably usually the case,* though the overseer intimated the owner had been displeased, and he "did not mean to be caught so bad again."

There were 135 slaves, big and little, of which 67 went to field regularly—equal, the overseer thought, to 60 able-bodied hands. Beside the field-hands, there were 3 mechanics (blacksmith, carpenter and wheelwright), 2 seamstresses, 1 cook, 1 stable servant, 1 cattle-tender, 1 hog-tender, 1 teamster, 1 house servant (overseer's cook), and one midwife and nurse. These were all first-class hands; most of them would be worth more, if they were for sale, the overseer said, than the best of field-hands. There was also a driver of the hoe-gang who did not labor personally, and a foreman of the plow-gang. These two acted as petty officers in the field, and alternately in the quarters.

There was a nursery for sucklings at the quarters, and twenty women at this time who left their work four times each day, for half an hour, to nurse their young ones, and whom the overseer counted as half-hands—that is, expected to do half an ordinary day's work.

DESERTERS AND DETECTIVES.

He had no runaways out at this time, but had just sold a bad one to go to Texas. He was whipping the fellow, when he turned and tried to stab him—then broke from

---

* "The bacon is almost entirely imported from the Northern States, as well as a considerable quantity of Indian corn. This is reckoned bad management by intelligent planters**** On this plantation as much Indian corn was raised as was needed, but little bacon, which was mostly imported from Ohio. The sum annually paid for this article was upward of eight hundred pounds. Large plantations are not suited to the rearing of hogs; for it is found almost impossible to prevent the negroes from stealing and roasting the young pigs." Mr. Russell, visiting the plantations of a friend near Natchez—*North America; its Agriculture, etc.,* p. 265.

him and ran away. He had him caught almost immediately
by the dogs. After catching him, he kept him in irons till
he had a chance to sell him. His niggers did not very often
run away, he said, because they were almost sure to be
caught. As soon as he saw that one was gone he put the
dogs on, and if rain had not just fallen, they would soon
find him. Sometimes, though, they would outwit the dogs,
but if they did they almost always kept in the neighborhood, because they did not like to go where they could
not sometimes get back and see their families, and he
would soon get wind of where they had been; they would
come round their quarters to see their families and to get
food, and as soon as he knew it, he would find their tracks
and put the dogs on again. Two months was the longest
time any of them ever kept out. They had dogs trained
on purpose to run after niggers, and never let out for any
thing else.

DRIVING.

We found in the field thirty plows, moving together,
turning the earth from the cotton plants, and from thirty
to forty hoers, the latter mainly women, with a black
driver walking about among them with a whip, which he
often cracked at them, sometimes allowing the lash to fall
lightly upon their shoulders. He was constantly urging
them also with his voice. All worked very steadily, and
though the presence of a stranger on the plantation must
have been rare, I saw none raise or turn their heads to look
at me. Each gang was attended by a "water-toter," that
of the hoe-gang being a straight, sprightly, plump little
black girl, whose picture, as she stood balancing the
bucket upon her head, shading her bright eyes with one
hand, and holding out a calabash with the other to maintain her poise, would have been a worthy study for
Murillo.

DAYS AND HOURS OF LABOR.

I asked at what time they began to work in the morning. "Well," said the overseer, "I do better by my niggers
than most. I keep 'em right smart at their work while they
do work, but I generally knock 'em off at 8 o'clock in

the morning Saturdays, and give 'em all the rest of the day to themselves, and I always gives 'em Sundays, the whole day. Pickin' time, and when the crap's bad in grass, I sometimes keep 'em to it till about sunset, Satudays, but I never work 'em Sundays."

"How early do you start them out in the morning, usually?"

"Well, I don't never start my niggers 'fore daylight except 'tis in pickin' time, then maybe I got 'em out a quarter of an hour before. But I keep 'em right smart to work through the day." He showed an evident pride in the vigilance of his driver, and called my attention to the large area of ground already hoed over that morning; well hoed, too, as he said.

"At what time do they eat?" I asked. They ate "their snacks" in their cabins, he said, before they came out in the morning (that is before daylight—the sun rising at this time at a little before five, and the day dawning, probably, an hour earlier); then at 12 o'clock their dinner was brought to them in a cart—one cart for the plow-gang and one for the hoe-gang. The hoe-gang ate its dinner in the field, and only stopped work long enough to eat it. The plow-gang drove its teams to the "weather houses" —open sheds erected for the purpose in different parts of the plantation, under which were cisterns filled with rain water, from which the water-toters carried drink to those at work. The mules were fed as much oats (in straw), corn and fodder as they would eat in two hours; this forage having been brought to the weather houses by another cart. The plowmen had nothing to do but eat their dinner in all this time. All worked as late as they could see to work well, and had no more food nor rest until they returned to their cabin.* At half past nine o'clock the drivers, each on an alternate night, blew a

---

* This would give at this season hardly less than sixteen hours of plodding labor, relieved by but one short interval of rest, during the daylight, for the hoe-gang. It is not improbable. I was accustomed to rise early and ride late, resting during the heat of the day, while in the cotton district, but I always found the negroes in the field when I first looked out, and generally had to wait for the negroes to come from the field to have my horse fed when I stopped for the night. I am told, however, and I believe, that it is usual in the hottest weather to give a rest of an hour or two to all hands at noon. I never happened to see it done. The legal limit of a slave's days work in S. Carolina is 15 hours.

horn, and at ten visited every cabin to see that its occupants were at rest, and not lurking about and spending
their strength in fooleries, and that the fires were safe—a
very unusual precaution; the negroes are generally at liberty after their day's work is done till they are called in
the morning. When washing and patching were done,
wood hauled and cut for the fires, corn ground, etc., I did
not learn: probably all chores not of daily necessity, were
reserved for Saturday. Custom varies in this respect. In
general, with regard to fuel for the cabins, the negroes are
left to look out for themselves, and they often have to go
to "the swamp" for it, or at least, if it has been hauled, to
cut it to a convenient size, after their day's work is done.
The allowance of food was a peck of corn and four pounds
of pork per week, each. When they could not get
"greens" (any vegetables) he generally gave them five
pounds of pork. They had gardens, and raised a good deal
for themselves; they also had fowls, and usually plenty of
eggs. He added, "the man who owns this plantation does
more for his niggers than any other man I know. Every
Christmas he sends me up a thousand or fifteen hundred
dollars' [equal to eight or ten dollars each] worth of molasses and coffee, and tobacco, and calico, and Sunday
tricks for 'em. Every family on this plantation gets a barrel of molasses at Christmas." (Not an uncommon practice
in Mississippi, though the quantity is very rarely so generous. It is usually made somewhat proportionate to the
value of the last crop sold.) *

Beside which, the overseer added, they are able, if they
choose, to buy certain comforts for themselves—tobacco
for instance—with money earned by Saturday and Sunday work. Some of them went into the swamps on Sunday
and made boards—"puncheons" made with the ax. One
man sold last year as much as fifty dollars' worth.

Finding myself nearer the outer gate than the "quarters," when at length my curiosity was satisfied, I did not
return to the house. After getting a clear direction how
to find my way back to the road I had been upon the previous day, I said to the overseer, with some hesitation

---

* I was told by a gentleman in North Carolina, that the custom of
supplying molasses to negroes in Mississippi, was usually mentioned to
those sold away from his part of the country, to reconcile to going
thither.

lest it should offend him, "You will allow me to pay you for the trouble I have given you?" He looked a little disconcerted by my putting the question in this way, but answered in a matter-of-course tone, "It will be a dollar and a quarter, sir."

This was the only large plantation that I had an opportunity of seeing at all closely, over which I was not chiefly conducted by an educated gentleman and slave owner, by whose habitual impressions and sentiments my own were probably somewhat influenced. From what I saw in passing, and from what I heard by chance of others, I suppose it to have been in no respect an unfavorable specimen of those plantations on which the owners do not reside. A merchant of the vicinity recently in New York tells me that he supposes it to be a fair enough sample of plantations of its class. There is nothing remarkable in its management that he had heard. When I asked about molasses and Christmas presents, he said he reckoned the overseer rather stretched that story, but the owner was a very good man. A magistrate of the district, who had often been on the plantation, said in answer to an inquiry from me, that the negroes were very well treated upon it, though not extraordinarily so. His comparison was with plantations in general.* He also spoke well of the overseer. He had been a long time on this plantation—I think he said, ever since it had begun to be cultivated. This is very rare; it was the only case I met with in which an overseer had kept the same place ten years, and it was a strong evidence of his comparative excellence, that his employer had been so long satisfied with him. Perhaps it was a stronger evidence that the owner of the negroes was a

* In Debow's Resources of the South, vol. i., p. 150, a table is furnished by a cotton planter to show that the expenses of raising cotton are "generally greatly underrated." It is to be inferred that they certainly are not underrated in the table. On "a well improved and properly organized plantation," the expense of feeding one hundred negroes, "as deduced from fifteen years' experience" of the writer, is asserted in this table to be $750 per annum, or seven dollars and a half each; in this sum is included, however, the expenses of the "hospital and the overseer's table." This is much less than the expense for the same purposes, if the overseer's account was true, of the plantation above described. Clothing, shoes, bedding, *sacks for gathering cotton, and so forth*, are estimated by the same authority to cost an equal sum— $7.50 for each slave. I have just paid on account of a day laborer on a farm in New York, his board bill, he being a bachelor living at the house of another Irish laborer with a family. The charge is twenty-one times as large as that set down for the slave.

man of good temper, systematic and thorough in the management of his property.*

The condition of the fences, of the mules and tools, and
tillage, which would have been considered admirable in
the best farming district of New York—the dress of the
negroes and the neatness and spaciousness of their "quarters," which were superior to those of most of the better
class of plantations on which the owners reside, all bore
strong testimony to a very unusually prudent and provi-
dent policy.

I made no special inquiries about the advantages for
education or means of religious instruction provided for
the slaves. As there seems to be much public desire for
definite information upon that point, I regret that I did
not. I did not need to put questions to the overseer to satisfy my own mind, however. It was obvious that all natural incitements to self-advancement had been studiously
removed or obstructed, in subordination to the general
purpose of making the plantation profitable. The machinery of labor was ungeared during a day and a half a week,
for cleaning and repairs; experience having proved here,
as it has in Manchester and New York, that operatives do
very much better work if thus privileged. During this interval, a limited play to individual qualities and impulses
was permitted in the culture of such luxuries as potatoes
and pumpkins, the repair of garments, and in other sordid recreations involving the least possible intellectual
friction. Regarding only the balance sheet of the owner's
ledger, it was admirable management. I am sorry to think
that it is rare, where this is the uppermost object of the
cotton-planter, that an equally frugal economy is maintained.

---

* "I was informed that some successful planters, who held several
estates in this neighborhood [Natchez] made it a rule to *change their
overseers every year*, on the principle that the *two* years' service system
is sure to spoil them."—*Russell's North America: its Agriculture, etc.*, p.
258.

"Overseers are changed every year; a few remain four or five years,
but the average time they remain on the same plantation does not exceed
two years."—*Southern Agriculturist*, vol. iv., p. 351.

CHAPTER II

------◆◈◆------

A TENNESSEE SQUIRE

❈   ❈   ❈

FORTUNATELY I did not have to go much further before I came to the best house I had seen during the day, a large, neat, white house, with negro shanties, and an open log cabin in the front yard. A stout, elderly, fine-looking woman, in a cool white muslin dress sat upon the gallery, fanning herself. Two little negroes had just brought a pail of fresh water, and she was drinking of it with a gourd, as I came to the gate. I asked if it would be convenient for her to accommodate me for the night, doubtingly, for I had learned to distrust the accommodations of the wealthy slaveholders.

"Oh yes, get down, fasten your horse there, and the niggers will take care of him when they come from their work. Come up here and take a seat."

I brought in my saddle-bags.

"Bring them in here, into the parlor," she said, "where they'll be safe."

The interior of the house was furnished with unusual comfort. "The parlor," however, had a bed in it. As we came out she locked the door.

We had not sat long, talking about the weather (she was suffering much from the heat), when her husband came. He was very hot also, though dressed coolly enough in merely a pair of short-legged, unbleached cotton trowsers and a shirt with the bosom spread open—no shoes nor stockings. He took his seat before speaking to me, and after telling his wife it was the hottest day he ever saw, squared his chair toward me, threw it back so as to recline against a post, and said gruffly, "Good evening, sir; you going to stay here to-night?"

I replied, and he looked at me a few moments without speaking. He was in fact so hot that he spoke with difficulty. At length he got breath and asked abruptly: "You a mechanic, sir, or a dentist, eh—or what?"

I presently asked what railroad it was that I had crossed

about six miles east of Chattanooga. I had not expected to find any railroad in this direction. He answered pompously that it was "the Atlantic and Pacific railroad. It began at Charleston and ended at Chattanooga, but was to be carried across to a place called Francisco in California."

Valuable information, but hardly as interesting as that which the old lady gave me soon afterward. We had been talking of Texas and the emigration. She said "there was a new country they had got annexed to the United States now, and she reckoned people would all be for going to that, now it was annexed. They called it Nebrasky; she didn't know much about it, but she reckoned it must be a powerful fine country, they'd taken so much trouble to get possession of it."

Supper was cooked by two young women, daughters of the master of the house, assisted by the two little negro boys. The cabin in front of the house was the kitchen, and when the bacon was dished up, one of the boys struck an iron triangle at the door. "Come to supper," said the host, and led the way to the kitchen, which was also the supper room. One of the young ladies took the foot of the table; the other seated herself apart by the fire, and actually waited on the table, though the two negro boys stood at the head and foot, nominally waiters, but always anticipated by the Cinderella, when any thing was wanted.

A big lout of a youth who came from the field with the negroes, looked in, but seeing me, retired. His father called, but his mother said, " 'twouldn't do no good—he was so bashful."

Speaking of the climate of the country, I was informed that a majority of the folks went barefoot all winter, though they had snow much of the time four or five inches deep, and the man said he didn't think most of the men about here had more than one coat, and they never wore any in winter except on holidays. "That was the healthiest way," he reckoned, "just to toughen yourself and not wear no coat; no matter how cold it was, he didn't wear no coat."

The master held a candle for me while I undressed, in a large room above stairs; and gave me my choice of the four beds in it. I found one straw bed (with, as usual, but one sheet), on which I slept comfortably. At midnight I was awakened by some one coming in. I rustled my straw, and a voice said, "Who is there in this room?"

"A stranger passing the night; who are you?"

"All right; I belong here. I've been away and have just come home."

He did not take his clothes off to sleep. He turned out to be an older son who had been fifty miles away, looking after a stray horse. When I went down stairs in the morning, having been wakened early by flies, and the dawn of day through an open window, I saw the master lying on his bed in the "parlor," still asleep in the clothes he wore at supper. His wife was washing herself on the gallery, being already dressed for the day; after drying her face on the family towel, she went into the kitchen, but soon returned, smoking a pipe, to her chair in the doorway.

Yet every thing betokened an opulent and prosperous farmer—rich land, extensive field crops, a number of negroes, and considerable herds of cattle and horses. He also had capital invested in mines and railroads, he told me. His elder son spoke of him as "the squire."

A negro woman assisted in preparing breakfast (she had probably been employed in the field labor the night before), and both the young ladies were at the table. The squire observed to me that he supposed we could buy hands very cheap in New York. I said we could hire them there at moderate wages. He asked if we couldn't buy as many as we wanted, by sending to Ireland for them and paying their passage. He had supposed we could buy them and hold them as slaves for a term of years, by paying the freight on them. When I had corrected him, he said, a little hesitatingly, "You don't have no black slaves in New York?" "No, sir." "There's niggers there, ain't there, only they're all free?" "Yes, sir." "Well, how do they get along so?" "So far as I know, the most of them live pretty comfortably." (I have changed my standard of comfort lately, and am inclined to believe that the majority of the negroes at the North live more comfortably than the majority of whites at the South.) "I wouldn't like that," said the old lady. "I wouldn't like to live where niggers was free, they are bad enough when they are slaves: it's hard enough to get along with them here, they're so bad. I reckon that niggers are the meanest critters on earth; they are so mean and nasty" (she expressed disgust and indignation very strongly in her face). "If they was to think themselves equal to we, I don't think white folks could abide it—they're such vile saucy things." A negro woman and two boys were in the room as she said this.

At night I was again troubled to find a house at which
my horse could be suitably fed, and was finally directed
to a place at some distance off my direct road. To reach it,
I followed a cart path up a pretty brook in a mountain
glen, till I came to an irregular-shaped cattle yard, in the
midst of which was a rather picturesque cabin, the roof
being secured by logs laid across it and held in place by
long upright pins. The interior consisted of one large
"living-room," and a "lean-to," used as a kitchen, with a
sleeping loft over half the living-room. For furniture, there
were two bedsteads, which occupied one-third of the
room; a large and a small table, on the latter of which lay
a big Bible, and other books; several hide-bottomed chairs,
two chests, shelves, with crockery, and a framed lithographic portrait of Washington on the white horse. Wom-
en's dresses hung as a curtain along the foot of one bed;
hides, hams and bunches of candles from the rafters. An
old man and his wife, with one hired man, were the occupants; they had come to this place from North Carolina
two years before. They were very good, simple people;
social and talkative, but at frequent intervals the old man,
often in the midst of conversation, interrupting a reply
to a question put by himself, would groan aloud and sigh
out, "Glory to God!" "Oh. my blessed Lord!" "Lord, have
mercy on us!" or something of the sort, and the old woman
would respond with a groan, and then there would be
silence for reflection for a few moments, as if a dead man
were in the house, and it had been forgotten for a time.
They talked with great geniality and kindness, however,
and learning that I was from New York, said that I had
reminded them, "by the way I talked," of some New York
people who had moved near to where they had lived in
North Carolina, and whom they seemed to have much
liked. "They was well larned people," the old man said;
"though they warn't rich, they was as well larned as any,
but they was the most friendly people I ever see. Most
of our country folks, when they is well larned, is too
proud, they won't hardly speak civil to the common; but
these Yorkers wasn't so, the least bit; they was the civilest
people I ever seed. When I seed the gals coming over to
our housen, I nat'rally rejoiced; they always made it so
pleasant. I never see no people who could talk so well."

He and his wife frequently referred to them afterwards,

and complimented me by saying that "they should have known me for a Yorker by my speeching so like them."

I said, in answer to their inquiry, that I had found the people of this part of the country remarkably friendly and sociable. The old man said he had "always heard this was so, and it was nat'ral it should be. There warn't no niggers here; where there was niggers, people couldn't help getting a cross habit of speaking." He asked if New York were not a free State, and how I liked that. I answered, and he said he'd always wished there hadn't been any niggers here (the old woman called out from the other room that she wished so, too), but he wouldn't like to have them free. As they had got them here, he didn't think there was any better way of getting along with them than that they had. There were very few in this district, but where they came from there were more niggers than whites. They had had three themselves; when they decided to move up here into the mountains, the niggers didn't want to come with them, and they sold them to a speculator.

I asked if it was possible they would prefer to be sold to a trader, who might take them off and sell them to a cotton planter.

"Oh, yes, they had a great fear of the mountains; they would rather, they said, be sent to a cotton farm, or a rice or sugar farm—any thing else; so we sold them to the first nigger-speculator that come along." The old woman called out again, that she wished they hadn't, for after all they was a great help to her, and it was very hard sometimes to do all the work she had to do, alone. "Those Yorkers didn't like slaves neither," she continued, coming into the room, "they said they couldn't bear to have 'em do any thing for 'em, they was so shacklin and lazy, but one of the gals married a man who owned a heap of niggers, for all that."

Their notions of geography were amusing. They thought Virginia lay to the southward, and was a cotton-growing State, and they supposed that one reason their niggers were willing to be sold, was that their mother came from Virginia, and they had heard her talk of it, and that they thought they might be sold to go back there upon a cotton farm. New York, they thought, lay west of Georgia, and between them and Texas. They asked about Indiana, and said that I must have passed through it com-

ing from Texas, confusing it, probably, with Louisiana;
and they asked if New York were not the country the Yankees came from—"the people that used to come peddling." They supposed also that New York had a much
warmer climate than Georgia. The younger man informed
me that "the United States had lately annexed a new
country that was called Nebrisky. It was large enough to
make thirteen States, and they had had a great commo-
tion as to whether it should be free or slave States. The
people here all wanted it to be slave States, because they
might want to move out there, and a fellow might get a
nigger and have to sell him. If a man moved into a free
State, he'd have to sell his niggers; if he didn't, they'd be
free as soon as he took 'em in. He didn't think that was
right; a man ought to be able to take his property wherever he pleased."

I replied that it would be a great deal better place for
nonslaveholders to move to, if slaves were excluded, to
which he made no reply.

We had for supper, cold corn bread, cold bacon and
hot coffee. The old woman remarked she had got so warm
she couldn't eat any thing, but she drank much coffee.
I was a good deal fatigued; about eight o'clock I intimated
that I would like to go to bed. The old man lighted a candle, for until then, we had been sitting by the firelight in
the chimney, and after groaning aloud for the space of
ten minutes, began to read in a very slow, monotonous
manner, spelling out the hard words, from the Bible. After
continuing this exercise for half an hour, he took a hymn
book, read two lines and commenced to sing, and thus
went on reading and singing the other two joining him at
the second verse, when we all rose. Thirteen verses were
sung, and then, after blowing out the candle, he kneeled
for prayer. He prayed with great fervor, much assisted
by the ejaculatory responses of his wife, for more than half
an hour. When we rose, the old woman took a single clean
sheet from a chest, spread it on one of the beds, and told
me that I could take that one. I began to undress, and she
stepped out of doors till I was under the counterpane. The
young man climbed into the loft, and the two old people
took the other bed. There was no window at all in the
house; they closed both doors and left a considerable fire
burning on the hearth. There did not, however, appear
to be any want of ventilation, the logs and roof being suf-

ficiently open. It was the first time, with only one exception, in more than a month, that I had been furnished with a clean sheet. (The luxury of two sheets I have never had in a private house since crossing the Mississippi); and I slept better than I have done before, for weeks.

When I came to breakfast, the old woman was much disappointed that I declined coffee. She had thought I would like it sweet, and had taken pains to boil in some sweetenin' (molasses) on my account; she said she did not think I could have strength to travel such hot weather without it. I replied that I thought that I had found that in hot weather, after a little while, its effect was rather debilitating. "Perhaps it was so," she said, "and that was the reason she felt so weak and sleepy in the afternoon. They didn't have no coffee for dinner, and she had thought she ought to have it, because in the afternoon she was always so tired and sleepy she could hardly drag about till supper time, and at supper she always drank a lot of coffee just to keep from going to sleep till after prayers. She didn't feel as though she could live without coffee."

She had taken much pains otherwise to get a good breakfast—thick griddle cakes of Indian meal, which I could really praise with a good conscience. This greatly elevated her, and she told me in a confidential whisper, "there were none of her neighbors ever had any thing nice, not even for company, because they didn't any of 'em know how to cook beyond the common."

Molasses they always used as if in the plural number (like oats), urging me to take "them molasses—but perhaps I wouldn't like them with my bacon."

My horse was well cared for, voluntarily, by the hired man; cleaned and fed generously with corn, fodder, hay and sheaf oats. Charge for all, including two of the notable Indian slap-jacks, which I carried away in my haversack, sixty-two and a half cents. When I wanted to wash, I was directed to "the spring," the old woman having the wash basin in use. In fact, she was mixing the cakes in it.

TENNESSEE COPPER MINING.

I have been visiting the mining region, which I approached through the pretty valley of the ———, where, for the first time in this journey, I met with hemlocks and laurels growing in great perfection.

The first discovery of ore was made ten years ago, soon after which specimens were taken to New York, but no mining was done, and nothing was known of it here, until a New York company bought a tract of land three years ago and immediately commenced operations. New veins were soon found and new companies formed, and the excitement continues, new discoveries being made up to this time. At the public house were ten or twelve gentlemen of wealth, who had come to sell or buy copper land, or to learn "the signs" that they might look for them on their own land elsewhere.

The mines in operation at present are owned almost entirely in New York and London. The miners employed are mostly white North Carolinians, who are paid twenty to twenty-five dollars a month, when digging perpendicular shafts, and twenty-five to thirty dollars, when working horizontally. There are here, however, several hundred Cornish men ("London miners," a native told me), and more are constantly coming. They are engaged in Cornwall, and have their expenses out paid, and forty dollars a month wages. They are said, at these wages, to be much more profitably employed than the natives. Two, whom I found at work together, one hundred and fifty feet from the surface, told me that they had been here about six weeks, and were well pleased. They each got forty dollars a month; in England, they had earned respectively but three and four pounds. Board costs here at the boarding houses seven dollars a month, but they thought that a man living "in a cottage" by himself, could live cheaper than in England. Corn-bread (though Cornish men), they had not yet eaten, and they did not believe that they should ever come to it. They must have wheaten bread. The only thing they much missed was ale; the people here did not know what it was, but drank whiskey. They would rather have one draught of Cornish swipes than a gallon of this whiskey.

Some of the miners, including some of the Cornish men, had been getting ready a pole, which they were to erect, and hoist a flag upon, on the fourth of July. I heard a report the day before I reached the mines, that the Englishmen at the mines were going to hoist the English flag and hurrah for the Queen on the fourth of July. The country people were much excited by this report, and on the third

I met a great many of them, armed with rifles, coming in "to see about it." I could not persuade them that the Englishmen were intending in good faith to celebrate the day, so strong was their belief in the continued hostility of the English people to American independence.

There were few settlers here when the mines were discovered. At present, the population is reported to be many thousand. If so, it must be remarkably scattered, for there is nothing like a village; the only houses, with two or three exceptions, being small log cabins. I stopped at what is considered the best public house. When I asked for a bed, I was pointed to a room in which there were seven beds, and told that I could take my pick. Two gentlemen immediately called out to inform me which of the beds they had used the night before, hoping that I would respect their claim to hold them. All the beds had been slept in by others, without change of sheet. Being the first to withdraw from the bar room, I had my choice, and found one straw bed among them, which, of course, I appropriated. Fortunately, I had no bed-fellow; the other beds were mostly doubly occupied.

At a public house, a few nights before, I heard the landlord, while conducting two men to their sleeping room, observe, that he supposed that they would like to sleep both in the same bed, as they came together, and I afterwards saw them together in a feather bed, notwithstanding there were several vacant beds in the same room. It was almost the hottest night I ever experienced out of the East Indies, and I sweltered upon the floor.

A SMART YANKEE.

Everybody at the mines took me for either a shrewd speculator, or a mineralogist who had come to make examinations for a speculator. I was several times stopped and asked if I did not wish to look at a good piece of mineral land, and often requested to give my opinion of specimens, nor could I make myself believed when I said I knew nothing about the matter. After I returned from visiting some of the mines, there was a room full of people at the public house. One asked me if I would tell them what I thought about those I had seen. I assured him that I was not in the least able to judge of their value, probably not half so much so as he was himself. He laughed, and another, laughing, asked, "What do you carry in that thing at your side?" and every body smiled.

"In this pouch, do you mean?"

"Yes, if it's no offense—no offense meant, no offense taken, you know."

"Certainly not; I'll tell you exactly what I've got in it." I opened it and looking in, as it were, read the contents, "a pair of gloves, a knife, a corkscrew, a fleam, a tooth brush, a box of tapers and, a ball of twine." All laughed aloud, being quite sure in their minds that the pouch contained a blow-pipe, tests, and specimens of ore, and that I was a very knowing fellow, who could keep his own counsel.

July 5th.—Last evening I rode several miles, constantly saying to myself, as I passed the miserable huts, "that, I can't put up with," and still going on to try further for something better, until, just as it was getting dark, I came to some larger cabins, one of which had creepers trained over a porch, for which sign of taste I selected it. It was occupied by a family, possessing a number of negro servants, and living in more comfort than I have seen for some time. My horse being brought out in the morning covered with mire, I asked the negro if he would not clean him. He picked up a piece of corn cob and began scraping him. "Hadn't he got a curry comb or card?" I asked, but he did not know what I meant, and laughed when I explained it to him, as you would laugh at some little article of pure foppery.

I passed through Murphy to-day, a pretty, shady town, surrounded by lovely scenery. I was a little surprised at the sight of a pillory and stocks, and to learn that a white man had been recently stripped, whipped, and branded with a red hot iron for some petty crime, by the officers of the law, in the presence of my informant, and of all of the inhabitants who could be called together to witness this solemn testimony of the legislative barbarism of their State.

While I stopped under a tree near a house as a heavy rain cloud was passing, a white man came out, and after greeting me with a single word, began calling: "Duke, Clary, Tom, Joe," etc., finally collecting seven little negroes and three white children; "Just look a here! here's a reg'lar nigger dog; have it to ketch niggers when they run away, or don't behave." (He got a piece of bread and threw it to Jude.) "There! did you see that! See what teeth she's got, she'd just snap a nigger's leg off. If you don't mind I'll get one—you Jule, if I hear you crying any more, I'll get this gentleman to send me one. See how strong its jaws be; he says all he's got to do when a nigger don't behave, is just to say the word, and it'll snap a nigger's head right off, just as easy as you'd take a chicken's head off with an ax." (The niggers look with dismay at Jude, who is watching them very closely expecting some more bread. The white children laugh foolishly.)

July 6.—I have to-day crossed the Tomahila mountain, having spent the night at an unusually comfortable house, known throughout all the country as "Walker's," situated at its western base. Apparently it is a house which the wealthy planters from the low country make a halting station on their journey to certain sulphur springs further north and east. There were plenty of negroes, under unusually good government, and the table supply was abundant and various. Yet every thing was greasy; even what we call simple dishes, such as boiled rice, and toast, were served soaking in a sauce of melted fat. I gave the stable boy a quarter of a dollar for thoroughly cleaning my horse, but rode away with less than usual scrutiny of the harness, and when I came to climb a steep pitch of the mountain, discovered that the rascal had unbuckled and kept the preventer-girth.

The road, which is excellent, and which was built by aid of a State appropriation, follows for some distance the slopes of a water-course, and then, tack and tack, up a steep mountain-side, until, at about twelve miles from Walker's, a small plateau and clearing is reached, on which stands a cabin occupied by a man, who, as he told me, gets his living by turning bed-posts of maple, which grows here abundantly and is scarce below.

After leaving this place, the road descends into a shallow valley in which flows the Tomahila river, a stream some twenty yards across, then follows for several miles along the crest of a deep dark gorge, at the bottom of which the river roars in frequent cascades, and then mounts another high ridge. From the summit there is a grand prospect, to the eastward. Directly below is a deep valley, surrounded on all sides by a succession of mountain peaks. With the exception of one bald prominence towering up on the left, these are all, notwithstanding their great height, densely wooded. Those directly opposite are some forty miles distant, and are among the highest elevations on the continent.

While I was resting my horse and looking at these distant summits, some thunder clouds drifted around and collected before them, and then floated forward, hovering over the minor peaks and pouring copious showers upon them. The thunder grew constantly more threatening, and I began to descend hastily. A zigzag road has been made with great labor, so that by traveling two miles upon a descending slope, never more rapidly than at the rate of perhaps six feet in one hundred, you accomplish with entire ease what would be, in a direct course down the steep side of the mountain, not more than a thousand feet. The entire distance to the valley is six miles.

A little boy on a mule, carrying a mail-bag, here overtook me. He said that he carried the mail from Ashville to Murphy, one hundred and fourteen miles, traveling each way once a week. He starts from Ashville Monday morning and returns there Saturday night, rests on Sunday, but during the week travels an average of nearly forty miles a day on a mule's back. Last winter, he said, the snow was often up to the mule's shoulders on the mountain, but he did not fail to accomplish his stated journey every day. When I asked him how old he was, he said "he believed that he should be about fifteen in three or four months." He had two mules, but only changed from one to the other on alternate weeks. He was paid $5 a month, and board.

Speaking of mountains, he asked if I "had ever been on Old Balsam?" He had; he was up on the top of it one morning at sunrise. I asked how he could sleep there—was there a cabin? No, but he had been coon hunting with some fellows all night, and toward daylight they got to running a wild-cat, for they had a dog that would kill any wild-cat if it could catch it. They did not succeed, however, and just at sunrise they gave it up and found themselves close to the top of Old Balsam. Then he had to go down the mountain and get up his mule, and ride forty miles with the mail before he could go to sleep. It was as much as he could do to keep awake that day.

Hearing that I belonged in New York, he asked if I knew a man there by the name of Poillon. Yes, I did;

he lived a little out of New York city, though—in the country. "The man I mean lives in New York center— right in the village itself," he replied. I knew that there was a man there of that name, I said. "Well he went from Ashville." "Yes, perhaps so." "Oh he did, he went from there two years ago. Do you know a man there by the name of Ogee?"

"No."

"There was a man at Ashville, came from somewhere in that country—Charleston, I believe 'twas—by that name."

"Charleston is not very near New York."

"Ain't it? well, 'twas Charleston he said, I believe; Charleston or New York, or some place out there."

Another man near Waynesville in this region, asked me if I knew Mr. White, of New York. I did not. "Why, he belongs in New York."

"Very likely, but New York is a large place. There are probably a hundred people of the name of White there, but I don't happen to know one of them."

"Reckon you'd know this man if he came from there, for he's a man of talent; must be one of the first men; I never see a man who knew so much about all sorts of things, and who could explain every thing out to you, as well as he. Expect he must have come from some other place. I thought he said he was raised in New York, too."

"Very possibly he was, but I know but very few indeed of all the men of talent in New York. You don't consider how many people there are there."

"It's a right smart business place, I know; it must be. You know Mr. ——, don't you?"

"Who is he?"

"Why the little man that keeps store in Waynesville; reckon you know him, he goes to New York every spring to buy goods; seen him there, hain't you?"

"I don't think that I have; you see, there are seven hundred thousand people in New York, and there are thousands and tens of thousands whom I never saw. It would be impossible for me to see one in a thousand of the people who come there every year. In fact, though I have lived in New York some years, I have but very few acquaintances there, not nearly as many as you have in this county probably."

"Such a big place; I suppose there's some people been

living there all their lives that don't know each other, and never spoke to one another once yet in their lives, ain't there?"

"Certainly—thousands of them."

" 'Tain't so here; people's more friendly, this country."

Ashville, July 11th.—This is a beautiful place among the hills, with a number of pretty country-seats about it, which, I suppose are summer residences of South Carolina planters. A great many of these "Southerners," as they are called here, are now traveling farther north, to spend the heat of summer at the numerous sulphur springs and other pleasure haunts where good boarding houses have been established for them along the cool region of the Blue Ridge. I passed one of these, a sulphur spring, yesterday. It was a white wooden building, with a long piazza for smokers, loungers and flirters, and a bowling alley and shuffle board; with coaches and trotting wagons at the stable; poor women picking blackberries, poor men bringing fowls, school girls studiously climbing romantic rocks and otherwise making themselves as pretty as possible, children fighting their black nurses, and old gold spectacles stopping me to inquire if I was the mail, and if I had not got a newspaper.

It is very odd, by the way, what old news one keeps getting in these places far from telegraphs. I inquired here for a late paper, and the clerk of the hotel went to a store to get one. It was the Ashville News, with the same articles copied from New York papers, which I had read a month before. All this country is to be netted by railroads soon, however, that is, as soon as they can be built after an appropriation to assist them passes Congress. I have crossed engineers' stakes every day, I believe, since I left Jackson, Mississippi, and generally, when I stop at night, the farmer tells me that a railroad, which will be *the* link which is wanting, either in a direct communication between the Atlantic and the Mississippi, or between New York and New Orleans, is to pass between his house and his corn-crib, and that in consequence land about him has lately become of great value, that is, from four to ten dollars an acre. He is in great perplexity, too, to conclude how much he can make the railroad company pay for damages.

Day before yesterday I ascended "Balsam Mountain," said to have been recently ascertained to be the highest peak of the Appalachian chain. A barometrical measurement of Professor W. D. Jones of Tennessee makes it ten thousand and three hundred feet above the sea, or one hundred and five feet higher than Black Mountain which has always had the reputation of being the highest. I was told that the ascent was easy, and could be made on horseback to within less than a quarter of a mile of the top. I was offered a guide, but preferred to go alone, leaving Belshazzar to rest and recruit below.

The mountain is one of a very lofty range, and the gap between it and the next peak is crossed by a (State) turnpike road. The distance to the top from this road is about four miles, and its elevation above the road, four thousand feet. A very rank growth of weeds and grass covers the ground on nearly all parts of the mountain to the top which is all used as a range for cattle, horses and hogs, and would be very profitably employed in this way but for the havoc committed on young cattle, and especially on swine and sheep, by bears, wolves and panthers.

The horses and cattle make so many paths that I was soon led astray from the one which leads directly to the top (if there is any such), and had to shape my course by the sun and the apparent feasibility of the ground in different directions before me. The mountain to within less than a mile from the top is entirely shaded by a forest of large trees, the chestnut predominating. The only change found as you ascend is in their height, the trunks continually becoming shorter and sturdier. At perhaps half a mile from the summit, the trees appear gradually more scattered; at length there is a nearly bald zone, covered, however, with grass and weeds waist high. Above this, at a quarter of a mile from the top, begins a forest of balsam firs (popularly called "balsams"). In the interval between the two forests the ascent was steep and fatiguing. Whether owing to the exertion of climbing altogether, or somewhat to the rarity of the atmosphere, I was obliged to stop frequently to rest, to relieve myself from a rush of blood to the head. The moment I entered the balsam forest, I was freed from this. These balsams are thirty or forty feet high, and under their shelter flourish a variety of smaller trees and shrubs. A great many of these trees have fallen down, and the nearer I came to the top the steeper became the ascent, the more frequent the prostrate trees, and the thicker and more impenetrable the undergrowth, a large part of it being blackberry briars. I crept under and climbed over and pulled myself along slowly, and at length came to a knob or pinnacle, across and upon which trees and shrubs and stumps with the roots uppermost seemed to have been hurled by a whirlwind. Supposing this to be the summit itself, I climbed among the roots and briars the best way I could, until I got my head above the wreck. It was very dark from the shade of the standing trees, and I perceived that the rocks rose still higher beyond. I worked my way down again and continued climbing until I reached a comparatively level surface of several yards in extent, from which a number of trees had been cut away so as to open a view in two or three directions. A dense cloud hung in a circle all around the peak, and though it was quite clear in the center where I stood, I could not see beyond it at all. Overhead, at a still vast apparent distance, were striæ, through which, at length, the sun came out for a few minutes, but the only effect was to give the cumulus below me a more mist-like and steamy appearance. At length came a slight breeze and set it in rapid motion, and rent and lifted and lowered it, so that I got a few glimpses across the neighboring mountains and saw their tops rising above rolling thunder heads, one of which was dark and probably discharging rain. I heard thunder, and conjectured that at a distance the cloud within which I stood would appear to be a thunder cloud, wooly and snowy, and gilded when the sun shone and dark and rainy below.

The peculiarity of this mountain-top, distinguishing it from all others I know of nearly equal height, is its moderate temperature and consequent abundant vegetation. It was so warm (it was half past one), that, heated as I became by my exertions, I felt no necessity for putting on my coat. The air was soft and agreeable. The ground, a dark, rich soil, with rocks protruding and shaly stones, bore luxuriant coarse herbage. Beside the thick growth of firs, I noticed black birch, chestnut, mountain ash, wild currant, whortleberry, blackberry, honeysuckle and a variety of cherry, all growing on the highest point. The air was of course, moist, and every thing damp, and this was evidently its usual condition. All the dead and broken-down trees and the rocks were covered thickly with mosses and lichens, which were charged with water like a soaked sponge.

I remained half an hour, hoping the cloud would clear away, but it only grew denser and darker. Beginning to descend, I found a path and endeavored to follow it, but as it soon ran into forks branching out in every direction, I determined to pursue a direct course down the mountain to the edge of the balsam forest, and then follow its lower line until I came to the path, or to the ridge along which I knew the path or way usually followed led. I got lost, however, in the cloud, and descended at a point where the lower forest extended up so as to meet the firs. I could not see out but turning to the left continued descending diagonally. The slope was very steep and the ground covered with shelving stones, so that it was difficult to keep my feet. At length on an inclination of about thirty-five degrees I slipped, caught myself with a quick motion of my foot, but at the next step, tripped on a protruding root or tangle of weeds, balanced for a moment and was then thrown down headlong. I was severely bruised, and for some minutes could not rise. Fortunately, at no great distance I found a deep gully with a stream of cold water, after bathing in which I entirely recovered my strength, though it was not till after several days that the contusions I received ceased to be inconvenient. I soon reached a more moderate slope, with a rich soil bearing large trees and very luxuriant tangled herbage.

Meanwhile the cloud on the pinnacle was muttering thunder, and growing darker and more threatening. As I hastened on, I saw at no great distance, waddling off through the weeds, two black bears, but was so fortunate as to meet no snakes, and nothing else at all memorable. At about half past six I reached the foot of the mountain, and shortly afterward the cloud on its summit swept downward and onward with heavy thunder and copious rain.

I was about five hours descending and reaching the house whence I started. The farmer said that he went nearly to the top to salt his cattle once a week, and he could go up and back again by his path in two hours. In going up I went leisurely, stopping to sketch, and made a very good course until I got to the firs; but in coming down I missed my way, and probably traveled over four times as much ground as was necessary. It was from carelessness or indifference at the start—I was willing to make a day of it.

The view from under the cloud was very beautiful. The general character of the scenery is less grand than that of the White Mountains, but it has impressive sublimity and repose. All the mountains are covered with trees, which, with the luxuriant herbage beneath them, secures softness of outline. Brooks of clear water are frequent. The mountain sides are often very steep, but actual precipices or even large ledges or masses of rock, I have not seen. These mountains would therefore be more pleasant to ramble over than the White Mountains, and will probably, when railroads are completed in their neighborhood, be much resorted to for pleasure. At present there is no public conveyance to any point within thirty-five miles of the base of "Balsam Mountain."

Mr. Buckley, a New York botanist, gives the following facts with regard to the mountains of this vicinity:

"The following are the heights of some mountains, and places among the mountains of North Carolina south and west of Ashville. These heights were ascertained by me with two of Green's standard barometers. Professor J. Le Conte, of Columbia, South Carolina observed the stationary barometer at Waynesville for the measurement of the highest Smoky mountains, and being called away by the duties of his professorship, Miss S. Cathey, with the same barometer, made observations at the Forks of Pigeon, Haywood county, while I was with another barometer on the tops of the other mountains measured. The highest are in the Great Smoky or Unaka range of mountains, on the line between the States of North Carolina and Tennessee near the head waters of the Oconaluftee and Little Pigeon rivers. You will observe that there are twelve peaks higher than Mount Washington and two higher than Mount Mitchell, 6711 feet high, which has long been considered the highest east of the Rocky Mountains, viz.: Mount Le Conte, 6670; Mount Guyot, 6734; Mount Buckley, 6755; Clingman's Peak, 6941.

"Those high mountains show us why western North Carolina and eastern Tennessee have a northern climate in a southern latitude.

"These late measurements show us that the highest mountains at the South are not at the sources of the largest rivers, as has generally been supposed.

"The highest mountains are covered with Abies Nigra

and Abies Fraseri, which are rarely found growing beneath an elevation of four thousand feet—the first being called by the inhabitants the he-balsam, and the latter the she-balsam. The Abies balsamica is not found there as stated by Michaux. A large moss (Hypnum splendens), often dotted with oxalis acetosella and Mitchella repens, almost invariably forms a thick, soft carpet beneath these balsam trees. Our little red squirrel (Sciurus Hudsonius), there called the mountain buma, sports and chatters among these balsam trees, feeding on their cones. He rarely descends to the base of the mountains."

July 13.—I rode last night, there being no cabins for several miles in which I was willing to spend the night, until I came to one of larger size than usual, with a gallery on the side toward the road and a good stable opposite it. A man on the gallery was about to answer (as I judged from his countenance), "I reckon you can," to my inquiry if I could stay, when the cracked voice of a worryful woman screeched out from within, "We don't foller takin' in people."

"No, sir," said the man, "we don't foller it."

"How far shall I have to go?"

"There's another house a little better than three quarters of a mile further on."

To this house I proceeded—a cabin of one room and a loft, with a kitchen in a separate cabin. The owner said he never turned anybody away, and I was welcome. He did not say that he had no corn until after supper, when I asked for it to feed my horse. The family were good-natured, intelligent people, but very ignorant. The man and his wife and the daughters slept below, the boys and I in the cock-loft. Supper and breakfast were eaten in the detached kitchen. Yet they were by no means poor people. The man told me that he had over a thousand acres of rich tillable land, besides a large extent of mountain range, the most of which latter he had bought from time to time as he was able, to prevent the settlement of squatters near his valley-land. "There were people who would be bad neighbors I knew," he said, "that would settle on most any kind of place, and every body wants to keep such as far away from them as they can." (When I took my bridle off, I hung it up by the stable door; he took it down and said he'd hang it in a safer place. "He'd never had any thing stolen from here, and he didn't mean to have—it was just as well not to put temptation before people," and he took it into the house and put it under his bed.)

Besides this large tract of land here, he owned another tract of two hundred acres with a house upon it, rented for one third the produce, and another smaller farm, similarly rented; he also owned a grist mill, which he rented to a miller for half the tolls. He had also a considerable stock of cattle and large crops of grain, so that he must be considered a very respectable capitalist for a mountaineer. He told me that he had thought a good deal formerly of moving to new countries, but he had been doing pretty well and had staid here now so long, he didn't much think he should ever budge. He reckoned he'd got enough to make him a living for the rest of his life, and he didn't know any use a man had for more'n that.

I did not see a single book in the house, nor do I think that any of the family could read. He said that many people here were talking about Iowa and Indiana; "was Iowa (Hiaway) beyond the Texies?" I opened my map to show him where it was, but he said he "wasn't scollar'd enough" to understand it, and I could not induce him to look at it. I asked him if the people here preferred Iowa and Indiana to Missouri at all because they were free States. "I reckon," he replied, "they don't have no allusion to that. Slavery is a great cuss, though, I think, the greatest there is in these United States. There ain't no account of slaves up here in the west, but down in the east part of this State about Fayetteville, there's as many as there is in South Carolina. That's the reason the West and the East don't agree in this State; people out here hates the eastern people."

"Why is that?"

"Why you see they vote on the slave basis, and there's some of them nigger counties where there ain't more'n four or five hundred white folks, that has just as much power in the Legislature as any of our mountain counties where there'll be some thousand voters."

He made further remarks against slavery and against slaveholders. When I told him that I entirely agreed with him, and said further that poor white people were usually far better off in the free States than in the slave, he seemed a little surprised and said, "New York ain't a free State, is it?"

Laborers' wages here, he stated, were from fifty cents to one dollar a day, or eight dollars a month. "How much by the year?" "They's never hired by the year."

"Would it be $75 a year?"

" 'Twouldn't be over that, any how, but 'tain't general for people to hire here only for harvest time; fact is, a man couldn't earn his board, let alone his wages, for six months in the year."

"But what do these men who hire out during harvest time do during the rest of the year; do they have to earn enough in those two or three months to live on for the other eight or nine?"

"Well they gets jobs sometimes, and they goes from one place to another."

"But in winter time, when you say there's not work enough to pay their board?"

"Well, they keeps a goin' round from one place to another, and gets their living somehow."

"The fact on't is," he said at length, as I pressed the enquiry, "there ain't anybody that ever means to work any in this country, except just along in harvest—folks don't keep working here as they do in your country, I expect."

"But they must put in their crops?"

"Yes, folks that have farms of their own, they do put in their craps and tend 'em, but these fellows that don't have farms, they won't work except in harvest, when they can get high wages [$8 a month]. I hired a fellow last spring for six months; I wanted him to help me plant and tend my corn. You see I had a short crap last year, and this spring I had to pay fifty cents a bushel for corn for bread, and I didn't want to get caught so again, not this year, so I gin this fellow $6 a month for six months—$36 I gin him in hard silver."

"Paid it to him in advance?"

"Yes, he wouldn't come 'less I'd pay him right then. Well, he worked one month, and maybe eight days—no, I don't think it was more than six days over a month, and then he went away, and I hain't seen a sight on him since. I expect I shall lose my money—reckon he don't ever intend to come back; he knows I'm right in harvest, and want him now, if ever I do."

"What did he go away for?"

"Why he said he was sick, but if he was, he got well mighty easy after he stopped working."

"Do you know where he is now?"

"Oh, yes, he's going round here."

"What is he doing?"

"Well, he's just goin' round."

"Is he at work for any one else?"

"Reckon not—no, he's just goin' round from one place to another."

At supper and breakfast surprise was expressed that I declined coffee, and more still that I drank water instead of milk. The woman observed, " 'twas cheap boarding me." The man said he must get home a couple more cows; they ought to drink milk more, coffee was so high now, and he believed milk would be just as healthy. The woman asked the price of coffee in New York; I could not tell her, but said I believed it was uncommonly high; the crops had been short. She asked how coffee grew. I told her as well as I was able, but concluded by saying I had never seen it growing. "Don't you raise coffee in New York?" she asked; "I thought that was where it came from."

The butter was excellent. I said so, and asked if they never made any for sale. The woman said she could make "as good butter as any ever was made in the yarth, but she couldn't get any thing for it; there warn't many of the merchants would buy it, and those that did would only take it at eight cents a pound for goods." The man said the only thing he could ever sell for ready money was cattle. Drovers bought them for the New York market, and lately they were very high—four cents a pound. He had driven cattle all the way to Charleston himself to sell them, and only got four cents a pound there. He had sold corn here for twelve and a half cents a bushel.

Although the man could not read, he had honored letters by calling one of his children "Washington Irving"; another was known as Matterson (Madison?). He had never tried manuring land for crops, but said, "I do believe it is a good plan, and if I live I mean to try it sometime."

A COLONIZATIONIST.

July 16th.—I stopped last night at the pleasantest house I have yet seen in the mountain: a framed house, painted white, with a log kitchen attached. The owner was a man of superior standing. I judged from the public documents and law books on his table that he had either been in the Legislature of the State or that he was a justice of the peace. There were also a good many other books and newspapers, chiefly of a religious character. He used, however, some singularly uncouth phrases common here. He had a store and carried on farming and stock raising. After a conversation about his agriculture, I remarked that there were but few slaves in this part of the country. He wished that there were fewer. They were not profitable property here, I presumed. They were not, he said, except to raise for sale; but there were a good many people here who would not have them if they were profitable, and yet who were abundantly able to buy them. They were horrid things, he thought; he would not take one to keep it if it should be given to him. 'Twould be a great deal better for the country, he believed, if there was not a slave in it. He supposed it would not be right to take them away from those who had acquired property in them, without any remuneration, but he wished they could all be sent out of the country—sent to Liberia. That was what ought to be done with them. I said it was evident that where there were no slaves, other things being equal, there was greater prosperity than where slavery supplied the labor. He didn't care so much for that, he said; there was a greater objection to slavery than that, in his mind. He was afraid that there was many a man who had gone to the bad world who wouldn't have gone there if he hadn't had any slaves. He had been down in the nigger counties a good deal, and he had seen how it worked on the white people. It made the rich people who owned the niggers passionate and proud and ugly, and it made the poor people mean. "People that own niggers are always mad with them about something; half their time is spent in swearing and yelling at them."

"I see you have 'Uncle Tom's Cabin' here," said I; "have you read it?"

"Oh, yes."

"And what do you think of it?"

"Think of it? I think well of it."

"Do most of the people here in the mountains think as you do about slavery?"

"Well, there's some thinks one way and some another, but there's hardly any one here that don't think slavery's a curse to our country, or who wouldn't be glad to get rid of it."

I asked what the people about here thought of the Nebraska Bill. He couldn't say what the majority thought. Would people moving from here to Nebraska now be likely to vote for the admission of slavery there? He thought not; "most people would much rather live in a free State." He told me that he knew personally several persons who had gone to California and taken slaves with them who had not been able to bring them back. There were one or two cases where the negroes had been induced to return, and these instances had been made much of in the papers as evidence that the slaves were contented.

"That's a great lie," he said; "they are not content, and nine tenths of 'em would do 'most any thing to be free. It's only now and then that slaves, who are treated unusual kind and made a great deal of, will choose to remain in slavery if freedom is put in their way." He knew one man (giving his name), who tried to bring two slaves back from California, and had got started with them when some white people suspecting it went on board the ship and told him it was against the law to hold negroes as slaves in California, and his negroes shouldn't go back with him unless they were willing to. Then they went to the slaves and told them they need not return if they preferred to stay, and the slaves said they had wanted very much to go back to North Carolina, yet they would rather remain in California if they could be free, and so they took them ashore. He had heard the slave owner himself relating this and cursing the men who interfered. He had told him that they did no more than Christians were obliged to do.

I overtook upon the road to-day three young men of the poorest class. Speaking of the price of land and the profit of farming, one of them said, believing me to be a southerner,

"We are all poor folks here; don't hardly make enough to keep us in liquor. Anybody can raise as much corn and hogs on the mountains as he'll want to live on, but there ain't no rich people here. Nobody's got any black ones— only three or four; no one's got fifty or a hundred, like as they have down in the East." "It would be better," interrupted another, somewhat fiercely, "if there warn't any at all, that's my mind about it; they're no business here; they ought to be in their own country and take care of themselves, that's what I believe, and I don't care who hears it." But let the reader not be deceived by these expressions; they indicate simply the weakness and cowardice of the class represented by these men. It is not slavery they detest; it is simply the negro competition, and the monopoly of the opportunities to make money by negro-owners, which they feel and but dimly comprehend.

HOW THEY TALK.

A man said to me to-day, "It's a heap warm."

The hail here, as in Texas, is "Travelin'?" after which "Traveled a good piece?" "What parts you been to?" etc.

If you meet a man without stopping, the salutation always is, "How d'ye do, sir," never "Good morning"; and on parting it is, "I wish you well, sir," more frequently than "Good bye." You are always commanded to appear at the table, as elsewhere throughout the South, in a rough, peremptory tone, as if your host feared you would try to excuse yourself.

"Come in to supper." "Take a seat. Some of the fry? Help yourself to any thing you see that you can eat."

They ask your name, but do not often call you by it, but hail you "Stranger," or "Friend."

Texas is always spoken of in the plural—"the Texies." "Bean't the Texies powerful sickly?"

"Ill" is used for "vicious." "Is your horse ill?" "Not that I am aware of. Does he appear so?" "No; but some horses will bite a stranger, if he goes to handling on 'em."

"Is your horse ill?" "No, I believe not." "I see he kind o' drapt his ears when I came up, 'zif he was playful."

Everybody I've met in the last three counties—after ascertaining what parts I came from, and which parts I'm going to, where I got my horse, what he cost, and of what breed he is, what breed the dog is, and whether she's followed me all the way from the Texies, if her feet ain't worn out, and if I don't think I'll have to tote her if I go much further, and if I don't want to give her away, how I

like the Texies, etc.—has asked me whether I didn't see a
man by the name of Baker in the Texies, who was sheriff
of —— county, and didn't behave exactly the gentleman,
or another fellow by the name of ———, who ran away
from the same county and cut to the Texies. I've been
asked if they had done fighting yet in the Texies, referring
to the war with Mexico.

THE

COTTON KINGDOM:

A TRAVELLER'S OBSERVATIONS ON COTTON AND
SLAVERY IN THE AMERICAN SLAVE STATES.

BASED UPON THREE FORMER VOLUMES OF JOURNEYS AND
INVESTIGATIONS BY THE SAME AUTHOR.

BY

FREDERICK LAW OLMSTED.

IN TWO VOLUMES.

VOL. 1

NEW YORK:
PUBLISHED BY MASON BROTHERS.
5 AND 7 MERCER STREET.
LONDON: SAMPSON LOW, SON & CO., 47 LUDGATE HILL
1861.

CHAPTER I

COTTON AND SLAVERY

INTRODUCTORY.—THE PRESENT CRISIS.

THE mountain ranges, the valleys and the great waters of America, all trend north and south, not east and west. An arbitrary political line may divide the north part from the south part, but there is no such line in nature: there can be none, socially. While water runs downhill, the currents and counter-currents of trade, of love, of consanguinity and fellowship, will flow north and south. The unavoidable comminglings of the people in a land like this, upon the conditions which the slavery of a portion of the population impose, make it necessary to peace that we should all live under the same laws and respect the same flag. No government could long control its own people, no government could long exist, that would allow its citizens to be subject to such undignities under a foreign government as those to which the citizens of the United States heretofore have been required to submit under their own, for the sake of the tranquillity of the South. Nor could the South, with its present purposes, live on terms of peace with any foreign nation, between whose people and its own there was no division, except such an one as might be maintained by means of forts, frontier-guards and custom-houses, edicts, passports and spies. Scotland, Wales and Ireland are each much better adapted for an independent government, and under an independent government would be far more likely to live at peace with England, than the South to remain peaceably separated from the North of this country.

It is said that the South can never be subjugated. It must be, or we must. It must be, or not only our American republic is a failure, but our English justice and our English law and our English freedom are failures. This Southern repudiation of obligations upon the result of an election is but a clearer warning than we have had before, that these cannot be maintained in this land any longer in such intimate association with slavery as we have hitherto tried to hope that they might. We now know that we must give them up, or give up trying to accommodate ourselves to what the South has declared, and demonstrated, to be the necessities of its state of society. Those necessities would not be less, but, on the contrary, far more imperative, were the South an independent people. If the South has reason to declare itself independent of our long-honoured constitution, and of our common court of our common laws, on account of a past want of invariable tenderness on the part of each one of our people towards its necessities, how long could we calculate to be able to preserve ourselves from occurrences which would be deemed to abrogate the obligations of a mere treaty of peace? A treaty of peace with the South as a foreign power would be a cowardly armistice, a cruel aggravation and prolongation of war.

Subjugation! I do not choose the word but take it and use it in the only sense in which it can be applicable. This is a Republic, and the South must come under the yoke of freedom, not to work for us, but to work with us, on equal terms, as a free people. To work with us, for the security of a state of society, the ruling purpose and tendency of which, spite of all its bendings heretofore, to the necessities of slavery; spite of the incongruous foreign elements which it has had constantly to absorb and incorporate; spite of a strong element of excessive backwoods individualism, has, beyond all question, been favourable to sound and safe progress in knowledge, civilization, and Christianity. To this yoke the head of the South must now be lifted, or we must bend our necks to that of slavery, consenting and submitting, even more than we have been willing to do heretofore, to labour and fight, and pay for the dire needs of a small portion of our people living in an exceptional state of society, in which Cowper's poems must not be read aloud without the precautions against the listening of family servants; in which it may be treated as a crime against the public safety to teach one of the labouring classes to write; in which the names of Wilberforce and Buxton are execrated; within which the slave trade is perpetuated, and at the capital of whose rebellion, black seamen born free, taken prisoners, in mer-

chant ships, not in arms, are even already sold into slavery
with as little hesitation as even in Barbary. One system or
the other is to thrive and extend, and eventually possess
and govern this whole land.

This has been long felt and acted upon at the South;
and the purpose of the more prudent and conservative
men, now engaged in the attempt to establish a new government in the South, was for a long time simply to obtain
an advantage for what was talked of as "reconstruction";
namely, a process of change in the form and rules of our
government that would disqualify us of the Free States
from offering any resistance to whatever was demanded
of our government, for the end in view of the extension
and eternal maintenance of slavery. That men to whom
the terms prudent and conservative can in any way be
applied, should not have foreseen that such a scheme
must be unsuccessful, only presents one more illustration of that, of which the people of England have had
many in their own history, the moral Myopism, to which
the habit of almost constantly looking down and never up
at mankind always predisposes. That the true people of
the United States could have allowed the mutiny to proceed so far before rising in their strength to resist it, is due
chiefly to the instructive reliance which every grumbler
really gets to have under our forms of society in the ul-
timate common-sense of the great body of the people, and
to the incredulity with which the report has been regarded that slavery had made such a vast difference between the character of the South and that of the country
at large. Few were fully convinced that the whole proceedings of the insurgents meant anything else than a
more than usually bold and scandalous way of playing the
game of brag to which we had been so long used in our
politics, and of which the people of England had a little
experience shortly before the passage of a certain Reform
Bill. The instant effect of the first *shotted*-gun that was
fired proves this. We knew then that we had to subjugate
slavery, or be subjugated by it.

Peace is now not possible until the people of the South
are well convinced that the form of society, to fortify
which is the ostensible purpose of the war into which they
have been plunged, is not worthy fighting for, or until
we think the sovereignty of our convictions of Justice,

Freedom, Law and the conditions of Civilization in this land to be of less worth than the lives and property of our generation.

From the St. Lawrence to the Mexican Gulf, freedom must everywhere give way to the necessities of slavery, or slavery must be accommodated to the necessary incidents of freedom.

Where the hopes and sympathies of Englishmen will be, we well know.

"The necessity to labour is incompatible with a high civilization, and with heroic spirit in those subject to it."

"The institution of African slavery is a means more effective than any other yet devised, for relieving a large body of men from the necessity of labour; consequently, states which possess it must be stronger in statesmanship and in war, than those which do not; especially must they be stronger than states in which there is absolutely no privileged class, but all men are held to be equal before the law."

"The civilized world is dependent upon the Slave States of America for a supply of cotton. The demand for this commodity has, during many years, increased faster than the supply. Sales are made of it, now, to the amount of two hundred millions of dollars in a year, yet they have a vast area of soil suitable for its production which has never been broken. With an enormous income, then, upon a steadily rising market, they hold a vast idle capital yet to be employed. Such a monopoly under such circumstances must constitute those who possess it the richest and most powerful people on the earth. The world must have cotton, and the world depends on them for it. Whatever they demand, that must be conceded them; whatever they want, they have but to stretch forth their hands and take it."

These fallacies, lodged in certain minds, generated, long ago, grand, ambitious, and bold schemes of conquest and wealth. The people of the North stood in the way of these schemes. In the minds of the schemers, labour had been associated with servility, meekness, cowardice; and they were persuaded that all men not degraded by labour at the North "kept aloof from politics," or held their

judgment in entire subjection to the daily wants of a working population of no more spirit and no more patriotism
than their own working men—slaves. They believed this
whole people to be really in a state of dependence, and
that they controlled that upon which they depended. So,
to a hitherto vague and inert local partisanship, they
brought a purpose of determination to overcome the
North, and, as this could not be safely avowed, there was
the necessity for a conspiracy, and for the cloak of a conspiracy. By means the most mendacious, the ignorant,
proud, jealous and violent free population of the cotton
States and their dependencies were persuaded that less
consideration was paid to their political demands than the
importance of their contentment entitled them to expect
from their government, and were at length decoyed into
a state of angry passion, in which they only needed leaders of sufficient audacity to bring them into open rebellion. Assured that their own power if used would be supreme, and that they had but to offer sufficient evidence
of a violent and dangerous determination to overawe the
sordid North, and make it submit to a "reconstruction" of
the nation in a form more advantageous to themselves,
they were artfully led along in a constant advance, and
constant failure of attempts at intimidation, until at length,
they must needs take part in a desperate rebellion, or accept a position which, after the declarations they had
made for the purpose of intimidation, they could not do
without humiliation.

The conspirators themselves have, until recently, been
able, either directly or by impositions upon patriotic, but
too confiding and generous instruments, to control the
treasury of the United States, its post-office, its army and
navy, its arsenals, workshops, dockyards and fortresses,
and, by the simple means of perjury, to either turn these
agencies against the government, or at least render them
ineffectual to aid it, and this at a time when its very existence, if it were anything but a democratic republican
government, and, as we think for all good purposes, by
far the strongest that ever existed, would have depended
on a perfect instant and unquestionable command of them.
Yet I doubt not that the conspirators themselves, trust at
this moment, as they ever have trusted, even less to the
supposed helpless condition of the government than to

the supposed advantages of the cotton monopoly to the Slave States, and to the supposed superiority of a community of privileged classes over an actual democracy.

"No! you dare not make war upon cotton; no power on earth dares to make war upon it. Cotton is king; until lately the Bank of England was king; but she tried to put her screws, as usual, the fall before the last, on the cotton crop, and was utterly vanquished. The last power has been conquered: who can doubt, that has looked at recent events, that cotton is supreme?"

These are the defiant and triumphant words of Governor Hammond, of South Carolina, addressed to the Senate of the United States, March 4th, 1858. Almost every important man of the South, has at one time or other, within a few years, been betrayed into the utterance of similar exultant anticipations; and the South would never have been led into the great and terrible mistake it has made, had it not been for this confident conviction in the minds of the men who have been passing for its statesmen. Whatever moral strength the rebellion has, abroad or at home, lies chiefly in the fact that this conviction is also held, more or less distinctly, by multitudes who know perfectly well that the commonly assigned reasons for it are based on falsehoods.

Recently, a banker, who is and always has been a loyal union man, said, commenting upon certain experiences of mine narrated in this book: "The South cannot be poor. Why their last crop alone was worth two hundred million. They must be rich": ergo, say the conspirators, adopting the same careless conclusion, they must be powerful, and the world must feel their power, and respect them and their institutions.

My own observation of the real condition of the people of our Slave States, gave me, on the contrary, an impression that the cotton monopoly in some way did them more harm than good; and, although the written narration of what I saw was not intended to set this forth, upon reviewing it for the present publication, I find the impression has become a conviction. I propose here, therefore, to show how the main body of the observations of the book arrange themselves in my mind with reference to this question, and also to inquire how far the conclusion to which I think they tend is substantiated by the Census returns of those States.°

Coming directly from my farm in New York to Eastern Virginia, I was satisfied, after a few weeks' observation, that the most of the people lived very poorly; that the proportion of men improving their condition was much less than in any Northern community; and that the natural resources of the land were strangely unused, or were used with poor economy. It was "the hiring season," and I had daily opportunities of talking with farmers, manufacturers, miners, and labourers, with whom the value of labour and of wages was then the handiest subject of conversation. I soon perceived that labour was much more readily classified and measured with reference to its quality than at the North. The limit of measure I found to be the ordinary day's work of a "prime field-hand," and a prime field-hand, I found universally understood to mean, not a man who would split two cords of wood, or cradle two acres of grain in a day, but a man for whom a "trader" would give a thousand dollars, or more, to take on South, for sale to a cotton planter. I do not mean that the alternative of a sale to a trader was always had in view in determining how a man should be employed. To be just, this seldom appeared to be the case —but that, in estimating the market value of his labour, he was viewed, for the time, from the trader's point of view, or, as if the question were—What is he worth for cotton?

I soon ascertained that a much larger number of hands, at much larger aggregate wages, was commonly reckoned to be required to accomplish certain results, than would have been the case at the North. Not all results, but certain results, of a kind in which it happened that I could most readily make a confident comparison. I have been in the habit of watching men at work, and of judging of their industry, their skill, their spirit; in short, of whatever goes to make up their value to their employers, or to the community, as instruments of production; and from day to day I saw that, as a landowner, or as a citizen, in a community

---

° I greatly regret, after visiting Washington for this purpose, to find that the returns of the Census of 1860 are not yet sufficiently verified and digested to be given to the public. I have therefore had to fall back upon those of 1850. The rate of increase of the slave population in the meantime is stated at 25 per cent.

largely composed, or dependent upon the productive industry, of working people of such habits and disposition as I constantly saw evinced in those of Virginia, I should feel disheartened, and myself lose courage, spirit, and industry. The close proximity of the better and cheaper labour —labour seeking a field of labour—which I had left behind me, added greatly to my interest in the subject, and stimulated close inquiry. It seemed, indeed, quite incredible that there really could be such a want of better labour in this region as at first sight there appeared to be, when a supply was so near at hand. I compared notes with every Northern man I met who had been living for some time in Virginia, and some I found able to give me quite exact statements of personal experience, with which, in the cases they mentioned, it could not be doubted that labourers costing, all things considered, the same wages, had taken four times as long to accomplish certain tasks of rude work in Virginia as at the North, and that in house service, four servants accomplished less, while they required vastly more looking after, than one at the North.

I left Virginia, having remained much longer than I at first intended, in trying to satisfy myself about this matter —quite satisfied as to the general fact, not at all satisfied with any theories of demand and supply which had been offered me, or which had occurred to me, in the way of explanation of it.

My perplexity was increased by certain apparent exceptions to the general rule; but they were, all things considered, unimportant, and rather served as affording contrasts, on the ground, to satisfy me of the correctness of my general conclusion.

I subsequently returned, and spent another month in Virginia, after visiting the cotton States, and I also spent three months in Kentucky and other parts of the Slave States where the climate is unsuitable for the production of cotton, and with the information which I had in the meantime obtained, I continued to study both the question of fact, and the question of cause. The following conclusions to which my mind tended strongly in the first month, though I did not then adopt them altogether with confidence, were established at length in my convictions.

1. The cash value of a slave's labour in Virginia is, practically, the cash value of the same labour minus the

cost of its transportation, acclimatizing, and breaking
in to cotton-culture in Mississippi.

2. The cost of production, or the development of natural
wealth in Virginia, is regulated by the cost of slave-
labour: (that is to say) the competition of white labour
does not materially reduce it; though it doubtless has
some effect, at least in certain districts, and with reference to certain productions or branches of industry.

3. Taking infants, aged, invalid, and vicious and knavish
slaves into account, the ordinary and average cost of
a certain task of labour is more than double in Virginia
what it is in the Free States adjoining.

4. The use of land and nearly all other resources of wealth
in Virginia is much less valuable than the use of similar property in the adjoining Free States, these resources having no real value until labour is applied to
them. (The Census returns of 1850 show that the sale
value of farm lands by the acre in Virginia is less than
one-third the value of farm lands in the adjoining Free
State of Pennsylvania, and less than one-fifth than that
of the farm lands of the neighbouring Free State of
New Jersey.)

5. Beyond the bare necessities of existence, poor shelter,
poor clothing, and the crudest diet, the mass of the
citizen class of Virginia earn very little and are very
poor—immeasurably poorer than the mass of the people of the adjoining Free States.

6. So far as this poverty is to be attributed to personal
constitution, character, and choice, it is not the result
of climate.

7. What is true of Virginia is measurably true of all the
border Slave States, though in special cases the resistance of slavery to a competition of free labour is more
easily overcome. In proportion as this is the case, the
cost of production is less, the value of production
greater, the comfort of the people is greater; they are
advancing in wealth as they are in intelligence, which
is the best form or result of wealth.

I went on my way into the so-called cotton States,
within which I travelled over, first and last, at least three
thousand miles of roads, from which not a cotton plant
was to be seen, and the people living by the side of which
certainly had not been made rich by cotton or anything

else. And for every mile of road-side upon which I saw
any evidence of cotton production, I am sure that I saw a
hundred of forest or waste land, with only now and then
an acre or two of poor corn half smothered in weeds; for
every rich man's house, I am sure that I passed a dozen
shabby and half-furnished cottages, and at least a hundred
cabins—mere hovels, such as none but a poor farmer
would house his cattle in at the North. And I think that,
for every man of refinement and education with whom I
came in contact, there were a score or two superior only in
the virtue of silence, and in the manner of self-compla-
cency, to the sort of people we should expect to find paying a large price for a place from which a sight could be
got at a gallows on an execution day at the North, and a
much larger number of what poor men at the North would
themselves describe as poor men: not that they were destitute of certain things which are cheap at the South,—
fuel for instance,—but that they were almost wholly destitute of things the possession of which, at the North,
would indicate that a man had begun to accumulate capital—more destitute of these, on an average, than our day-
labourers. In short, except in certain limited districts, mere
streaks by the side of rivers, and in a few isolated spots of
especially favoured soil away from these, I found the same
state of things which I had seen in Virginia, but in a more
aggravated form.

At least five hundred white men told me something of
their own lives and fortunes, across their own tables, and
with the means of measuring the weight of their words
before my eyes; and I know that white men seldom want
an abundance of coarse food in the cotton States: the proportion of the free white men who live as well in any respect as our working classes at the North, on an average,
is small, and the citizens of the cotton States, as a whole,
are poor. They work little, and that little, badly; they
earn little, they sell little; they buy little, and they have
little—very little—of the common comforts and consola-
tions of civilized life. Their destitution is not material
only; it is intellectual and it is moral. I know not what
virtues they have that rude men everywhere have not; but
those which are commonly attributed to them, I am sure
that they lack: they are not generous or hospitable; and,
to be plain, I must say that their talk is not the talk of even
courageous men elsewhere. They boast and lack self-re-

straint, yet, when not excited, are habitually reserved and guarded in expressions of opinion very much like cowardly men elsewhere.

But, much cotton is produced in the cotton States, and by the labour of somebody; much cotton is sold and somebody must be paid for it; there are rich people; there are good markets; there is hospitality, refinement, virtue, courage, and urbanity at the South. All this is proverbially true. Who produces the cotton? who is paid for it? where are, and who are, the rich and gentle people?

I can answer in part at least.

I have been on plantations on the Mississippi, the Red River, and the Brazos bottoms, whereon I was assured that ten bales of cotton to each average prime field-hand had been raised. The soil was a perfect garden mould, well drained and guarded by levees against the floods; it was admirably tilled; I have seen but few Northern farms so well tilled: the labourers were, to a large degree, tall, slender, sinewy, young men, who worked from dawn to dusk, not with spirit, but with steadiness and constancy. They had good tools; their rations of bacon and corn were brought to them in the field, and eaten with efficient despatch between the cotton plants. They had the best sort of gins and presses, so situated that from them cotton bales could be rolled in five minutes to steamboats, bound direct to the ports on the gulf. They were superintended by skilful and vigilant overseers. These plantations were all large, so large as to yet contain much fresh land, ready to be worked as soon as the cultivated fields gave out in fertility. If it was true that ten bales of cotton to the hand had been raised on them, then their net profit for the year had been, not less than two hundred and fifty dollars for each hand employed. Even at seven bales to the hand the profits of cotton planting are enormous. Men who have plantations producing at this rate, can well afford to buy fresh hands at fourteen hundred dollars a head. They can even afford to employ such hands for a year or two in clearing land, ditching, leveeing, fencing, and other preparatory work, buying, meantime, all the corn and bacon they need, and getting the best kind of tools and cattle, and paying fifteen per cent. per annum interest on all the capital required for this, as many of them do. All this can be well afforded to establish new plantations favourably situated, on fresh soil, if there is a reasonable probability that they can after all be made to produce half a dozen seven-bale crops. And a great many large plantations do produce seven bales to the hand for years in succession. A great many more produce seven bales occasionally. A few produce even ten bales occasionally, though by no means as often as is reported.

Now, it is not at a Roman lottery alone that one may see it, but all over the world, where a few very large prizes are promised and many very small ones, and the number of tickets is limited; these are always speculated on, and men will buy them at third and fourth hand at prices which, it is useless to demonstrate to them, must be extravagant. They go to the Jews and pledge the clothes on their back to get another biacchi to invest; they beggar themselves; they ruin their families; they risk damnation in their passionate eagerness to have a chance, when they know perfectly well that the average of chances is not worth a tithe of what they must pay for it.

The area of land on which cotton may be raised with profit is practically limitless; it is cheap; even the best land is cheap; but to the large planter it is much more valuable when held in large parcels, for obvious reasons, than when in small; consequently the best land can hardly be obtained in small tracts or without the use of a considerable capital. But there are millions of acres of land yet untouched, which if leveed and drained and fenced, and well cultivated, might be made to produce with good luck seven or more bales to the hand. It would cost comparatively little to accomplish it—one lucky crop would repay all the outlay for land and improvements—if it were not for "the hands." The supply of hands is limited. It does not increase in the ratio of the increase of the cotton demand. If cotton should double in price next year, or become worth its weight in gold, the number of negroes in the United States would not increase four per cent. unless the African slave-trade were re-established. Now step into a dealer's "jail" in Memphis, Montgomery, Vicksburg, or New Orleans, and you will hear the Mezzano of the cotton lottery crying his tickets in this way: "There's a cotton nigger for you! Genuine! Look at his toes! Look at his fingers! There's a pair of legs for you! If you have got the right sile and the right sort of overseer, buy him, and put your trust in Providence! He's just as good for ten bales as I am for a julep at eleven o'clock." And this is

just as true as that any named horse is sure to win the
Derby. And so the price of good labourers is constantly
gambled up to a point, where, if they produce ten bales to
the hand, the purchaser will be as fortunate as he who
draws the high prize of the lottery; where, if they produce seven bales to the hand, he will still be in luck;
where, if rot, or worm, or floods, or untimely rains or
frosts occur, reducing the crop to one or two bales to the
hand, as is often the case, the purchaser will have drawn a
blank.

That, all things considered, the value of the labour of
slaves does not, on an average, by any means justify the
price paid for it, is constantly asserted by the planters, and
it is true. At least beyond question it is true, and I think
that I have shown why, that there is no difficulty in finding purchasers for all the good slaves that can be got by
traders, at prices considerably more than they are worth
for the production of cotton *under ordinary circumstances*.
The supply being limited, those who grow cotton on the
most productive soils, and with the greatest advantages in
all other respects, not only can afford to pay more than
others, for all the slaves which can be brought into market,
but they are driven to a ruinous competition among themselves, and slaves thus get a fictitious value like stocks "in
a corner." The buyers indeed are often "cornered," and
it is only the rise which almost annually has occurred in
the value of cotton that has hitherto saved them from
general bankruptcy. Nearly all the large planters carry a
heavy load of debt from year to year, till a lucky crop co-
incident with a rise in the price of cotton relieves them.

The whole number of slaves engaged in cotton culture
at the Census of 1850 was reckoned by De Bow to be
1,800,000,* the crops at 2,400,000 bales, which is a bale
and a third to each head of slaves. This was the largest
crop between 1846 and 1852. Other things being equal,
for reasons already indicated, the smaller the estate of
slaves, the less is their rate of production per head; and,
as a rule, the larger the slave estate the larger is the production per head. The number of slaves in cotton plantations held by owners of fifty and upwards is, as nearly as
it can be fixed by the Census returns, 420,000.

If these produce on an average only two and a half
bales per head (man, woman, and child), and double

* Official Census—Compend., p. 94.

this is not extraordinary on the large plantations of the South-west,† it leaves an average for the smaller plantations of seven-eighths of a bale per head. These plantations are mostly in the interior, with long haulage and boatage to market. To the small planter in the interior, his cotton crop does not realize, as an average plantation price, more than seven cents a pound, or thirty dollars the bale.‡ Those who plant cotton in this small way usually raise a crop of corn, and some little else, not enough, take the country through, one year with another, to supply themselves and their slaves with food; certainly not more than enough to do so, on an average. To this the Southern agricultural periodicals frequently testify. They generally raise nothing *for sale,* but cotton. And of cotton their sale, as has been shown, amounted in 1849—a favourable year —to less than the value of twenty-five dollars for each slave, young and old, which they had kept through the year.* Deducting those who hold slaves only as domestic servants from the whole number of slaveholders returned by the Census, more than half of all the slaveholders, and fully half of all the cotton-sellers, own each, not more than one family, on an average, of five slaves of all ages.†† The ordinary total cash income, then, in time of peace, of fully half our cotton-planters, cannot be reckoned at more than one hundred and twenty-five dollars, or, in extraordinary years, like the last, at, say, one hundred and fifty dollars. From this they must purchase whatever clothing and other necessaries they require for the yearly supply of an average of more than ten persons (five whites and five slaves), as well as obtain tools, mechanics' work and materials, and whatever is necessary for carrying on the work

---

† Messrs. Neill Brothers, cotton merchants of New Orleans, the most painstaking collectors of information about the cotton crop in the country, state, in a recent circular, that many of the Mississippi cotton plantations last year, after an extraordinary fertilizing flood, produced sixteen bales to the hand. The slaves on these plantations being to a large extent picked hands, as I elsewhere show, the production per head was fully eight bales.

‡ In a careful article in the *Austin State Gazette,* six and a quarter cents is given as the average net price of cotton in Texas. The small planters, having no gins or presses of their own, usually have their cotton prepared for market by larger planters, for which service they of course have to pay.

* There have been much larger aggregate crops since, and the price may be a cent more to the planter, but the number of slaves drawn to the larger plantations in the meantime has increased in quite equal proportion.

†† Census Compend., p. 95.

of a plantation, usually of some hundred acres,‡ and must
yet save enough to pay the fees of doctors, clergy, and
lawyers, if they have had occasion to employ them, and
their county and state taxes (we will say nothing of the
education of their children, or of accumulations for the
war expenses of the Confederation). My personal experience of the style of living of the greater number of cotton-planters leads me to think this not an unfair estimate.
It is mainly based upon the official returns and calculations of the United States Census of 1850, as prepared
by Mr. De Bow, a leading secessionist, and it assumes
nothing which is not conceded in the article on cotton in
his Resources of the South. A majority of those who sell
the cotton crop of the United States must be miserably
poor—poorer than the majority of our day-labourers at
the North.

A similar calculation will indicate that the planters who
own on an average two slave families each, can sell
scarcely more than three hundred dollars' worth of cotton
a year, on an average; which also entirely agrees with my
observations. I have seen many a workman's lodging at
the North, and in England too, where there was double
the amount of luxury that I ever saw in a regular cotton-
planter's house on plantations of three cabins.

The next class of which the Census furnishes us means
of considering separately, are planters whose slaves occupy, on an average, seven cabins, lodging five each on
an average, including the house servants, aged invalids,
and children. The average income of planters of this
class, I reckon from similar data, to be hardly more than
that of a private of the New York Metropolitan Police
Force. It is doubtless true that cotton is cultivated profitably, that is to say, so as to produce a fair rate of interest
on the capital of the planter, on many plantations of this
class; but this can hardly be the case on an average, all
things considered.

It is not so with many plantations of the next larger
class even, but it would appear to be so with these on an
average; that is to say, where the quarters of a cotton plantation number half a score of cabins or more, which
method of classification I use that travellers may the more

‡ The average size of plantations in the South-west, including the
farms and "patches" of the non-slaveholders, is 273 acres (p. 170, C.
Compend.). Cotton plantations are not generally of less than 400 acres.

readily recall their observations of the appearance of such plantations, when I think that their recollections will confirm these calculations. There are usually other advantages for the cultivation, cleaning, pressing, shipping and disposing of cotton, by the aid of which the owner obtains a fair return for the capital invested, and may be supposed to live, if he knows how, in a moderately comfortable way. The whole number of slaveholders of this large class in all the Slave States is, according to De Bow's Compendium of the Census, 7,929, among which are all the great sugar, rice and tobacco-planters. Less than seven thousand, certainly, are cotton-planters.

A large majority of these live, when they live on their plantations at all, in districts, almost the only white population of which consists of owners and overseers of the same class of plantations with their own. The nearest other whites will be some sand-hill vagabonds, generally miles away, between whom and these planters, intercourse is neither intimate nor friendly.

It is hardly worth while to build much of a bridge for the occasional use of two families, even if they are rich. It is less worth while to go to much pains in making six miles of good road for the use of these families. A schoolhouse will hardly be built for the children of six rich men who will all live on an average six miles away from it, while private tutors or governesses can be paid by the earnings of a single fieldhand. If zeal and fluency can be obtained in a preacher coming occasionally within reach, the interest on the cost of a tolerable education is not likely to be often paid by all who would live within half a day's journey of a house of worship, which can be built anywhere in the midst of a district of large plantations. It is not necessary to multiply illustrations like these. In short, then, if all the wealth produced in a certain district is concentrated in the hands of a few men living remote from each other, it may possibly bring to the district comfortable houses, good servants, fine wines, food and furniture, tutors and governesses, horses and carriages, for these few men, but it will not bring thither good roads and bridges, it will not bring thither such means of education and of civilized comfort as are to be drawn from libraries, churches, museums, gardens, theatres, and assembly rooms; it will not bring thither local newspapers, telegraphs, and so on. It will not bring thither that subtle

force and discipline which comes of the myriad relations
with and duties to a well-constituted community which
every member of it is daily exercising, and which is the
natural unseen compensation and complement of its more
obvious constraints and inconveniences. There is, in fact,
a vast range of advantages which our civilization has made
so common to us that they are hardly thought of, of which
the people of the South are destitute. They chiefly come
from or connect with acts of co-operation, or exchanges of
service; they are therefore possessed only in communities,
and in communities where a large proportion of the people
have profitable employment. They grow, in fact, out of
employments in which the people of the community are
associated, or which they constantly give to and receive
from one another, with profit. The slaves of the South,
though often living in communities upon plantations, fail
to give or receive these advantages because the profits of
their labour are not distributed to them; the whites, from
not engaging in profitable employment. The whites are
not engaged in profitable employment, because the want
of the advantages of capital in the application of their
labour, independently of the already rich, renders the
prospective result of their labour so small that it is inoper-
ative in most, as a motive for exerting themselves further
than is necessary to procure the bare means of a rude sub-
sistence; also because common labour is so poorly re-
warded in the case of the slaves as to assume in their
minds, as it must in the minds of the slaves themselves, a
hateful aspect.

In the late act of treason of the usurpers of government
in Louisiana, the commercial demand which induces a
man to go to work is considered to be equivalent to slavery; and the fear that the election of Lincoln, by its tend
ency to open a way for the emancipation of the negroes
may lead on to a necessity for the whites to go to work, is
gravely set forth as a justification for the surrender of the
State to the conspiracy. Thus:—

"Fully convinced as we are that slavery. . . . leaves to
the *black labourer* a more considerable sum of comfort,
happiness and liberty than the inexorable labour required
from the free servants of the whole universe, and that
each emancipation of an African, without being of any
benefit to him, would necessarily *condemn to slavery* one
of our own race, etc."

To work industriously and steadily, especially under directions from another man, is, in the Southern tongue, to "work like a nigger": and, from childhood, the one thing in their condition which has made life valuable to the mass of whites has been that the niggers are yet their inferiors. It is this habit of considering themselves of a privileged class, and of disdaining something which they think beneath them, that is deemed to be the chief blessing of slavery. It is termed "high tone," "high spirit," and is supposed to give great military advantages to those who possess it. It should give advantages of some sort, for its disadvantages are inexpressibly great.

But if the poor whites were ever so industriously disposed, the rich planter has a natural distaste to exchange absolute for partial authority over the instruments by which he achieves his purpose; and the employment of free and slave labour together, is almost as difficult as working, under the same yoke, an unbroken horse and a docile ox. Again, however repugnant it may be to the self-esteem, and contrary to the habits of the rich man to treat his labourers with respect, he has to do it when employing white men, from motives of self-interest which lie below the surface, and he consequently habitually avoids arranging his affairs in such a way as will make it necessary for him to offer them employment.

It may be said that on the more profitable cotton plantations where little is raised except cotton, supplies for the maintenance of the slaves and for carrying on the work of the plantation, are largely bought which are raised elsewhere at the South; and that those who supply the commodities thus required by the cotton-planter draw from his profits which are thus distributed throughout the South, even to the non-cotton-producing States, the people of which are thus enriched. As far as all articles are concerned, in the production of which labour is a comparatively unimportant item of cost,—mules for instance, and in certain circumstances, within certain limits, swine,— this is true. But these are of small consequence. It is constantly assumed by nearly all writers on this subject that the labour directed to the cultivation of Indian corn for the necessary sustenance of slaves engaged in cotton culture must be just as profitably directed as if it were devoted to the cultivation of cotton itself. This is not true, although the Southern agricultural journals, and to a

large extent our national agriculture reports, have for
years been assuming it to be so. It is frequently spoken
of indeed, as a mystery, that the cotton-planters cannot be
induced to raise the food required by their force. The reason of it is a very simple one, namely, that in the cultivation of corn their labour must come into competition with
the free labour of the Northern States, as it does not in the
production of cotton: and the corn-raisers of the Northern
Slave States, without enjoying any monopoly of production like that of the cotton-raisers, have to share with
these, all the manifold inconveniences which result from
the scarcity of good workmen, and the necessary concen-
tration of all the effective working force of the country,
limited as it is, upon the one purpose of getting cotton.

The interests of the owners of all soil in the Slave States
which is not adapted to cotton culture, and of all capital
not engaged in cotton culture, or in supplying slaves for
it, are thus injured by the demand for cotton, they being,
in fact, forced to be co-partners in an association in which
they do not share the profits.

And as to what are commonly called the Cotton States,
if we assume that cotton cultivation is profitable only
where the production is equal to two bales for each slave
employed, it will be seen that wherever the land will not
yield as much as this, the owner of it suffers all the disadvantages of the difficulty of getting good labourers as
much as the owner of the land which produces seven or
ten bales to the hand, although none of the profits of supplying the cotton demand, which gives this extraordinary
price to labour, come to him.

According to the Census,* the whole crop of cotton is
produced on 5,000,000 acres. It could be produced, at the
rate common on good South-western plantations, on less
than half that area. The rest of the land of the Slave States,
which amounts to over 500,000,000 acres, is condemned,
so far as the tendencies I have indicated are not over-
weighed here and there by some special advantages, to
non-cultivation, except for the hand-to-mouth supply of
its people. And this is true not only of its agricultural but
of all other of its resources.

That for all practical purposes this is not an exaggerated statement is clearly enough shown by the differ-

* Compendium, p. 176.

ence in the market value of land, which as officially given by De Bow, as, notwithstanding the extraordinary demand of the world upon the cotton land, between four and five hundred per cent. higher in the Free than in the Slave States, the frontier and unsettled districts, Texas, California and the territories not being considered.

One of the grand errors out of which this rebellion has grown came from supposing that whatever nourishes wealth and gives power to an ordinary civilized community must command as much for a slave-holding community. The truth has been overlooked that the accumulation of wealth and the power of a nation are contingent not merely upon the primary value of the surplus of productions of which it has to dispose, but very largely also upon the way in which the income from its surplus is distributed and reinvested. Let a man be absent from almost any part of the North twenty years, and he is struck, on his return, by what we call the "improvements" which have been made: better buildings, churches, schoolhouses, mills, railroads, etc. In New York city alone, for instance, at least two hundred millions of dollars have been reinvested merely in an improved housing of the people; in labour-saving machinery, waterworks, gasworks, etc., as much more. It is not difficult to see where the profits of our manufacturers and merchants are. Again, go into the country, and there is no end of substantial proof of twenty years of agricultural prosperity, not alone in roads, canals, bridges, dwellings, barns and fences, but in books and furniture, and gardens, and pictures, and in the better dress and evidently higher education of the people. But where will the returning traveller see the accumulated cotton profits of twenty years in Mississippi? Ask the cotton-planter for them, and he will point in reply, not to dwellings, libraries, churches, school-houses, mills, railroads, or anything of the kind; he will point to his negroes—to almost nothing else. Negroes such as stood for five hundred dollars once, now represent a thousand dollars. We must look then in Virginia and those Northern Slave States which have the monopoly of supplying negroes for the real wealth which the sale of cotton has brought to the South. But where is the evidence of it? where anything to compare with the evidence of accumulated profits to be seen in any Free State? If certain por-

tions of Virginia have been a little improving, others un-
questionably have been deteriorating, growing shabbier,
more comfortless, less convenient. The total increase in
wealth of the population during the last twenty years
shows for almost nothing. One year's improvements of
a Free State exceed it all.

It is obvious that to the community at large, even in
Virginia, the profits of supplying negroes to meet the
wants occasioned by the cotton demand have not compen-
sated for the bar which the high cost of all sorts of human
service, which the cotton demand has also occasioned,
has placed upon all other means of accumulating wealth;
and this disadvantage of the cotton monopoly is fully experienced by the negro-breeders themselves, in respect to
everything else they have to produce or obtain.

I say all sorts of human service. What the South will
have to pay for the service of true statesmanship, the
world has now to see.

Whither the profits of cotton go, it is not my purpose,
here, to undertake to show. I will barely notice the hypo-
critical statement made for the English market as an apology for this mad crime of the slaveholders, that they are
greatly absorbed in contributions made by the planting
States to our national treasury in payment of duties on importations. The cotton-planters pay duties only on what
they consume of foreign goods. A very large part of our
duties are collected on a class of goods for which there is
almost no demand at all from the South, either directly or
indirectly—woollen and fur goods, for instance: of the
goods required for the South not a few have been practically free. The whole slave population of the South con-
sumes almost nothing imported (nor would it, while slave,
under any circumstances). The majority of the white population habitually makes use of no foreign production except chickory, which, ground with peas, they call coffee.
I have never seen reason to believe that with absolute free
trade the cotton States would take a tenth part of the value
of our present importations. And as far as I can judge from
observation of the comparative use of foreign goods at the
South and at the North, not a tenth part of our duties
have been defrayed by the South in the last twenty years.
The most indefensible protective duty we have is one
called for by the South, and which has been maintained

solely to benefit the South. Our protective system had a Southern origin; its most powerful advocates have been Southerners; and there has not been a year in the last twenty, in which it could have been maintained but for Southern votes.

CHAPTER II

SLAVERY IN ITS PROPERTY ASPECT

In a hilly part of Alabama, fifty miles north of the principal cotton-growing districts of that State, I happened to have a tradesman of the vicinity for a travelling companion, when, in passing an unusually large cluster of negro cabins, he called my attention to a rugged range of hills behind them which, he said, was a favourite lurking-ground for runaway negroes. It afforded them numerous coverts for concealment during the day, and at night the slaves of the plantation we were passing would help them to find the necessaries of existence. He had seen folks who had come here to look after niggers from plantations two hundred miles to the southward. "I suppose," said he, "'t would seem kind o' barbarous to you to see a pack of hounds after a human being?"

"Yes, it would."

"Some fellows take as much delight in it as in runnin' a fox. Always seemed to me a kind o' barbarous sport." [A pause.] "It's necessary, though."

"I suppose it is. Slavery is a custom of society which has come to us from a barbarous people, and, naturally, barbarous practices have to be employed to maintain it."

"Yes, I s'pose that's so. But niggers is generally pretty well treated, considering. Some people work their niggers too hard, that's a fact. I know a man at ——; he's a merchant there, and I have had dealings with him; he's got three plantations, and he puts the hardest overseers he can get on them. He's all the time a' buying niggers, and they say around there he works 'em to death. On these small plantations, niggers ain't very often whipped bad; but on them big plantations, they've got to use 'em hard to keep any sort of control over 'em. The overseers have to always go about armed; their life wouldn't be safe, if they didn't. As 't is, they very often get cut pretty bad." (Cutting is knifing; it may be stabbing, in south-western parlance).

He went on to describe what he had seen on some large plantations which he had visited for business purposes—indications, as he thought, in the appearance of "the people," that they were being "worked to death." "These rich men," he said, "are always bidding for the overseer who will make the most cotton; and a great many of the overseers didn't care for anything but to be able to say they've made so many bales in a year. If they make plenty of cotton, the owners never ask how many niggers they kill."

I suggested that this did not seem quite credible; a negro was a valuable piece of property. It would be foolish to use him in such a way.

"Seems they don't think so," he answered. "They are always bragging—you must have heard them—how many bales their overseer has made, or how many their plantation has made to a hand. They never think of anything else. You see, if a man did like to have his niggers taken care of, he couldn't bear to be always hearing that all the plantations round had beat his. He'd think the fault was in his overseer. The fellow who can make the most cotton always gets paid the best."

Overseers' wages were ordinarily from $200 to $600, but a real driving overseer would very often get $1,000. Sometimes they'd get $1,200 or $1,500. He heard of $2,000 being paid one fellow. A determined and perfectly relentless man—I can't recall his exact words, which were very expressive—a real devil of an overseer, would get almost any wages he'd ask; because, when it was told round that such a man had made so many bales to the hand, everybody would be trying to get him.

The man who talked in this way was a native Alabamian, ignorant, but apparently of more than ordinarily reflective habits, and he had been so situated as to have unusually good opportunities for observation. In character, if not in detail, I must say that his information was entirely in accordance with the opinions I should have been led to form from the conversations I heard by chance, from time to time, in the richest cotton districts. That his statements as to the bad management of large plantations, in respect to the waste of negro property, were not much exaggerated, I find frequent evidence in southern agricultural journals. The following is an extract from one of a series of essays published in *The Cotton Planter*, the chief object of which is to persuade planters that they are under no necessity to employ slaves exclusively in the production of cotton. The writer, Mr. M. W. Phillips, is a well-known, intelligent, and benevolent planter, who resides constantly on his estate, near Jackson, Mississippi:—

"I have known many in the rich planting portion of Mississippi especially, and others elsewhere, who, acting on the policy of the boy in the fable, who 'killed the goose for the golden egg,' accumulated property, yet among those who have relied solely on their product in land and negroes, I doubt if this be the true policy of plantation economy. With the former everything has to bend, give way to large crops of cotton, land has to be cultivated wet or dry, negroes to work, cold or hot. Large crops planted, and they must be cultivated, or done so after a manner. When disease comes about, as, for instance, cholera, pneumonia, flux, and other violent diseases, these are more subject, it seemeth to me, than others, or even if not, there is less vitality to work on, and, therefore, in like situations and similar in severity, they must sink with more certainty; or even should the animal economy rally under all these trials, the neglect consequent upon this 'cut and cover' policy must result in greater mortality. Another objection, not one-fourth of the children born are raised, and perhaps not over two-thirds are born on the place, which, under a different policy, might be expected. And this is not all: hands, and teams, and land must wear out sooner; admitting this to be only one year sooner in twenty years, or that lands and negroes are less productive at forty than at forty-two, we see a heavy loss. Is this not so? I am told of negroes not over thirty-five to forty-five, who look older than others at forty-five to fifty-five. I know a man now, not short of sixty, who might readily be taken for forty-five; another on the same place full fifty (for I have known both for twenty-eight years, and the last one for thirty-two years), who could be sold for thirty-five, and these negroes are very leniently dealt with. Others, many others, I know and have known twenty-five to thirty years, of whom I can speak of as above. As to rearing children, I can point to equally as strong cases; ay, men who are, 'as it were,' of one family, differing as much as four and eight bales in cropping, and equally as much in raising young negroes. The one scarcely paying expenses by his crop, yet in the past twenty-five years raising over seventy-five to a hundred negroes, the other buying more than raised, and yet not as many as the first.

"I regard the 'just medium' to be the correct point. Labour is conducive to health; a healthy woman will rear most children. I favour good and fair work, yet not over-worked so as to tax the animal economy, that the woman cannot rear healthy children, nor should the father be over-wrought, that his vital powers be at all infringed upon.

"If the policy be adopted, to make an improvement in land visible, to raise the greatest number of healthy children, to make an abundance of provision, to rear a portion at least of work horses, rely on it we will soon find by our tax list that our country is improving.   *   *   *

"Brethren of the South, we must change our policy. *Overseers are not interested in raising children, or meat, in improving land, or improving productive qualities of seed, or animals. Many of them do not care whether property has depreciated or improved, so they have made a crop [of cotton] to boast of.*

"As to myself, I care not who has the credit of making crops at Log Hall; and I would prefer that an overseer, who has been one of my family for a year or two, or more, should be benefited; but this thing is to be known and well understood. I plant such fields in such crops as I see fit; I plant acres in corn, cotton, oats, potatoes, etc., as I select, and the general policy of rest, cultivation, etc., must be preserved which I lay down. A self-willed overseer may fraudulently change somewhat in the latter, by not carrying out orders—that I cannot help. What I have written, I have written, and think I can substantiate."

From the *Southern Agriculturist*, vol. iv., page 317:—

"OVERSEERS.

*   *   *   "When they seek a place, they rest their claims entirely on the number of bags they have heretofore made to the hand, and generally the employer unfortunately recognizes the justice of such claims.

"No wonder, then, that the overseer desires to have entire control of the plantation. No wonder he opposes all experiments, or, if they are persisted in, neglects them; *presses everything at the end of the lash; pays no attention to the sick, except to keep them in the field as long as possible; and drives them out again at the first moment, and forces sucklers and breeders to the utmost. He has no other interest than to make a big cotton crop.* And if this does not please you, and induce you to increase his wages, he knows men it will please, and secure him a situation with."

From the Columbia *South Carolinian:*—

*   *   *   "Planters may be divided into two great classes, viz., those who attend to their business, and those

who do not. And this creates corresponding classes of
overseers. The planter who does not manage his own
business must, of course, surrender everything into the
hands of his overseer. Such a planter usually rates the
merits of the overseer exactly in proportion to the number
of bags of cotton he makes, and of course the overseer
cares for nothing but to make a large crop. To him it is of
no consequence that the old hands are worked down, or
the young ones overstrained; that the breeding women
miscarry, and the sucklers lose their children; that the
mules are broken down, the plantation tools destroyed,
the stock neglected, and the lands ruined: *so that he has
the requisite number of cotton bags, all is overlooked;* he
is re-employed at an advanced salary, and his reputation
increased. Everybody knows that by such a course, a crop
may be increased by the most inferior overseer, in any
given year, unless his predecessors have so entirely exhausted the resources of the plantation, that there is no
part of the capital left which can be wrought up into current income.   °   °   °   Having once had the sole management of a plantation, and imbibed the idea that the
only test of good planting is to make a large crop of cotton,
an overseer becomes worthless. He will no longer obey
orders; he will not stoop to details; he scorns all improvements, and *will not* adopt any other plan of planting than
simply to work lands, negroes, and mules to the top of
their bent, which necessarily proves fatal to every employer
who will allow it.

"It seems scarcely credible, that any man owning a
plantation will so abandon it and his people on it entirely
to a hireling, no matter what his confidence in him is.
Yet there are numbers who do it habitually; and I have
even known overseers to stipulate that their employers
should not give any order, nor interfere in any way with
their management of the plantation. There are also some
proprietors of considerable property and pretension to being
planters, who give their overseer a proportion of the crop
for his wages; thus bribing him by the strongest induce-
ments of self-interest, to overstrain and work down everything committed to his charge.

"No planter, who attends to his own business, can dispense with agents and sub-agents. It is impossible, on a
plantation of any size, for the proprietor to attend to all
the details, many of which are irksome and laborious, and
he requires more intelligence to assist him than slaves
usually possess. To him, therefore, a good overseer is a
blessing. But an overseer who would answer the views of
such a planter is most difficult to find. The men engaged
in that occupation who combine the most intelligence,

industry, and character, are allured into the service of those who place all power in their hands, and are ultimately spoiled."

An English traveler writes to the London *Daily News* from Mississippi (1857):—

"On crossing the Big Block river, I left the sandhills and began to find myself in the rich loam of the valley of the Mississippi. The plantations became larger, the clearings more numerous and extensive, and the roads less hilly, but worse. Along the Yazoo river one meets with some of the richest soil in the world, and some of the largest crops of cotton in the Union. My first night in that region was passed at the house of a planter who worked but few hands, was a fast friend of slavery, and yet drew for my benefit one of the most mournful pictures of a slave's life I have ever met with. He said, and I believe truly, that the negroes of small planters are, on the whole, well treated, or at least as well as the owners can afford to treat them. Their master not unfrequently works side by side with them in the fields. * * * But on the large plantations, where the business is carried on by an overseer, and everything is conducted with military strictness and discipline, he described matters as being widely different. *The future of the overseer depends altogether on the quantity of cotton he is able to make up for the market.* Whether the owner be resident or nonresident, if the plantation be large, and a great number of hands be employed upon it, the overseer gets credit for a large crop, and blame for a small one. His professional reputation depends in a great measure upon the number of bales or hogsheads he is able to produce, and neither his education nor his habits are such as to render it likely that he would allow any consideration for the negroes to stand in the way of his advancing it. His interest is to get as much work out of them as they can possibly perform. His skill consists in knowing exactly how hard they may be driven without incapacitating them for future exertion. The larger the plantation the less chance there is, of course, or the owner's softening the rigour of the overseer, or the sterness of discipline by personal interference. So, as Mr. H ——— said, a vast mass of the slaves pass their lives, from the moment they are able to go afield in the picking season till they drop worn out into the grave, in incessant labour, in all sorts of weather, at all seasons of the year, without any other change or relaxation than is furnished by sickness, without the smallest hope of any improvement either in their condition, in their food, or in their clothing, which are of the plainest and coarsest kind, and indebted solely to the forbearance or good temper of the overseer for exemption from terrible physical suffering. They are rung to bed at nine o'clock, almost immediately after bolting the food which they often have to cook after coming home from their day's labour, and are rung out of bed at four or five in the morning. The interval is one long round of toil. Life has no sunny spots for them. Their only refuge or consolation in this world is in their own stupidity and grossness. The nearer they are to the beast, the happier they are likely to be. Any mental or moral rise is nearly sure to bring unhappiness with it."

The same gentleman writes from Columbus:—

"One gets better glimpses of the real condition of the negroes from conversations one happens to overhear than from what is told to one's-self—above all, when one is known to be a stranger, and particularly an Englishman. The cool way in which you hear the hanging of niggers, the shooting of niggers, and the necessity for severe discipline among niggers talked of in bar-rooms, speaks volumes as to the exact state of the case. A negro was shot when running away, near Greensboro, a small town on my road, the day before I passed through, by a man who had received instructions from the owner to take him alive, and shoot him if he resisted. I heard the subject discussed by some 'loafers' in the bar, while getting my horse fed, and I found, to my no small—I do not know whether to say horror or amusement—that the point in dispute was not the degree of moral guilt incurred by the murderer, but the degree of loss and damage for which he had rendered himself liable to the owner of the slave in departing from the letter of his commission. One of the group summed up the arguments on both sides, by exclaiming, 'Well, this shootin' of niggers should be put a stop to, that's a fact.' The obvious inference to be deduced from this observation was, that a 'nigger shootin'' was a slight contravention of police regulations—a little of which might be winked at, but which, in this locality, had been carried to such an extent as to call for the interference of the law."

I do not think that I have ever seen the sudden death of a negro noticed in a Southern newspaper, or heard it referred to in conversation, that the loss of property, rather than the extinction of life, was not the evident occasion of interest. Turning over several Southern papers at this moment, I fall at once upon these examples:—

"We are informed that a negro man, the property of Mr. William Mays, of this city, was killed last Thursday by a youth, the son of Mr. William Payne, of Campbell county. The following are the circumstances, as we have received them. Two sons of Mr. Payne were shooting pigeons on the plantation of Mr. Mays, about twenty miles from this place, and went to the tobacco-house, where the overseer and hands were housing tobacco; one of the boys had a string of pigeons and the other had none. On reaching the house, the negro who was killed asked the boy who had no pigeons, 'where his were.' He replied that he killed none, but could kill him (the negro), and raised his gun and fired. The load took effect in the head, and caused death in a few hours. *The negro was a valuable one. Mr. Mays had refused* $1,200 *for him.*"—*Lynchburg Virginian.*

"*A valuable negro boy, the property of* W. A. Phipps, living in the upper end of this county, was accidentally drowned in the Holston river a few days ago."—*Rogersville Times.*

"Mr. Tilgham Cobb's barn at Bedford, Va., was set fire to by lightning on Friday, the 11th, and consumed. Two negroes and three horses perished in the flames."— *New Orleans Daily Crescent.*

I have repeated these accounts, not to convey to the reader's mind the impression that slaves are frequently shot by their masters, which would be, no doubt, a mistaken inference, but to show in what manner I was made to feel, as I was very strongly in my journey, that what we call the sacredness of human life, together with a great range of kindred instincts, scarcely attaches at all, with most white men, to the slaves, and also in order to justify the following observation:—that I found the lives and the comfort of negroes, in the rich cotton-planting districts especially, habitually regarded, by all classes, much more from a purely pecuniary point of view than I had ever before supposed they could be; and yet that, as property, negro life and negro vigour were generally much less carefully economized than I had always before imagined them to be.

As I became familiar with the circumstances, I saw reasons for this, which, in looking from a distance, or through the eyes of travellers, I had not been able adequately to appreciate. I will endeavour to state them:—

It is difficult to handle simply as property, a creature possessing human passions and human feelings, however debased and torpid the condition of that creature may be; while, on the other hand, the absolute necessity of dealing with property as a thing, greatly embarrassed a man in any attempt to treat it as a person. And it is the natural result of his complicated state of things, that the system of slave-management is irregular, ambiguous, and contradictory; that it is never either consistently humane or consistently economical.

As a general rule, the larger the body of negroes on a plantation or estate, the more completely are they treated as mere property, and in accordance with a policy calculated to insure the largest pecuniary returns. Hence, in part, the greater proportionate profit of such plantations, and the tendency which everywhere prevails in the planting districts to the absorption of small, and the augmentation of large estates. It may be true, that among the wealthier slave-owners there is oftener a humane disposition, a better judgment, and a greater ability to deal with their dependents indulgently and bountifully, but the effects of this disposition are chiefly felt, even on those plantations where the proprietor resides permanently, among the slaves employed about the house and stables, and perhaps a few old favourites in the quarters. It is more than balanced by the difficulty of acquiring a personal interest in the units of a large body of slaves, and an acquaintance with the individual characteristics of each. The treatment of the mass must be reduced to a system, the ruling idea of which will be, to enable one man to force into the same channel of labour the muscles of a large number of men of various and often conflicting wills.

The chief difficulty is to overcome their great aversion to labour. They have no objection to eating, drinking, and resting, when necessary, and no general disinclination to receive instruction. If a man own many slaves, therefore, the faculty which he values highest, and pays most for, in an overseer, is that of making them work. Any fool could see that they were properly supplied with food, clothing, rest, and religious instruction.

The labourers we see in towns, at work on railroads and steamboats, about stations and landings; the menials of our houses and hotels, are less respectable, moral, and intelligent that the great majority of the whole labouring class of the North. The traveller at the South has to learn that there the reverse is the case to a degree which can hardly be sufficiently estimated. I have been obliged to think that many amiable travellers who have received impressions with regard to the condition of the slaves very different from mine, have failed to make a sufficient allowance for this. The rank-and-file plantation negroes are not to be readily made acquaintance with by chance or through letters of introduction.

I have described in detail, in former chapters, two large plantations, which were much the best in respect to the happiness of the negroes, of all that I saw in the South. I am now about to describe what I judged to be the most profitable estate that I visited. In saying this I do not compare it with others noticed in this chapter, my observations of which were too superficial to warrant a comparison. It was situated upon a tributary of the Mississippi, and accessible only by occasional steamboats; even this mode of communication being frequently interrupted at low stages of the rivers. The slaves upon it formed about one twentieth of the whole population of the county, in which the blacks considerably outnumber the whites. At the time of my visit, the owner was sojourning upon it, with his family and several invited guests, but his usual residence was upon a small plantation, of little productive value, situated in a neighbourhood somewhat noted for the luxury and hospitality of its citizens, and having a daily mail, and direct railroad and telegraphic communication with New York. This was, if I am not mistaken, his second visit in five years.

The property consisted of four adjoining plantations, each with its own negro-cabins, stables, and overseer, and each worked to a great extent independently of the others, but all contributing their crop to one gin-house and warehouse, and all under the general superintendence of a bailiff or manager, who constantly resided upon the estate, and in the absence of the owner, had vice-regal power over the overseers, controlling, so far as he thought fit, the economy of all the plantations.

The manager was himself a gentleman of good education, generous and poetic in temperament, and possessing a capacity for the enjoyment of nature and a happiness in the bucolic life, unfortunately rare with Americans. I found him a delightful companion, and I have known no man with whose natural tastes and feelings I have felt, on so short acquaintance, a more hearty sympathy. The gang of toiling negroes to him, however, was as essential an element of the poetry of nature as flocks of peaceful sheep and herds of lowing kine, and he would no more appreciate the aspect in which an Abolitionist would see them, than would Virgil have honoured the feelings of a vegetarian, sighing at the sight of flocks and herds destined to feed the depraved appetite of the carnivorous savage of modern civilization. The overseers were superior to most of their class, and, with one exception, frank, honest, temperate, and industrious, but their feelings toward negroes were such as naturally result from their occupation. They were all married, and lived with their families, each in a cabin or cottage, in the hamlet of the slaves of which he had especial charge. Their wages varied from $500 to $1,000 a year each.

These five men, each living more than a mile distant from either of the others, were the only white men on the estate, and the only others within several miles of them were a few skulking vagabonds. Of course, to secure their own personal safety and to efficiently direct the labour of such a large number of ignorant, indolent, and vicious negroes, rules, or rather habits and customs, of discipline, were necessary, which would in particular cases be liable to operate unjustly and cruelly. It is apparent, also, that, as the testimony of negroes against them would not be received as evidence in court, that there was very little probability that any excessive severity would be restrained by fear of the law. A provision of the law intended to secure a certain privilege to slaves, was indeed disregarded under my own observation, and such infraction of the law was confessedly customary with one of the overseers, and was permitted by the manager, for the reason that it seemed to him to be, in a certain degree, justifiable and expedient under the circumstances, and because he did not like to interfere unnecessarily in such matters.

In the main, the negroes appeared to be well taken care of and abundantly supplied with the necessaries of vigorous physical existence. A large part of them lived in commodious and well-built cottages, with broad galleries in front, so that each family of five had two rooms on the lower floor, and a loft. The remainder lived in log huts, small and mean in appearance, but those of their overseers were little better, and preparations were being made to replace all of these by neat boarded cottages. Each family had a fowl-house and hog-sty (constructed by the negroes themselves), and kept fowls and swine, feeding the latter during the summer on weeds and fattening them in the autumn on corn, *stolen* (this was mentioned to me by the overseers as if it were a matter of course) from their master's corn-fields. I several times saw gangs of them eating the dinner which they had brought, each man for himself, to the field, and observed that they generally had plenty, often more than they could eat, of bacon, corn-bread, and molasses. The allowance of food is weighed and measured under the eye of the manager by the drivers, and distributed to the head of each family weekly: consisting of —for each person, 3 pounds of pork, 1 peck of meal; and from January to July, 1 quart of molasses. Monthly, in addition, 1 pound tobacco, and 4 pints salt. No drink is ever served but water, except after unusual exposure, or to ditchers working in water, who get a glass of whisky at night. All hands cook for themselves after work at night, or whenever they please between nightfall and daybreak, each family in its own cabin. Each family has a garden, the products of which, together with eggs, fowls, and bacon, they frequently sell, or use in addition to their regular allowance of food. Most of the families buy a barrel of flour every year. The manager endeavours to encourage this practice; and that they may spend their money for flour instead of liquor, he furnishes it to them at rather less than what it costs him at wholesale. There are many poor whites within a few miles who will always sell liquor to the negroes, and encourage them to steal, to obtain the means to buy it of them. These poor whites are always spoken of with anger by the overseers, and they each have a standing offer of much more than the intrinsic value of their land, from the manager, to induce them to move away.

The negroes also obtain a good deal of game. They set traps for raccoons, rabbits, and turkeys; and I once heard the stock-tender complaining that he had detected one of the vagabond whites stealing a turkey which had been caught in his pen. I several times partook of game, while on the plantation, that had been purchased of the negroes. The stock-tender, an old negro, whose business it was to ride about in the woods and keep an eye on the stock cattle that were pastured in them, and who was thus likely to know where the deer ran, had an ingenious way of supplying himself with venison. He lashed a scythe blade or butcher's knife to the end of a pole so that it formed a lance; this he set near a fence or fallen tree which obstructed a path in which the deer habitually ran, and the deer in leaping over the obstacle would leap directly on the knife. In this manner he had killed two deer the week before my visit.

The manager sent to him for some of this venison for his own use, and justified himself to me for not paying for it on the ground that the stock-tender had undoubtedly taken time which really belonged to his owner to set his spear. Game taken by the field-hands was not looked upon in the same light, because it must have been got at night when they were excused from labour for their owner.

The first morning I was on the estate, while at breakfast with the manager, an old negro woman came into the room and said to him, "Dat gal's bin bleedin' agin' dis mornin'."

"How much did she bleed?"

"About a pint, sir."

"Very well; I'll call and see her after breakfast."

"I come up for some sugar of lead, masser; I gin her some powdered alum 'fore I come away."

"Very well; you can have some."

After breakfast the manager invited me to ride with him on his usual daily round of inspection through the plantations.

On reaching the nearest "quarters," we stopped at a house, a little larger than the ordinary cabins, which was called the loom-house, in which a dozen negroes were at work making shoes, and manufacturing coarse cotton stuff for negro clothing. One of the hands so employed was insane, and most of the others were cripples, invalids with chronic complaints, or unfitted by age, or some infirmity, for field-work.

From this we went to one of the cabins, where we found the sick woman who had been bleeding at the lungs, with the old nurse in attendance upon her. The manager examined and prescribed for her in a kind manner. When we came out he asked the nurse if any one else was sick.

"Oney dat woman Carline."

"What do you think is the matter with her?"

"Well, I don't tink dere's anyting de matter wid her, masser; I mus' answer you for true, I don't tink anyting de matter wid her, oney she's a little sore from dat whippin' she got."

We went to another cabin and entered a room where a woman lay on a bed, groaning. It was a dingy, comfortless room, but a musquito bar, much patched and very dirty, covered the bed. The manager asked the woman several times what was the matter, but could get no distinct reply. She appeared to be suffering great pain. The manager felt her pulse and looked at her tongue, and after making a few more inquiries, to which no intelligible reply was given, told her he did not believe she was ill at all. At this the woman's groans redoubled. "I have heard of your tricks," continued the manager; "you had a chill when I came to see you yesterday morning; you had a chill when the mistress came here, and you had a chill when the master came. I never knew a chill to last the whole day. So you'll just get up now and go to the field, and if you don't work smart, you'll get a dressing; do you hear?"

We then left. The manager said that he rarely—almost never—had occasion to employ a physician for the people. Never for accouchements; the women, from their labour in the field, were not subject to the difficulty, danger, and pain which attended women of the better classes in giving birth to their offspring. (I do not suppose that there was a physician within a day's journey of the plantations.)

Near the first quarters we visited there was a large blacksmith's and wheelwright's shop, in which a number of mechanics were at work. Most of them, as we rode up, were eating their breakfast, which they warmed at their fires. Within and around the shop there were some fifty ploughs which they were putting in order. The manager inspected the work, found some of it faulty, sharply reprimanded the workmen for not getting on faster, and threatened one of them with a whipping for not paying closer attention to the directions which had been given him.

The overseer of this plantation rode up while we were at the shop, and in a free and easy style, reported to the manager how all his hands were employed. There were so many at this and so many at that, and they had done so much since yesterday. "There's that girl, Caroline," said the manager; "she's not sick, and I told her she must go to work; put her to the hoeing; there's nothing the matter with her, except she's sore with the whipping she got.

You must go and get her out." A woman passing at the time, the manager told her to go and tell Caroline she must get up and go to work, or the overseer would come and start her. She returned in a few minutes, and reported that Caroline said she could not get up. The overseer and manager rode toward the cabin, but before they reached it, the girl, who had probably been watching us from the window, came out and went to the field with her hoe. They then returned to me and continued their conversation. Just before we left the overseer, he said, "I think that girl who ran away last week was in her cabin last night." The manager told me, as we rode on, that the people often ran away after they have been whipped, or something else had happened to make them angry. They hide in the swamp, and come in to the cabins at night to get food. They seldom remain away more than a fortnight, and when they come in they are whipped. The woman, Caroline, he said, had been delivered of a dead child about six weeks before, and had been complaining and getting rid of work ever since. She was the laziest woman on the estate. This shamming illness gave him the most disagreeable duty he had to perform. Negroes were famous for it. "If it was not for her bad character," he continued, "I should fear to make her go to work to-day; but her pulse is steady, and her tongue perfectly smooth. We have to be sharp with them; if we were not, every negro on the estate would be a-bed."

We rode on to where the different gangs of labourers were at work, and inspected them one after another. I observed, as we were looking at one of the gangs, that they were very dirty. "Negroes are the filthiest people in the world," said the manager; "there are some of them who would not keep clean twenty-four hours at a time if you gave them thirty suits a year." I asked him if there were any rules to maintain cleanliness. There were not, but sometimes the negroes were told at night that any one who came into the field the next morning without being clean would be whipped. This gave no trouble to those who were habitually clean, while it was in itself a punishment to those who were not, as they were obliged to spend the night in washing.

They were furnished with two suits of summer, and one of winter clothing each year. Besides which, most of them got presents of holiday finery (calico dresses, handkerchiefs, etc.), and purchased more for themselves, at Christmas. One of the drivers now in the field had on a uniform coat of an officer of artillery. After the Mexican war, a great deal of military clothing was sold at auction in New Orleans, and much of it was bought by the planters at a low price, and given to their negroes, who were greatly pleased with it.

Each overseer regulated the hours of work on his own plantation. I saw the negroes at work before sunrise and after sunset. At about eight o'clock they were allowed to stop for breakfast, and again about noon, to dine. The length of these rests was at the discretion of the overseer or drivers, usually, I should say, from half an hour to an hour. There was no rule.

The number of hands directed by each overseer was considerably over one hundred. The manager thought it would be better economy to have a white man over every fifty hands, but the difficulty of obtaininng trustworthy overseers prevented it. Three of those he then had were the best he had ever known. He described the great majority as being passionate, careless, inefficient men, generally intemperate, and totally unfitted for the duties of the position. The best overseers, ordinarily, are young men, the sons of small planters, who take up the business temporarily, as a means of acquiring a little capital with which to purchase negroes for themselves.

The ploughs at work, both with single and double mule teams, were generally held by women, and very well held, too. I watched with some interest for any indication that their sex unfitted them for the occupation. Twenty of them were ploughing together, with double teams and heavy ploughs. They were superintended by a negro man who carried a whip, which he frequently cracked at them, permitting no dawdling or delay at the turning; and they twitched their ploughs around on the head-land, jerking their reins, and yelling to their mules, with apparent ease, energy, and rapidity. Throughout the South-west the negroes, as a rule, appear to be worked much harder than in the Eastern and Northern Slave States. I do not think they accomplish as much in the same time as agricultural labourers at the North usually do, but they certainly labour much harder, and more unremittingly. They are constantly and steadily driven up to their work, and the stupid, plodding, machine-like manner in which they labour, is painful to witness. This was especially the case with the hoe-gangs. One of them numbered nearly two hundred hands (for the force of two plantations was working together), moving across the field in parallel lines, with a considerable degree of precision. I repeatedly rode through the lines at a canter, with other horsemen, often coming upon them suddenly, without producing the smallest change or interruption in the dogged action of the labourers, or causing one of them, so far as I could see, to lift an eye from the ground. I had noticed the same thing with smaller numbers before, but here, considering that I was a stranger, and that strangers could but very rarely visit the plantation, it amazed me very much. I think it told a more painful story than any I had ever heard, of the cruelty of slavery. It was emphasized by a tall and powerful negro who walked to and fro in the rear of the line, frequently cracking his whip, and calling out in the surliest manner, to one and another, "Shove your hoe, there! shove your hoe!" But I never saw him strike any one with the whip.

The whip was evidently in constant use, however. There were no rules on the subject, that I learned; the overseers and drivers punished the negroes whenever they deemed it necessary, and in such manner, and with such severity, as they thought fit. "If you don't work faster," or "If you don't work better," or "If you don't recollect what I tell you, I will have you flogged," I often heard. I said to one of the overseers, "It must be disagreeable to have to punish them as much as you do?" "Yes, it would be to those who are not used to it—but it's my business, and I think nothing of it. Why, sir, I wouldn't mind killing a nigger more than I would a dog." I asked if he had ever killed a negro? "Not quite that," he said, but overseers were often obliged to. Some negroes are determined never to let a white man whip them, and will resist you, when you attempt it; of course you must kill them in that case.* Once a negro, whom he was about to whip in the field, struck at his head with a hoe. He parried the blow with his whip,

---

* "On Monday last, as James Allen (overseer on Prothro's plantation at St. Maurice) was punishing a negro boy named Jack, for stealing hogs, the boy ran off before the overseer had chastised him sufficiently for the offence. He was immediately pursued by the overseer, who succeeded in catching him, when the negro drew a knife and inflicted a terrible gash in his abdomen. The wounds of the overseer were dressed by Dr. Stephens, who pronounces it a very critical case, but still entertains hope of his recovery. '—*Nichitoches Chronicle.*

and, drawing a pistol, tried to shoot him; but the pistol missing fire, he rushed in and knocked him down with the butt of it. At another time, a negro whom he was punishing insulted and threatened him. He went to the house for his gun, and as he was returning, the negro, thinking he would be afraid of spoiling so valuable a piece of property by firing, broke for the woods. He fired at once, and put six buck-shot into his hips. He always carried a bowie-knife, but not a pistol unless he anticipated some unusual act of insubordination. He always kept a pair of pistols ready loaded over the mantel-piece, however, in case they should be needed. It was only when he first came upon a plantation that he ever had much trouble. A great many overseers were unfit for their business, and too easy and slack with the negroes. When he succeeded such a man, he had hard work for a time to break the negroes in; but it did not take long to teach them their place. His conversation on the subject was exactly like what I have heard said, again and again, by northern shipmasters and officers, with regard to seamen.

I happened to see the severest corporal punishment of a negro that I witnessed at the South while visiting this estate. I suppose, however, that punishment equally severe is common; in fact, it must be necessary to the mantenance of adequate discipline on every large plantation. It is much more necessary than on shipboard, because the opportunities of hiding away and shirking labour, and of wasting and injuring the owner's property without danger to themselves, are far greater in the case of the slaves than in that of the sailors, but, above all, because there is no real moral obligation on the part of the negro to do what is demanded of him. The sailor performs his duty in obedience to a voluntary contract; the slave is in an involuntary servitude. The manner of the overseer who inflicted the punishment, and his subsequent conversation with me about it, indicated that it was by no means unusual in severity. I had accidentally encountered him, and he was showing me his plantation. In going from one side of it to the other, we had twice crossed a deep gully, at the bottom of which was a thick covert of brushwood. We were crossing it a third time, and had nearly passed through the brush, when the overseer suddenly stopped his horse exclaiming, "What's that? Hallo! who are you, there?"

It was a girl lying at full length on the ground at the bottom of the gully, evidently intending to hide herself from us in the bushes.

"Who are you, there?"

"Sam's Sall, sir."

"What are you skulking there for?"

The girl half rose, but gave no answer.

"Have you been here all day?"

"No, sir."

"How did you get here?"

The girl made no reply.

"Where have you been all day?"

The answer was unintelligible.

After some further questioning, she said her father accidentally locked her in, when he went out in the morning.

"How did you manage to get out?"

"Pushed a plank off, sir, and crawled out."

The overseer was silent for a moment, looking at the girl, and then said, "That won't do; come out here." The girl arose at once, and walked towards him. She was about eighteen years of age. A bunch of keys hung at her waist, which the overseer espied, and he said, "Your father locked you in; but you have got the keys." After a little hesitation, she replied that these were the keys of some other locks; her father had the door-key.

Whether her story were true or false, could have been ascertained in two minutes by riding on to the gang with which her father was at work, but the overseer had made up his mind.

"That won't do;" said he, "get down." The girl knelt on the ground; he got off his horse, and holding him with his left hand, struck her thirty or forty blows across the shoulders with his tough, flexible, "raw-hide" whip (a terrible instrument for the purpose). They were well laid on, at arm's length, but with no appearance of angry excitement on the part of the overseer. At every stroke the girl winced and exclaimed, "Yes, sir!" or "Ah, sir!" or "Please, sir!" not groaning or screaming. At length he stopped and said, "Now tell me the truth." The girl repeated the same story. "You have not got enough yet," said he; "pull up your clothes—lie down." The girl without any hesitation, without a word or look of remonstrance or entreaty, drew closely all her garments under her shoulders, and lay down upon the ground with her face toward the overseer, who continued to flog her with the raw hide, across her naked loins and thighs, with as much strength as before. She now shrunk away from him, not rising, but writhing, grovelling, and screaming, "Oh, don't sir! oh, please stop, master! please, sir! please, sir! oh, that's enough, master! oh, Lord! oh, master, master! oh, God master do stop! oh, God, master! oh, God, master!"

A young gentleman of fifteen was with us; he had ridden in front, and now, turning on his horse, looked back with an expression only of impatience at the delay. It was the first time I had ever seen a woman flogged. I had seen a man cudgelled and beaten, in the heat of passion, before, but never flogged with a hundredth part of the severity used in this case. I glanced again at the perfectly passionless but rather grim business-like face of the overseer, and again at the young gentleman, who had turned away; if not indifferent he had evidently not the faintest sympathy with my emotion. Only my horse chafed. I gave him rein and spur and we plunged into the bushes and scrambled fiercely up the steep acclivity. The screaming yells and the whip strokes had ceased when I reached the top of the bank. Choking, sobbing, spasmodic groans only were heard. I rode on to where the road, coming diagonally up the ravine, ran out upon the cottonfield. My young companion met me there, and immediately afterward the overseer. He laughed as he joined us, and said:

"She meant to cheat me out of a day's work, and she has done it, too."

"Did you succeed in getting another story from her?" I asked, as soon as I could trust myself to speak.

"No; she stuck to it."

"Was it not perhaps true?"

"Oh no, sir; she slipped out of the gang when they were going to work, and she's been dodging about all day, going from one place to another as she saw me coming. She saw us crossing there a little while ago, and thought we had gone to the quarters, but we turned back so quick, we came into the gully before she knew it, and she could do nothing but lie down in the bushes."

"I suppose they often slip off so."

"No, sir; I never had one do so before—not like this; they often run away to the woods, and are gone some time, but I never had a dodge-off like this before."

"Was it necessary to punish her so severely?"

"Oh yes, sir," (laughing again.) "If I hadn't, she would have done the same thing again to-morrow, and half the people on the plantation would have followed her example. Oh, you've no idea how lazy these niggers are; you Northern people don't know anything about it. They'd never do any work at all if they were not afraid of being whipped."

We soon afterward met an old man, who, on being closely questioned, said that he had seen the girl leave the gang as they went to work after dinner. It appeared that she had been at work during the forenoon, but at dinner-time the gang was moved, and as it passed through the gully she slipped out. The driver had not missed her. The overseer said that when he first took charge of this plantation, the negroes ran away a great deal—they disliked him so much. They used to say, 'twas hell to be on his place; but after a few months they got used to his ways, and liked him better than any of the rest. He had not had any run away now for some time. When they ran away they would generally return within a fortnight. If many of them went off, or if they stayed out long, he would make the rest of the force work Sundays, or deprive them of some of their usual privileges until the runaways returned. The negroes on the plantation could always bring them in if they chose to do so. They depended on them for their food, and they had only to stop the supplies to oblige them to surrender.

Accepting the position of the overseer, I knew that his method was right, but it was a red-hot experience to me, and has ever since been a fearful thing in my memory. Strangely so, I sometimes think, but I suppose the fact that the delicate and ingenuous lad who was with me betrayed not even the slightest flush of shame, and that I constrained myself from the least expression of feeling of any kind, made the impression in my brain the more intense and lasting.

Sitting near a gang with an overseer and the manager, the former would occasionally call out to one and another by name, in directing or urging their labour. I asked if he knew them all by name. He did, but I found that the manager did not know one in five of them. The overseer said he generally could call most of the negroes on a plantation by their names in two weeks after he came to it, but it was rather difficult to learn them on account of there being so many of the same name, distinguished from each other by a prefix. "There's a Big Jim here, and a Little Jim, and Eliza's Jim, and there's Jim Bob, and Jim Clarisy."

"What's Jim Clarisy?—how does he get that name?"

"He's Clarisy's child, and Bob is Jim Bob's father. That fellow ahead there, with the blue rag on his head, his name is Swamp; he always goes by that name, but his real name is Abraham, I believe; is it not, Mr. [Manager]?"

"His name is Swamp on the plantation register—that's all I know of him."

"I believe his name is Abraham," said the overseer; "he told me so. He was bought of Judge ——, he says, and he told me his master called him Swamp because he ran away so much. He is the worst runaway on the place."

I inquired about the increase of the negroes on the estate, and the manager having told me the number of deaths and births the previous year, which gave a net increase of four per cent.—on Virginia estates it is often twenty per cent.—I asked if the negroes began to have children at a very early age. "Sometimes at sixteen," said the manager. "Yes, and at fourteen," said the overseer; "that girl's had a child"—pointing to a girl that did not appear older than fourteen. "Is she married?" "No." "You see," said the manager, "negro girls are not remarkable for chastity; their habits indeed rather hinder them from having children. They'd have them younger than they do, if they would marry or live with but one man, sooner than they do.* They often do not have children till they are twenty-five years old." "Are those who are married true to each other?" I asked. The overseer laughed heartily at the idea, and described a disgusting state of things. Women were almost common property, though sometimes the men were not all inclined to acknowledge it; for when I asked: "Do you not try to discourage this?" the overseer answered: "No, not unless they quarrel." "They get jealous and quarrel among themselves sometimes about it," the manager explained, "or come to the overseer and complain, and he has them punished." "Give all hands a

---

* Mr. Russell makes an observation to the same effect with regard to the Cuba plantations, p. 230. On these large cotton plantations there are frequently more men than women, men being bought in preference to women for cotton picking.

The contrary is usually the case on the small plantations, where the profits of breeding negroes are constantly in view.

damned good hiding," said the overseer. "You punish for
adultery, then, but not for fornication?" "Yes," answered
the manager, but "No," insisted the overseer, "we punish
them for quarrelling; if they don't quarrel I don't mind
anything about it, but if it makes a muss, I give all four of
'em a warning."

Riding through a large gang of hoers, with two of the
overseers, I observed that a large proportion of them appeared to be thorough-bred Africans. Both of them
thought that the "real black niggers" were about three-
fourths of the whole number, and that this would hold
as an average on Mississippi and Louisiana plantations.
One of them pointed out a girl—"That one is pure white;
you see her hair?" (It was straight and sandy.) "She is
the only one we have got." It was not uncommon, he
said, to see slaves so white that they could not be easily
distinguished from pure-blooded whites. He had never
been on a plantation before, that had not more than one
on it.* "Now," said I, "if that girl should dress herself
well, and run away, would she be suspected of being a
slave?" (I could see nothing myself by which to distinguish her, as she passed, from an ordinary poor white
girl.)

---

* "A woman, calling herself Violet Ludlow, was arrested a few days
ago, and committed to jail, on the supposition that she was a runaway
slave belonging to A. M. Mobley, of Upshur county, Texas, who had
offered through our columns a reward of fifty dollars for her apprehension. On being brought before a justice of the peace, she stated that
she was a white woman, and claimed her liberty. She states that she is a
daughter of Jeremiah Ludlow, of Pike county, Alabama, and was brought
from that country in 1853, by George Cope, who emigrated to Texas.
After arriving in Texas, she was sold by George Cope to a Doctor Terry,
in Upshur county, Texas, and was soon after sold by him to a Mrs.
Hagen, or Hagens, of the same county. Violet says that she protested
against each sale made of her, declaring herself a free woman. She
names George Gilmer, Thomas Rogers, John Garret, and others, residents
of Pike county, Alabama, as persons who have known her from infancy
as the daughter of one Jeremiah Ludlow and Rene Martin, a widow at
the time of her birth, and as being a free white woman, and her father
a free white man. Violet is about instituting legal proceedings for her
freedom."—*Shreveport Southwestern.*

"Some days since, a woman named Pelasgie was arrested as a fugitive
slave, who has lived for more than twelve years in this city as a free
woman. She was so nearly white that few could detect any traces of her
African descent. She was arrested at the instance of a man named Riley,
who claimed her as belonging to an estate of which he is heir-at-law.
She was conveyed to the First District guardhouse for safe keeping, and
while there she stated to Acting Recorder Filleul that she was free, had
never belonged to Riley, and had been in the full and unquestioned enjoyment of her freedom in this city for the above-mentioned period. She
also stated that she had a house, well furnished, which she was in the
habit of letting out in rooms."—*New Orleans Picayune.*

"Oh, yes; you might not know her if she got to the North, but any of us would know her."

"How?"

"By her language and manners."

"But if she had been brought up as house-servant?"

"Perhaps not in that case."

The other thought there would be no difficulty; you could always see a slave girl quail when you looked in her eyes.

I asked if they thought the mulattoes or white slaves were weaker or less valuable than the pure negroes.

"Oh, no; I'd rather have them a great deal," said one. "Well, I had not," said the other; "the blacker the better for me." "The white ones," added the first, "are more active, and know more, and I think they do the most work." "Are they more subject to illness, or do they appear to be of weaker constitutions?" One said they were not, the other that they did not seem to bear the heat as well. The first thought that this might be so, but that, nevertheless, they would do more work. I afterwards asked the manager's opinion. He thought they did not stand excessive heat as well as the pure negroes, but that, from their greater activity and willingness, they would do more work. He believed they were equally strong and no more liable to illness; had never had reason to think them of weaker constitution. They often had large families, and he had not noticed that their children were weaker or more subject to disease than others. He thought that perhaps they did not have so many children as the pure negroes, but he had supposed the reason to be that they did not begin bearing so young as the others, and this was because they were more attractive to the men, and perhaps more amorous themselves. He knew a great many mulattoes living together, and they generally had large and healthy families.

Afterwards, at one of the plantation nurseries, where there were some twenty or thirty infants and young children, a number of whom were evidently the offspring of white fathers, I asked the nurse to point out the healthiest children to me, and of those she indicated more were of the pure than of the mixed breed. I then asked her to show me which were the sickliest, and she did not point to any of the latter. I then asked if she noticed any difference in this respect between the black and the yellow children. "Well, dey do say, master, dat de yellow ones is de sickliest, but I can't tell for true dat I ever see as dey was. . . ."

In spite of the constant denunciations by the Southern newspapers, of those who continued to patronize Northern educational institutions, I never conversed with a cultivated Southerner on the effects of slavery, that he did not express a wish or intention to have his own children educated where they should be free from demoralizing association with slaves. That this association is almost inevitably corrupting and dangerous, is very generally (I may say, excepting by the extremest fanatics of South Carolina, universally) admitted. Now, although the children of a few wealthy men may, for a limited period, be preserved from this danger, the children of the million cannot be. Indeed it requires a man of some culture, and knowledge of the rest of the world, to appreciate the danger sufficiently to guard at all diligently against it. If habitual intercourse with a hopelessly low and immoral class is at all bad in its effects on young minds, the people of the South are, as a people, educated subject to this bad influence, and must bear the consequences. In other words, if the slaves must not be elevated, it would seem to be a necessity that the citizens should steadily degenerate.

Change and grow more marked in their peculiarities with every generation, they certainly do, very obviously. "The South" has a traditional reputation for qualities and habits in which I think the Southern people, as a whole, are to-day more deficient than any other nation in the world. The Southern gentleman, as we ordinarily conceive him to be, is as rare a phenomenon in the South at the present day as is the old squire of Geoffrey Crayon in modern England. But it is unnecessary to argue how great must be the influence, upon people of a higher origin, of habitual association with a race systematically kept at the lowest ebb of intellect and morals. It has been elaborately and convincingly described by Mr. Jefferson, from his personal experience and observation of his neighbours. What he testified to be the effect upon the Virginians, in his day, of owning and associating with slaves, is now to be witnessed to a far greater and more deplorable extent throughout the whole South, but most deplorably in districts where the slave population predominates, and where, consequently, the action of slavery has been most unimpeded.*

What proportion of the larger cotton plantations are resided upon by their owners, I am unable to estimate with confidence. Of those having cabin accommodations for fifty slaves each, which came under my observation from the road, while I was travelling through the rich cotton district bordering the Mississippi river, I think more than half were unprovided with a habitation which I could suppose to be the ordinary residence of a man of moderate wealth. I should judge that a large majority of all the slaves in this district, were left by their owners to the nearly unlimited government of hireling overseers the greater part of the time. Some of these plantations are owned by capitalists, who reside permanently and constantly in the North or in Europe. Many are owned by wealthy Virginians and Carolinians, who reside on the "show plantations" of those States—country seats, the exhausted soil of which will scarcely produce sufficient to feed and clothe the resident slaves, whose increase is constantly removed to colonize these richer fields of the West.

A still larger number are merely occasional sojourning places of their owners, who naturally enough prefer to live, as soon as they can afford to do so, where the conveniences and luxuries belonging to a highly civilized state of society are more easily obtained than they can ever be in

---

* Jefferson fails to enumerate, among the evils of slavery, one of its influences which I am inclined to think as distinct and as baneful to us nationally as any other. How can men retain the most essential quality of true manhood who daily, without remonstrance or interference, see men beaten, whose position renders effective resistance totally impracticable—and not only men, but women, too! Is it not partially the result of this, that self-respect seldom seems to suggest to an angry man at the South that he should use anything like magnanimity? that he should be careful to secure fair play for his opponent in a quarrel? A gentleman of veracity, now living in the South, told me that among his friends he had once numbered two young men, who were themselves intimate friends, till one of them, taking offence at some foolish words uttered by the other, challenged him. A large crowd assembled to see the duel, which took place on a piece of prairie ground. The combatants came armed with rifles, and at the first interchange of shots the challenged man fell disabled by a ball in the thigh. The other, throwing down his rifle, walked toward him, and kneeling by his side, drew a bowie knife, and deliberately butchered him. The crowd of bystanders not only permitted this, but the execrable assassin still lives in the community, has since married, and, as far as my informant could judge, his social position has been rather advanced than otherwise, from thus dealing with his enemy. In what other English—in what other civilized or half-civilized community would such cowardly atrocity have been endured?

a country of large plantations. It is rare that a plantation of this class can have a dozen intelligent families residing within a day's ride of it. Any society that a planter enjoys on his estate must, therefore, consist in a great degree of permanent guests. Hence the name for hospitality of wealthy planters. A large plantation is necessarily a retreat from general society, and is used by its owner, I am inclined to think, in the majority of cases, in winter, as Berkshire villas and farms are in summer by rich people of New York and Boston. I have never been on a plantation numbering fifty field-hands, the owner of which was accustomed to reside steadily through the year upon it. Still I am aware that there are many such, and possibly it is a minority of them who are regularly absent with their families from their plantations during any considerable part of the year.

The summer visitors to our Northern watering places, and the European tourists, from the South, are, I judge, chiefly of the migratory, wealthy class. Such persons, it is evident, are much less influenced in their character and habits, by association with slaves, than any other at the South.

The number of the very wealthy is, of course, small, yet as the chief part of the wealth of these consists in slaves, no inconsiderable proportion of all the slaves belong to men who deputize their government in a great measure to overseers. It may be computed, from the census of 1850, that about one half the slaves of Louisiana and one third that of Mississippi, belong to estates of not less than fifty slaves each, and of these, I believe, nine-tenths live on plantations which their owners reside upon, if at all, but transiently.

The number of plantations of this class, and the proportion of those employed upon them to the whole body of negroes in the country, is, as I have said, rapidly increasing. At the present prices of cotton the large grower has such advantages over the small, that the owner of a plantation of fifty slaves, favourably situated, unless he lives very recklessly, will increase in wealth so rapidly and possess such a credit that he may very soon establish or purchase other plantations, so that at his death his children may be provided for without reducing the effective force of negroes on any division of his landed estate. The excessive credit given to such planters by negro dealers and

tradesmen renders this the more practicable. The higher
the price of cotton the higher is that of negroes, and the
higher the price of negroes the less is it in the power of
men of small capital to buy them. Large plantations of
course pay a much larger per centage on the capital invested in them than smaller ones; indeed the only plaus-
ible economical defence of slavery is simply an explanation of the advantages of associated labour, advantages
which are possessed equally by large manufacturing establishments in which free labourers are brought together
and employed in the most effective manner, and which I
can see no sufficient reason for supposing could not be
made available for agriculture did not the good results
flowing from small holdings, on the whole, counterbalance
them. If the present high price of cotton and the present
scarcity of labour at the South continues, the cultivation
of cotton on small plantations will by-and-by become unusual, for the same reason that hand-loom weaving has
become unusual in the farm houses of Massachusetts.

But whatever advantages large plantations have, they
accrue only to their owners and to the buyers of cotton;
the mass of the white inhabitants are dispersed over a
greater surface, discouraged and driven toward barbarism
by them, and the blacks upon them, while rapidly degen-
erating from all that is redeeming in savage-life, are, it is to
be feared, gaining little that is valuable of civilization.

In the report of the Grand Jury of Richland District,
South Carolina, in eighteen hundred and fifty-four, calling for a re-establishment of the African slave trade,* it is
observed: "As to the morality of this question, it is scarcely
necessary for us to allude to it; when the fact is remarked
that the plantations of Alabama, Mississippi, Louisiana,
and Texas have been and are daily settled by the removal
of slaves from the more northern of the Slave States, and
that in consequence of their having been raised in a more
healthy climate and in most cases trained to pursuits totally different, the mortality even on the best-ordered
farms is so great that in many instances the entire income
is expended in the purchase of more slaves from the same
source in order to replenish and keep up those plantations,
while in *every case* the condition of the slave, if his life is

---

* Richland District contains seven thousand white, and thirteen
thousand slave population. The Report is published in the *Charleston
Standard*, October 12th, 1854.

spared, is made worse both physically and morally. * * *
And if you look at the subject in a religious point of view,
the contrast is equally striking, for when you remove a
slave from the more northern to the more southern parts
of the slaveholding States, you thereby diminish his religious opportunities."

I believe that this statement gives an exaggerated and
calumnious report of the general condition of the slaves
upon the plantations of the States referred to—containing,
as they do, nearly one half of the whole slave population
of the South—but I have not been able to resist the conviction that in the districts where cotton is now grown most
profitable to the planters, the oppression and deteriora-
tion of the negro race is much more lamentable than is
generally supposed by those who like myself have been
constrained, by other considerations, to accept it as a duty
to oppose temperately but determinately the modern policy of the South, of which this is an immediate result. Its
effect on the white race, I still consider to be infinitely
more deplorable.

CAPRICORN TITLES